OLD DEVON

The detail from the Blaeu map of Devon (1650),
is reproduced on the cover by kind permission of
Baynton-Williams, 70 Old Brompton Road, London, SW7

The David & Charles Series

OLD DEVON

W. G. HOSKINS

UNABRIDGED

PAN BOOKS LTD : LONDON

First published 1966 by David & Charles (Publishers) Ltd.
This edition published 1971 by Pan Books Ltd,
33 Tothill Street, London, S.W.1.

ISBN 0 330 02682 8

Printed in Great Britain by
Cox & Wyman Ltd, London, Reading and Fakenham

CONTENTS

ILLUSTRATIONS IN PHOTOGRAVURE

(between pages 106 and 107)

MAPS AND PLANS

N

Holland

nowstone

itheridge Clayhanger

SOMERSET

Blackdown Hills

Tiverton

Halberton Uffculme

Kentisbeare

Cadbury Bradninch

Plymtree Luppitt

Thorverton Silverton Honiton

Shobrooke Ottery Yarway Axminster

rediton Newton St. Cyres St. Mary

R. Otter

Colyton Uplyme

EXETER Sidbury Axmouth

R. Exe Topsham R. Axe

Teign Exminster Marsh Barton

Bridford Kenn Woodbury

anaton Kenton Budleigh (Salterton)

Hennock Exmouth

Bovey Tracey Starcross

aytor

Teigngrace Teignmouth

Newton Abbot Stoke-in-Teignhead

uckfastleigh Torre

R. Dart Torquay

otnes Paignton ENGLISH

Harbertonford Brixham CHANNEL

Tuckenhay

Dartmouth

Stoke Fleming Start Bay

ACKNOWLEDGEMENTS

Some of the foregoing essays were originally published by Jonathan Cape in *Devonshire Studies* (1952). This book has long been unobtainable. The essay on 'The Study of Old Farmhouses' originally appeared in the form of three articles in *The Western Morning News*. 'The Winter of 1963' also appeared in that newspaper, as did 'Industrial Archaeology in Devon'. I am indebted to *The Western Morning News* for permission to reprint these essays here, generally in a revised and extended form.

'The Elizabethan Merchants of Exeter' was first published in *Elizabethan Government and Society* in 1961, a *festschrift* for Sir John Neale; and I am grateful to the Athlone Press of the University of London for their ready permission to reprint this essay here.

Preface

Old Devon is a book of ten studies concerned with many varied aspects of the history of Devon. The county is rich in old buildings, a great number of them still unrecognized at the end of narrow lanes; and I have written about this side of Devon history in two of the following essays. On quite another theme, the social history of the county has still to be properly written. I have included three essays on apparently widely different subjects, which in fact are related to each other in the sense that they all deal with social classes. One is about the Elizabethan merchants of Exeter, at a period when the city was one of the leading commercial cities in England; another is a study of three families who originated in the Devon countryside in early medieval times, tracing their fortunes through almost to the present day; and the third is a study of the farm-labourer and his varying fortunes – or lack of them – from the sixteenth century to the nineteenth.

A new field of local history is discussed in the short essay on Industrial Archaeology, for Devon has a long industrial history – not only in textiles, mining, and fishing, but in many minor industries also such as tanning and shipbuilding – and the visible remains of these dead industries (save in a few small instances) are numerous in most parts of the county and provide a richly rewarding field of work which has scarcely been touched as yet.

Yet another new field of local history is that of public health. How many local historians have ever given any thought to this kind of history? Yet illness and disease are one of the major preoccupations of the human race even today and were more so in the past. So the essay on 'Epidemics in Tudor Devon', which only purports to be a short pioneer study, should open the way for a number of local historians to do their own studies over a longer period of time.

Another major preoccupation of the human race, in England at least, is the weather, about which surprisingly little has been written from an historical point of view. I have put on record here in the essay entitled 'The Winter of 1963' some of the basic facts about the hardest winter in the South West for 223 years, the worst since that of 1740. The year 1963 may not sound like 'history' as it is commonly understood, but it was indeed, and is therefore worth recording. Some local historian ought to collect all the weather records and references, scattered in various places – in newspapers and parish registers to name only two very different sources – and make a short book on the subject, treating it as scientifically as possible.

Five of the essays that follow were originally published in a book, written in collaboration with Professor H. P. R. Finberg, entitled *Devonshire Studies*. This was published by Jonathan Cape in 1952, quickly went out of print, and is now quite unobtainable. I have therefore put most of my essays in that book into this one, so that they can be made available again to students of local history. The reprinted essays are: 'Some Old Devon Bartons', 'A Sheaf of Modern Documents', 'The Wealth of Medieval Devon', 'The Farm-Labourer through Four Centuries', and 'Three Studies in Family History' (here renamed 'Three Devon Families'). These essays have been revised where necessary. I have, however, omitted most of the footnote references that appeared in the original version, as making for easier reading. The few readers who may wish to trace the sources for any statement are referred to the original book *Devonshire Studies*, which can be seen in any good library.

Some of the other essays originally appeared in *The Western Morning News*, to whom I am indebted for permission to reprint them. They have been revised and slightly extended in most cases. As they contained a good deal of original material, I thought it worth while to rescue them from newspaper files where they were likely to sink into oblivion.

The essay on 'The Elizabethan Merchants of Exeter' was

originally written as my contribution to the *festschrift* for Sir
John Neale, the distinguished historian of Elizabethan England. It appeared in a volume of essays in 1961 entitled
Elizabethan Government and Society. I wish someone would
write a similar study of the Tudor merchants of Totnes, for
which ample materials exist. Totnes was second only to Exeter
as a prosperous cloth town in the sixteenth century, and it
housed some of the richest merchants in Devon. What is more,
a remarkable number of their houses still stand in the High
Street and Fore Street, and await a study of their own. The city
of Exeter, on the other hand, has been busily engaged in de-
stroying most of the evidence of its rich past, and there is little
left to study. What the Germans failed to destroy in May 1942,
the city council have been systematically demolishing ever
since. Most of what remains is under constant threat.

I was tempted to conclude this book with an historical survey
entitled The Exeter Mentality, beginning with Southey's
remarks after his visit to the city in September 1799, as printed
in his *Letters from England* (see the Cresset Press edition,
1951). Or one might have gone back to the nasty anti-Method-
ist riots by the religious bigots of Exeter in May 1745. Bigotry
has been an outstanding feature of Exeter life ever since that
date. In an essay in this book on The Lysons Correspondence
I quote what an eminent antiquary wrote to Lysons, the historian, warning him as long ago as 1820 that he would get little
help from the authorities at Exeter. 'As to the Chamber of
Exeter, you will find them jealous and illiberal in all their
measures ...' Alas, this is still true. The bigotry of modern
Exeter is still unbelievable to civilized people. As for their
politics, they are savage. Perhaps 'The Exeter Mentality' deserves a short book rather than a mere essay, for the materials –
in the records, in newspaper files, and in private sources – are
copious.

One essay in *Devonshire Studies* which is not reprinted here
is that entitled 'The Making of the Agrarian Landscape'. I have omitted this, rather reluctantly, for two reasons.
One is that it required considerable revision in the light of my

own later work on the antiquity of Devon farms. Some of these later conclusions are set out in my book *Provincial England* (1963). The other reason is that I still hope to write – in the not too-distant future – a full-length book on *The Making of the Devon Landscape*, covering not only the countryside and farming but also the towns, the industrial landscape, and the impact of communications on the landscape: in other words, a complete picture of the manner in which the Devonshire landscape has evolved over the past two thousand years. This book will complete all I want to say about Devon. But the subject is inexhaustible. However much I and others may have written about Devon, there remain vast tracts of almost untouched historical work waiting to be explored. I have indicated some of these in this preface, but many others will occur to the discerning reader. A visit to the Devon County Record Office will disclose mountains of virgin material to work upon; not least the veritable Matterhorn of the Duke of Bedford's archives relating to almost every aspect of South-Western history over a period of many centuries.

CHAPTER ONE

The Study of Old Farmhouses

WE ARE surprisingly ignorant in this country about the dwelling-houses of ordinary people and the way they have evolved in the past thousand years. Probably every country-house and manor-house has been recorded and written about somewhere. But below that social level the interested explorer of the English countryside and towns will find no book to enlighten him about the old houses he comes across in his travels.

With luck he may find a special article like the late Mr Hansford Worth's essay on 'The Dartmoor House', which was republished in 1953 in the volume of his collected papers entitled *Dartmoor*. Even this essay only scratched the surface. One wishes that Hansford Worth, with his vast and unrivalled knowledge of the moor, had made as systematic and complete a survey of Dartmoor farmhouses as he did of the other granite monuments within his chosen field.

As for the rest of Devon, with its many hundreds of ancient farmhouses of various plans and social types, dating from the fifteenth century onwards, there is practically nothing in print to help the intelligent explorer to understand what he is looking at.

Dartmoor, with its surrounding granite foothills, is one of the richest regions in England and Wales for the study of the development of the ordinary dwelling-house. It produces, of course, a particular type of house, built for a certain social class and a particular sort of farming economy, and what we find on the moor may not apply to farmhouses elsewhere in Devon. Or if it applies, then the chronology may be very different. Nevertheless, the moor contains one of the most instructive collections of ancient farmhouses south of the Scottish Highlands,

possibly in the whole of Great Britain, and as such deserves a
detailed study of its own. Such a study might take about two
years to accomplish.

The University of Exeter recently appointed a full-time Research Fellow to study the medieval and sub-medieval houses
of Exeter, many of which are in great danger of destruction for
the usual specious reasons.* The completion of this study
might well be followed by an expert survey of the granite
homesteads of Dartmoor and its foothills, for even these are in
some danger. It is not so long since the Duchy of Cornwall
destroyed the highly interesting Elizabethan farmstead of Bellever (Illus. 1). Fortunately this was one of the houses of which
Hansford Worth made a plan, reproduced opposite. It has gone
with only the most meagre record of its long existence.

What makes Dartmoor such a treasure-house for the study of
ancient farmstead types is its granite. Granite walls are almost
imperishable (though ivy can pull them down in time), unlike
nearly every other building material. Cob walls will last for 400
or 500 years if kept dry; theoretically a granite-walled house
should last for ever. But fashions change, even among Dartmoor farmers, in the course of the centuries, and the old house
would be modernized, or a new house built and the old one
abandoned to the labourers or the stock. This important social
change occurred widely in Devon and elsewhere in England
during the hundred years after about 1550.

Usually the farmer modernized his old house rather than
build a completely new one, but on Dartmoor he had plenty of
surface stone for a new building, free for the gathering, and
plenty of space in which to put it up, unlike the farmer who
lived in a village street and had to buy stone from a quarry. So
on Dartmoor the old house was often left standing. There was
no need to demolish it for the precious stone, and it was simply
put to other uses. Hence we find fourteenth- or fifteenth-century dwelling-houses tucked away behind the present house or
left somewhere up the yard as a farm building. Occasionally we

* The results of this survey were published in 1966 by Derek Port-
man, *Exeter Houses*, 1400—1700.

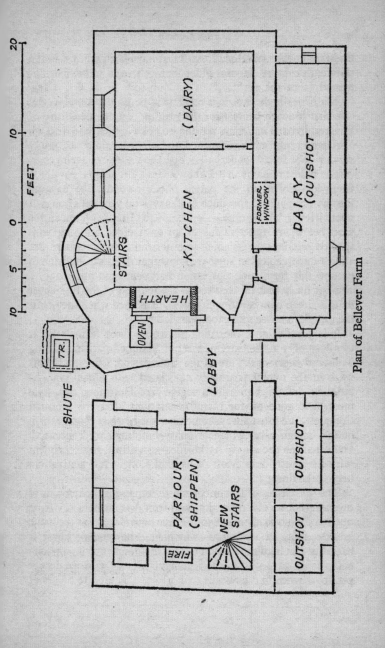

Plan of Bellever Farm

find the remains of a house that must have been erected in the
thirteenth century. Houses older than this seem to have disappeared from the surface, but undoubtedly lie buried a few
inches beneath the soil. No other part of England and Wales
offers such a rich harvest for discovering how the peasantry of
England lived. Though no farmhouse of an earlier date than the
thirteenth century has yet turned up in Devon, almost certainly
some will be found sooner or later on Dartmoor or its fringes.

The oldest remains that I know are the fragmentary walls at
Cholwich Town, in the parish of Cornwood. The existing
farmhouse is a good specimen of a moorland yeoman's house of
about Henry VIII's time – say 1500–40 (Illus. 3) – but in the
yard below are the remains of an even older building with
splayed windows in its thick granite walls. Such remains are
almost undateable, but since we know that the first Cholwich to
occupy this farm took possession between 1200 and 1230, I
think it likely that this represents the remains of the first house
on this site, a homestead which was abandoned when they built
their modern house some 300 years later.

It is possible that the ruins of two or three farmsteads at
Challacombe, in the extreme west of Manaton parish, showing
'long-and-short work', are of the same period. Long-and-short
work in the quoins is usually associated with Saxon church-
building, but in a primitive region like Dartmoor this style
must have gone on for many generations after the Norman
Conquest. We must always remember the marked conservatism
of the human race, where ordinary buildings are concerned.
Only the rich (now local authorities) can afford to experiment
with the latest ideas. Most of us plod along a few generations
behind the times.

The hut-circles of Dartmoor mostly represent the remains of
dwelling-houses of Bronze Age and Iron Age farmers, say from
about 1500 BC to about AD 500. These houses were, as the name
implies, more or less circular in plan. The modern house is
basically rectangular or square. At some point in time, the circular house gave way to the rectangular house, and we do not
yet know when and how this took place. The granite moors of

Devon and Cornwall, and their outer fringes, are the likeliest region in Britain to supply the clues for answering these questions. Professor Charles Thomas, who excavated Gwithian in West Cornwall, one of the most remarkable sites ever to be excavated in this country, believes that the rectangular house-plan was introduced into the South West by the Romans, and to some extent in Cornwall by the Irish. The houses of Roman origin are double-square in plan, with a doorway in the long side. Later we find an elongated plan in which the internal length varies from 2.4 to 2.8 times the internal width. These houses, though rectangular inside, have rounded corners externally, and additional doorways, and are probably the result of the Saxon invasions from the middle of the seventh century onwards in Devon and the eighth century in Cornwall.

The oldest Dartmoor house of which we have any record so far was excavated about the year 1901. The excavation naturally fell far short of that required by modern standards and the report (in the *Transactions of the Devonshire Association* for 1902) is vague on important details. The house was found at Greyhound Marsh, near Postbridge, close to the West Dart. It was rectangular in plan, with rounded corners externally, and seems to have consisted of one room only, with a door at one of the narrow ends. Fragments of pottery suggested that it was occupied during the thirteenth and fourteenth centuries, possibly somewhat earlier. Indeed, if it was a single-roomed house, and the traces of a second room were not missed in the process of excavation, it may be appreciably older than the thirteenth century in origin.

The house is baffling. There is an entire absence of provision for any animals or even for the sort of small family unit required to run a medieval holding. It may well represent the house of a medieval tinner, as the Rev S. Baring-Gould suggested at the time of excavation. Nearby are the sites of two blowing-houses. Tin-working began on Dartmoor in the twelfth century (as far as we know at present) and this house may well be of that period.

The Saxons had reached the fringes of the moor by the end

of the seventh century or the early eighth. Their earliest farmsteads will one day be found. In the meantime, a small settlement in the sheltered hollow between Hound Tor and Great
Tor has been located by the Ordnance Survey, and has now received a full-scale investigation. There seem to be five pounds
or small enclosures, and about twelve rectangular buildings,
some of them houses and some byres and kilns. The walls are
built of large blocks of uncut granite, without mortar and earth-
banked. Each building has an entrance, and there are accommo-
dation roads. These houses are more primitive than anything
recorded by Hansford Worth, and may indeed represent a late
Saxon settlement. Beneath the granite houses, which are
probably of thirteenth-century date, earlier structures have
been found which would take us well back into pre-Conquest
times. At the lowest level were small buildings with sunk floors.
These were succeeded by turf-walled houses of more than one
period; and finally the turf walls were replaced by stone
walls.

The change-over from turf to stone on Dartmoor can be
dated roughly from the very interesting old house at Stiniel, in
the parish of Chagford. This is recorded in a document of *c*
1224 as *Stenenhalle*, meaning 'the Stone Hall'. Hence stone-
built houses were rare enough at that date to give this house a
distinctive name. I have suggested above that the earliest buildings at Cholwich Town, which are of stone, date from 1200–30.
The change-over from turf and timber to stone probably began
on Dartmoor in the latter part of the twelfth century, but we
must await additional evidence before we can be quite certain.
In the meantime the old house at Stiniel, which again has some
unique features in its plan and is certainly medieval in part,
ought to be carefully surveyed, drawn, and photographed. It is
an almost unaltered specimen of its kind.

In the summer of 1956 Lady Aileen Fox excavated a medieval homestead on Dean Moor before it was inundated by the
making of the Avon Dam. This was of a type not hitherto
known on Dartmoor, consisting of a dwelling-house with two
rooms, and, across an enclosed yard, a large cattle-byre. The

scanty remains of pottery showed that this homestead was occupied only during the thirteenth century and perhaps the early fourteenth. It was probably abandoned at the time of the Black Death (1349–50) when we know the majority of Dartmoor farms were left tenantless. Some were re-occupied, but many were abandoned for good. The Dean Moor farmstead was probably a special type, as Lady Fox suggests, a homestead occupied by lay brothers from Buckfast Abbey. This would explain among other things the complete absence of any evidence that women lived here.

At Neadon, in Manaton parish, but off the moor proper, is another homestead which is so far unique in plan. It is now used as a shippon with hay-loft above, the present farmhouse being across the lane. The remarkable feature here is that the original shippon was always on the ground level, but the dwelling-house was above the cows on the first floor. A good traceried window in one gable-end shows that the house was built in the second half of the fifteenth century, and that it represents a considerable advance on the primitive structures of the twelfth to fourteenth centuries. That it was a dwelling-house is proved by the presence of two good fireplaces on the first floor, and also, at one end, the perfect remains of the garderobe, ie, the sanitary arrangements of the time, which discharged through a buttressed shaft into the ground outside. There were clearly two rooms, a hall and a solar, which were reached by means of an external stone stairway, now no longer to be seen.

The Neadon house is puzzling as a type. None like it has yet been found, but others may well be discovered in outhouses on other farms by a systematic search. It was evidently a good-class house, the home of a 'franklin' or free tenant, with its traceried window and its indoor sanitation.

An ancient farmhouse of the standard Dartmoor type, ie, a 'long house' with the dwelling at one end and the shippon at the other, may be found at the top of the yard at Yardworthy Farm in the parish of Chagford. The massive granite-covered porch suggests a very early date for the building, possibly about 1400. The dwelling-end probably had two rooms, one of which was a hall used for all the common purposes of living, including the cooking. The other, a small room beyond it, was probably used by the women of the house. It is almost certain that the fundamental improvement in the dwelling-house, its development into two rooms from the original one, was due to the need for some privacy for the women of the household. Left to themselves the majority of men would go on living in one room until doomsday.

Very rarely do we get a firm date for these rough granite houses on the moor, but the ancient structure (now used as farm buildings) behind the present farmhouse at Cudlipptown, near Tavistock, can be dated to about the first quarter of the sixteenth century. We know this by a fortunate chance. In February 1541, Stephen Coodlyp, of Coodlyp Town, yeoman, granted to his son, Roger, *inter alia* 'the Newe House in Coodlyp Towne'. This was evidently the ancestral house of the Cudlipp family, rebuilt shortly before the date of the grant. A similar old dwelling-house lies behind the present farmhouse at Clannaborough, in Throwleigh parish, again a two-roomed dwelling with a loft over.

For centuries the Dartmoor farmer lived in the same house as his animals. At some date, varying according to the class of farmer and the individual circumstances, the animals were turned out and housed in a building in the yard, and the old shippon was converted into another kitchen or a parlour. Often, however, we can see the old arrangement preserved, though the cows ceased to occupy it long ago. Lower Tor, in Widecombe parish (Illus. 13), has a granite porch dated 1707, but the house is essentially a structure of about 1500. Here the shippon is still plain to see, though I would guess that the cows were evicted in the year 1707 when the house was given a new face more befitting a prosperous Dartmoor yeoman. At Uppacott also, not far from Lower Tor, the open shippon-end with its drain and cobbled floor is still to be seen, and in bad winters the cows are still brought in for shelter.

At Yeo, in the parish of Chagford, stands a fascinating group of farmhouses and ancillary buildings. They probably represent successive periods of rebuilding on one farm. The present farmhouse, still owned and occupied by the Perrymans who have been there without a break since 1545, is mainly of eighteenth-century date. But in the yard is a large granite building now used for a barn which has a fireplace on the upper floor, so revealing that it was a dwelling-house when it was built in the fifteenth century. And farther up the yard stands an even older and decidedly primitive building, now used as a cowhouse, where another and much cruder fireplace indicates its original use as a dwelling. This, all on one ground floor, may well date from the fourteenth century, and could have been the home of the Walter-atte-Yo who is named in a tax assessment of 1332. Even this was probably not the first house on the site; I think it highly likely that Yeo was one of the Domesday farmsteads in the manor of Chagford. Somewhere in this little complex of ancient buildings there must lie the remains of the eleventh-century farmstead and possibly of one or two predecessors.

As elsewhere, there was much rebuilding of farmhouses in Queen Elizabeth's time, and for half a century afterwards. Robert Furse modernized his old house at Morshead, in Dean Prior, extensively during the 1580s and 90s, and of course other farmers, like the owner of Bellever, seem to have built entirely anew. The fact that neither Morshead nor Bellever now exist, both destroyed within living memory, is a sufficient indication of the need to examine and make a detailed record of all the Dartmoor houses while there is yet time.

If one systematically explored almost any rural parish in Devon, going down every lane and looking at every farmhouse and cottage, one would discover an extraordinary number of houses which were built in the last quarter of the sixteenth century and the first half of the seventeenth. The majority of these interesting houses are still not recorded anywhere, certainly not in Pevsner's two volumes on Devon in his *Buildings of England*. These are far from being a complete survey, though I continually come across people who imagine that the task of recording has been finished, and that there are no more discoveries to be made. It is the duty of the local historian, writing about his chosen parish or village, to make this record – for who else can, in a county with nearly 12,000 surviving farmhouses and probably 10,000 miles of roads and lanes?

Cottages are not to be ignored in such an exploration. What is now a farm-worker's cottage often originated as the farm-house of a husbandman or small farmer. Most of what we call 'old farmhouses' today were the homes of yeomen, solidly built in the first place, and on the whole well kept up through the centuries. The houses of Elizabethan and Jacobean husband-men, being smaller and less well built, have tended to sink in the social scale and to become cottages. (When they lie near large towns, of course, they have also tended to rise again as weekend residences for prosperous townspeople.) Even the humblest cottage may well be a small farmhouse of considerable age, and very probably less altered from its original state because its occupiers have always had limited means.

It is necessary to get inside every house, for the exterior, in these days of asbestos and concrete, may be totally unrevealing. Many times in Devon I have discovered a hitherto-unknown medieval house beneath the most unpromising exterior, as at Yard in Rose Ash parish. One should also explore upstairs. The true age of a house, more often than not, is to be found in the timbers of the roof structure, which, being so substantial, were the last part of any house to be renewed, except where the roof has been destroyed by fire.

If Devon farmhouses could be classified by periods, I think we would find that the commonest period of all was the two or three generations between about 1570 and 1640, though the eighteenth century would probably run it close. The reason for this is mainly a matter of money. About the year 1540 the general price-level began to rise steadily in England. This rise continued at a varying pace for the next eighty years, flattening out about 1620 into relative stability. For farmers generally this happy time meant ever-rising prices for their products in the local markets while their costs remained more or less con-stant. Rents were fixed, or moved only with extreme slowness.

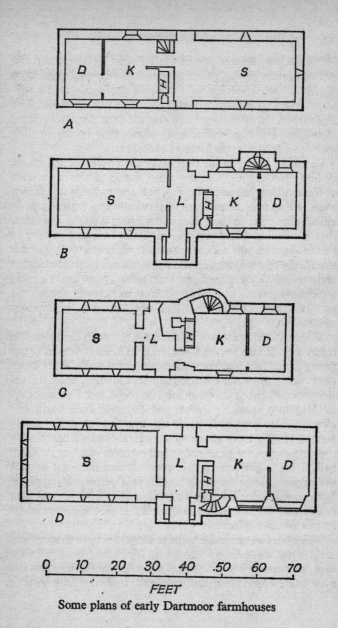

Some plans of early Dartmoor farmhouses

Many Devon farmers owned their farms. Labour costs also
moved up very slowly, partly because many farms depended on
family labour involving no wages, or on farm-servants who
lived in and were provided with all the necessities of life. The
Devonshire farmers, like farmers all over England, found
themselves steadily accumulating more ready money in their
coffers than their forefathers had ever seen.

Richard Carew, in his *Survey of Cornwall*, written in the
closing years of the sixteenth century, refers to 'the larger store
of coinage than our ancestors enjoyed' and to the fact that men
were falling over themselves to purchase long leases (usually
ninety-nine years or three lives in the South West) of any farms
that were going. What was true of Cornwall was even truer of
Devon, for this was a richer county in all respects. It was this
abundance of ready money that led so many farmers to enlarge
and modernize their medieval farmhouses, or to build a completely new house, in the two generations between about 1570
and the outbreak of the Civil War, which put a temporary stop
to all this activity.

Where an old house was modernized, the main change was to
insert a floor into the high medieval hall, so giving an upper
floor divided into bedrooms by thin internal walls, and a lower
floor containing a small hall, a parlour, a kitchen, and the usual
domestic offices. This gave the household more rooms, each
devoted to a special purpose, and easier to keep warm and
clean. Nearly everybody made this change; but at the lonely
farm of Hill, in Loxhore parish, it never took place. To this day
the kitchen remains as an untouched example of a late medieval
hall, rising to perhaps 16 ft or more. Across the front court is
the original detached kitchen. Hill is a remarkable survival
from round about the year 1500, showing all its original plan
and rooms. One would like to know if there are any other farmhouses like this in Devon.

The insertion of a floor helps to explain why in so many old
farmhouses the ceilings are so low in the ground-floor rooms: it
was not there in the first place, and therefore head-room was
inadequate when it came to be inserted. It also explains why we

often find a fifteenth-century roof upstairs above ground-floor ceilings of about 1600.

Extra rooms were also added at this period. In the household inventories that survive we often read of 'the old kitchen' and 'the new kitchen' in the Devon farmhouse, and there were other additions. Thus many houses are of more than one date, as their present owners frequently suspect. It is possible to trace the original core and to work out how the additions were made.

Besides being enlarged or rebuilt, farmhouses were made more comfortable. One of the greatest comforts was the coming of cheap glass for windows in place of horn or lattice, or even a rough wooden shutter such as one sees at Bartonbury farm-house (in Down St Mary), built about 1540. Church windows had glass at an earlier date (for example the magnificent windows at St Neot in Cornwall, put in during the 1520s, or the late medieval windows at Doddiscombsleigh in Devon). Glass began to appear in the windows of rich Exeter and Totnes merchants in the 1570s, imported from Rouen and London. One Exeter merchant owned a farm in Broad Clyst, now called Brockhill, and had glazed its windows before he died early in 1580; another early record of glass in farmhouse windows occurs at Morshead (now destroyed) in Dean Prior, where Robert Furse tells us in his notebook he 'seled the hall and glaste all the wyndoes', probably shortly before 1593. But very few farmhouses had glazed windows by 1600. Glass was still fairly expensive, and in the early seventeenth century, until it became cheaper through mass production, it was often left by will to the widow or a favourite son or daughter.

Henry Bidlake of Bidlake, gentleman, in his will dated March 28th, 1604, left to Jane his wife 'the glasinge and glasse of all my glass windows in Combe (in Bradstone parish) so long as she shall dwell in Combe . . . the said glasinge and glasse not to be removed, but repaired by her from time to time'. The inventory values 'glass in the farmhouse at Combe' at £3 6s 8d, a considerable sum of money at that time.

Ann Burrough, a farmer's widow at Luppitt in East Devon, in her will dated August 30th, 1606, left to her son 'the glass in the windows of the house where I dwell and all the sealing in the hall about the walls of the said house'. The 'sealing' was the wainscoting, still a feature of the best rooms in old farmhouses. Like glass windows, it came in as a modern comfort, indeed a luxury at first, at the end of the sixteenth century, though one occasionally finds some slightly earlier in date. As we have seen, Robert Furse 'seled' his hall, the principal living-room, shortly before 1593. Both the wainscoting and the glass were at first regarded as removable – they could be taken away to another house. This was possible because the earliest windows consisted of small panes of glass which were separately attached to the iron casement bars by means of thin lead tapes. I once saw such a window in a Devon farmhouse, preserved because it had been covered up by panelling shortly after it had been glazed. I never noted at the time where this farmhouse was and now I have forgotten.

One should always remember the old advice, 'When found, make a note of'. It is the details of any subject that matter. Any idiot can generalize, as William Blake once observed. There remain thousands of old farmhouses in Devon of which detailed surveys need to be made. Only after this shall we be in a position to generalize.

CHAPTER TWO

Industrial Archaeology in Devon

IN THE past few years a new field of historical inquiry has come into official existence – the study of the surviving remains of past industrial activity. It covers such things as industrial buildings – mills, warehouses, furnaces, etc, – industrial housing, the mechanical processes of industry and their machinery, and even the earthworks produced by industrial activity, such as the canals, railways, quarries, and mine-workings.

This field of inquiry is so newly recognized that there is still argument about what it can properly be called, and also about what it can legitimately cover. The orthodox archaeologists are deeply pained by the appropriation of their hallowed title to a field of inquiry which, almost without exception, dispenses with excavation, and indeed regards it as something to be done only as a last resort when one cannot discover the meaning of a site in any other way. They complain also of the modernity of the remains under study. But, with all our thought, no better title for the new field of inquiry can be found than industrial archaeology. There is no valid reason why the definition of archaeology should be narrowly restricted to the Romano-British period and earlier, or even to the recent field of medieval archaeology, or that it should necessarily involve digging.

As Kenneth Hudson said in the first comprehensive book to be written in this field, 'the label industrial archaeology has come under equally heavy fire from economists, historians, and archaeologists, partly from reasons of sheer conservatism, partly from resentment against an upstart, and partly because of serious and genuine doubts that industrial archaeology can be made into a satisfactory academic discipline'.

Nevertheless, it is here to stay. The label industrial

archaeology is here to stay, too, and South-Western England
will prove one of the most rewarding regions in the British Isles
for this new field of historical-archaeological inquiry.

As with all new subjects, there have been pioneers who
worked upon them, and wrote about them, without giving their
activities a specific name, just like Molière's M. Jourdain, who
was amazed to hear that 'for more than 40 years I have been
speaking prose without knowing it'. As long ago as 1878 a Mr
Isaac Fletcher wrote a paper in the *Transactions of the Cumberland and Westmorland Antiquarian and Archaeological
Society* on the Archaeology of the West Cumberland Coal
Trade, and may be regarded as the pioneer in this new territory.

The essence of his work was the use of all the documents he
could lay his hands on for the eighteenth and nineteenth centuries, and also personal visits to mines, inspections of drawings
of old machinery, and conversations with men who had spent a
lifetime in the industry. It is the combination of the documentary evidence with the visual evidence drawn from surviving buildings, machinery, and earthworks that distinguished
Fletcher's work from that of the more orthodox local historian;
and this is the essential approach today.

We now realize that documents leave many questions un-
answered or not even hinted at; and that the visual evidence
can start us off on something entirely new and unsuspected by
those who think that the final truth lies in libraries and record
offices. There are profoundly important discoveries to be made
by those who have learnt to use their eyes intelligently. Most of
us are visually illiterate, and our education has helped to make
us so.

Some of the West Midland and Northern counties are obviously very rich in the visible remains of the classic Industrial
Revolution, deeply involved as they were in that cataclysm, but
it would be wrong to write off Devon and Cornwall as any less
rewarding. Cornwall itself, with its long and important mining
industry, has attracted a considerable amount of attention,
chiefly from Cornishmen. The recent attention to Cornish

engine-houses as industrial monuments, many of them as worthy of preservation as good domestic architecture, is only one example of the work being done.

Devon has attracted far less notice, yet it has perhaps a more varied industrial history than Cornwall. Its mining history is not as long, but it is as varied in its visible remains. Then, too, Devon was an important textile county from the sixteenth century in the mid-nineteenth, and there remain many monuments of that industry, chiefly in the form of mills, waiting to be recorded before it is too late. There may be machinery in some of these old mills, if it has not already been scrapped during the last war.

The fishing industry, flourishing since the fifteenth century, had its own type of specialized buildings, such as the fish-cellars first built by Squire Cary at Clovelly in the last years of the reign of Elizabeth I. Do these still exist on the shore?

Mining, textiles, and fishing all left behind their characteristic types of 'monuments' and in some cases their characteristic earthworks. One can study the visible remains of mining at North Molton, for example, over a period of about a thousand years. The only mining activity hinted at in Devon in Domesday Book (1086) is the existence of four iron workers recorded under the royal manor of North Molton, on the southern edge of Exmoor. How much further back their activities could be traced we do not know.

An iron mine is referred to in Kent in a Saxon charter as early as the year 689; it is possible that the iron ore of North Molton was also known in Saxon times. What is more, one can actually trace the earliest iron-workings in the form of three series of pits, called Barton Pits, about 1½ miles NNW of the village. Each set of pits is about 350 yards long, but two are now overgrown. They are marked on the 2½-inch map but not identified for what they really are. A valuable clue is provided by the name: 'Barton' in Devon almost invariably indicates a demesne farm. These pits, then, belonged to the lord's de-mesne, and were worked on behalf of the King as lord of the manor of North Molton.

The next mention of mining activity in this parish appears to be of the King's copper mine in 1346. This was apparently a failure, but can the workings be traced on the ground today? Another copper mine is referred to in 1528. Forty years later German miners and their families were brought to North Molton to exploit the iron-workings. There are adits below Tabor Hill which may be the relics of this Elizabethan activity. These iron-workings, too, had ceased by the time that Westcote wrote (in the early seventeenth century), but at the very end of the century there was an influx of Cornish miners who worked the Florence and Marcia mines for iron and the Bampfylde mine for iron and copper.

These mines were abandoned in turn about 1773; but in 1840 or thereabouts another rich copper mine was found. And to complete the story, though there is much more to it, the Florence mine was re-opened in 1942 and worked for a few years to help meet the acute wartime mineral shortage. It is now abandoned, and the ivy-clad buildings already look as though nothing had happened for the last hundred years.

The large-scale maps of this fascinating parish are dotted with clues about old adits and mines, the workings and the tramways, and one can still trace some of the old buildings in various places. This parish alone would make a splendid subject for a detailed survey along industrial-archaeological lines. What one would like to see in Devon is something like the work of Mr Hamilton Jenkin on *Mines and Miners of Cornwall*, which combines a vast knowledge of all the documents with a flair for fieldwork. What he has to say about clues on the ground applies equally well to our own county: '. . . the patient search has brought its small rewards – as when in some secluded valley the course of an old miners' leat has guided one to their wheel-pit, shaft, and adjacent adit, all nearly concealed today amidst the encroaching undergrowth. Elsewhere, the indications may be even less evident. A trace of ochreous water oozing from a hillside, a slight irregularity in the surface of a field, sometimes a mere discoloration of the grass, now constitute the sole remaining traces of what was once a mine.'

To return for a moment to North Molton, mining does not exhaust its industrial-archaeological interest. It had a woollen mill at Heasley, a nineteenth-century brickworks near Marsh Farm, and water mills (for corn?) in at least three different places. One can still trace the ancient leats.

A parish of even greater possibilities for industrial archaeology is Tavistock in West Devon. Mining has been carried on since the thirteenth century, possibly the twelfth, if not in the parish then in its immediate vicinity. Here and there in the woods one can trace leats cut in the rock, probably in the fifteenth century, and no doubt these would direct one to a contemporary working. The modern 2½-inch map, especially of the small piece of country between Tavistock and the Tamar valley to the west, is thick with clues for the industrial archaeology of the relatively modern period: disused mines, derelict quays on the river, shafts, and quarries, an 'old canal'. But even the map does not show all there is to be seen on the ground: the canal tunnel under Morwell Down is not marked, nor is the railway from the Devon Great Consols mine down to Morwellham, nor the canal aqueduct over the Lumburn valley or the inclined planes at Morwellham. These have disappeared from the map within the last fifty or sixty years, with the final collapse of copper mining in the Tavistock district. Much has disappeared from the ground also, especially the machinery and buildings at the Devon Great Consols mine; and the buildings at Morwellham quay (Illus. 4) are fast falling into ruin.

Morwellham, on the Tamar, had long been a river-port for the copper mines of the Tavistock district. During the Napoleonic Wars, copper prices soared and new mines were being opened up rapidly. Cheaper transport to the navigable Tamar became essential. In 1803 a four-mile canal from Tavistock to Morwellham was proposed, but it was some thirteen years before it opened for traffic (in 1816). It involved some difficult engineering, including the aqueduct over the river Lumburn followed almost at once by a 2,560-yard tunnel through Morwell Down. Emerging high above the Tamar, the canal ends with an inclined plane dropping 237 ft to the quay at Morwellham, the greatest drop in Southern England. A branch of the canal ran up the Lumburn valley to the slate quarries at Millhill, but though completed this was closed in or shortly after 1831. In 1844 a railroad was laid from the slate quarries down to the main canal. This was strictly a tramway, and was closed in the late 1860s. A short stretch of the Millhill branch of the canal is visible to the south of the Tavistock-Gunnislake road, as far as the Lumburn aqueduct. The main Tavistock canal slowly faded out as a waterway, some time between 1883 and 1898, but its course can easily be traced and makes a pleasant walk for some miles.

In the meantime dramatic discoveries of copper were made in one of the Duke of Bedford's pheasant woods, at Blanch-down high above the Tamar valley. There had already been some prospecting in this wood without result. In March 1844 the Duke of Bedford leased the ground to a group known as the Devonshire Great Consolidated Copper Mining Company, a name later shortened to Devon Great Consols. In November of the same year a rich copper lode was struck, the beginning of an enterprise that was to produce more than £4,000,000 worth of minerals and to pay £1,250,000 in dividends.

The first mine was named Wheal Maria. It is actually in Grenoven Wood, four miles due west of the town of Tavistock. Morris's Shaft, so marked on the 2½-inch map, is named after Mr William Morris, father of William Morris, the poet and artist. He had taken 272 of the original 1,024 £1 shares. Another big shareholder was Mr Richard Gard, who was MP for Exeter and, like William Morris senior, a London discount broker. Gard took 288 shares, and when the first dividend was declared at £71 per share for the year he netted well over £20,000 on this investment alone. The earliest shaft was named after him – Gard's Shaft – and can be found a little to the west of Morris's Shaft. West of that again is Castle's Shaft, and to the south of this, on the old leat, is the remains of the iron foundry. The Devon Great Consols was unusual in having its own foundry for manufacturing and erecting steam-engines, employing nine men and two boys. The first leat, two miles long and 18ft wide, was cut about 1849 or 1850. It led to a water-wheel 40 ft in diameter and 12 ft wide (Illus. 5), which worked at five strokes a minute and lifted 52,000 lb of water with each stroke.*

This wheel was located on the banks of the river, and drained shafts at Wheal Maria and Wheal Josiah. A line of flat rods nearly half a mile long transmitted power from the great wheel to the pumps in the shafts. Another great wheel, 35 ft in diameter and 4 ft wide, was built to drive the machinery at the foundry.

Other mines were opened up eastwards from Wheal Maria: Wheal Fanny, Wheal Anna Maria (named after the Duchess of Bedford), Wheal Josiah, and Wheal Emma (named after Mrs William Morris). These five were known collectively as Devon Great Consols. They rapidly became one of the richest copper mines in the world, and indeed the production of ore out-stripped both the available power and the transport. In the spring of 1856 the ore completely filled the three quays at Gawton, Newquay, and Morwellham, with a consequent serious restriction on the sales of the Company. All these quays are worth visiting today for they contain a good deal of indus-trial-archaeological interest.

As a result of this situation, two further elements made their appearance in the local scene. A railway was built to link the mines with Morwellham Quay, 4½ miles away. Begun in 1857, it was open for traffic by November 1858. It was standard gauge, worked by steam locomotives drawing eight to ten wagons. Its course is marked on the 2½-inch map but not as a railway: it appears as a double line, rather like a minor lane, but its origin can be recognized in the way it follows the con-tours of the steep hillside. It runs underneath the main Tav-istock-Gunnislake road a few yards south of the third milestone from Tavistock and thence by sweeping curves to the top of Morwell Wood, some 240 ft above Morwellham Quay. The

* See J. C. Goodridge, 'Devon Great Consols' in *Trans. Devon Ass.*, vol 96 (1964) on which this account of the Blanchdown mines is largely based.

steep descent – one in three – is made by means of an inclined plane half a mile long, down which trucks were lowered two at a time by a 4-inch rope. At the same time large improvements were made to the quay at Morwellham. A new dock was completed in 1858, capable of taking six vessels of 300 tons each, and floors covering several acres laid out for receiving the ore from the laden trucks. Copper ore was sent out from Morwellham and coal and timber came in. Another visual change in the scene was the building of miners' cottages, some of them at the mines and some in the town of Tavistock.*

This industrial housing is itself worthy of study by open-minded archaeologists. Nothing could be more purblind than to believe that hut-circles of 500 BC are worth close attention and description, and to ignore miners' houses of the 1840s and 50s as 'not archaeology'. The study, survey, and drawing of houses is a part of archaeology whatever their 'period', provided they have passed out of current fashion. The Exeter merchants' houses described in a later essay in this book are certainly a kind of archaeology, and they become industrial archaeology when, as at Totnes, they survive within a complete arrangement of dwelling-house, offices, and warehouses.†

Further changes took place at Devon Great Consols during the late 1860s and early 70s. The phenomenally rich copper lodes were beginning to fail by the mid-60s, and in 1866 it was decided to erect works for the purpose of extracting arsenic from the pyrites which occurred abundantly on the walls of the lodes. This process is described by Goodridge in the article already referred to. Among the Bedford records now at the

* The site of Morwellham is now (1970) being scientifically cleared and tidied up by the Dartington Amenity Research Trust, and Mr Frank Booker has published *The Story of Morwellham*, a model guide to the whole complex. In 1967 he also published a larger work on *The Industrial Archaeology of the Tamar Valley* (David & Charles).

† At Totnes, No 70 Fore Street, rescued from decay and demolition by a far-sighted little town council, is a particularly complete example of this type of sixteenth-century housing complex, now used as a splendid local museum. Mr Michael Laithwaite is at present (1970) making a complete study of the vernacular buildings of Totnes.

Devon County Record Office is an agreement between the Duke and the company dated September 21st, 1866, for the construction of an arsenic works, giving details of flues, chambers, and cisterns. A later plan, dated August 1874, shows the works, with buildings, leats, and railway.

Altogether the Devon Great Consols was the largest and most extensive mine in the South West of England, covering about eight acres. Now it is represented by massive spoil heaps, broken flues, ruined buildings, empty cuttings and embankments; and down at Morwellham, which once resounded to the shouts and cries of busy industry, are a few roofless cottages, and a reed-filled dock basin with granite bollards round its edge. The end had come in the spring of 1903, but Blanchdown remains as one of the most remarkable sites in the country for the study of industrial archaeology.

Another industrial settlement of quite a different kind is Tuckenhay, on Bow Creek which opens into the estuary of the Dart. It has a most varied history, which has still to be worked out. Local historians so far have displayed little interest, if any, in this kind of subject: looking up the available material for Ashprington parish, in which Tuckenhay lies, one finds endless repetition about the church, the descent of the manor, and all the usual antiquarian matters. These are worthy subjects, but the total silence in most parish histories about visible remains of the past such as mills and mines is ample testimony to the origins of local history writing – in the squire's library and the parson's study.

The earliest reference to Tuckenhay is comparatively late by Devonshire standards. It occurs as *Tokenhey* in a document of 1550, a form which misleads the editors of *The Place Names of Devon* into saying that it possibly means 'at the oak enclosure', 'hay' being an enclosed field in this part of England. It means in fact the field where tucking or fulling was carried on, a process in the cloth industry, and is the first evidence of industrial activity here. A deed dated February 27th, 1568, refers to a dispute over a leat or watercourse of a tucking mill and a grist mill in Ashprington belonging to John Giles, esquire. It is not certain that this tucking mill was at Tuckenhay, but in all probability it was. The manor of Ashprington had belonged to Totnes priory for centuries, but at the Dissolution it was bought by John Giles of Totnes, the richest merchant in the town. He and his son William acquired it on June 27th, 1542. Unfortunately no detailed particulars are given in the public records of this grant.*

White's *Directory* for 1850 says that there was at Tuckenhay 'a large paper mill, a corn mill, and quarries of hard stone' large quantities of which were exported to London and elsewhere in vessels of 160 tons for macadamizing roads. There were quays along the Harbourne river and extensive buildings connected with the busy trade of this small riverside settlement. There was also an old gas-house erected about 1806 by Mr Abraham Tucker for lighting the village. We hear no more anywhere of this remarkable experiment, or whether it ever materialized. The first place to be lit by gas was the engineering works of Boulton & Watt near Birmingham in 1802, and the first public street lighting in London was in 1807. Does anything survive of this early attempt to introduce gas-lighting into Devon? Exeter was not lit by gas until 1817.

Shorter's great work on the history of the paper industry in this country shows that there was no paper mill at Tuckenhay by 1800. Presumably the fulling mill was converted to a paper mill by about 1830 when a 'paper worker' is recorded in the register of Cornworthy, the adjacent parish. The large paper mills now on the Cornworthy side of the river Wash came comparatively late: they were not there when White wrote in 1850.

The hamlet of Tuckenhay still retains its quays and warehouses. The whole complex of buildings would repay a detailed study before there are any further changes. In this search the first edition of the 25-inch Ordnance map, made as long ago as 1882, will be found to be a valuable document. The tithe map of Ashprington made in 1843 is of limited value as the build-

* Joyce Youings: *Devon Monastic Lands, Calendar of Particulars for Grants* 1536–58, p 15.

ings are not named. Nevertheless the layout of the hamlet as revealed in that map is of some interest.

Mention has been made of the remarkable engineering works of the Tavistock Canal (1803–16). Other canals in Devon are also worthy of study by the industrial archaeologist. The Torrington or Rolle Canal in North Devon has a particularly interesting history.* After some years of fruitless discussion, Lord Rolle began this canal at his own expense in 1823, with the object of linking the tide-water of the Torridge with the town of Torrington. It began at a sea-lock and basin below Wear Giffard, ran alongside the river for nearly a mile, and was then carried by an inclined plane to its summit level. A five-arched aqueduct carried the canal over the Torridge at Beam. Thence the canal followed the other bank of the river to the warehouses at the bottom of Mill Street in Torrington, and ended at New Manor Mill a mile above the town.

In the autumn of 1854 the railway reached Bideford, but not until 1870 was work begun on an extension to Torrington. The canal closed (probably) in 1871 and part of its bed was used for the railway. Very little remains to be seen of the canal except the inclined plane and the Beam aqueduct, now dry and used as the driveway to Beam House. This fine memorial of the old canal was built by James Green, who was also responsible for the beautiful Cowley Bridge near Exeter, built in 1813 and already listed as an ancient monument.

Another North Devon canal (in part) was the Bude Canal. After the usual abortive discussions and changes of plan, work began in 1820, and three years later the canal had been opened from Bude to near Holsworthy. Once again James Green was the engineer. 'The canal was a remarkable piece of engineering, both the longest tub-boat canal in Britain, and also that with the most inclined planes' (Hadfield). There were six inclines in the 35½-mile length, each with a double line of rails. Details of these will be found in Charles Hadfield's book. Most of the canal closed down in 1891. The canal reservoir – now called

* For this and all other canals, see Charles Hadfield, *The Canals of Southern England* (1955), now the standard work on the subject.

Tamar Lake – and about nine miles of the old waterway to the top of the Venn incline are still used for water-supply.

In South and East Devon there are remains of other small canals. The Grand Western Canal, from the Tone at Taunton to Tiverton, was opened in 1838, only a few years before the coming of the railway along almost the same route. After the usual chequered history, the eastern (Somerset) part of the canal closed in 1867, but the western part did not close until 1924.

The Exeter ship-canal deserves to be mentioned, though it is not yet archaeological. Opened as long ago as 1566, it is the oldest ship-canal in England and was the first to use the device of the pound-lock. Again, it has a complicated history of enlargements, extensions, and abortive extensions. It is still in use, though its future is now uncertain.

In South Devon, the Stover Canal and the Hackney Canal, both associated with the river Teign, have a good deal to show of archaeological interest. The former was begun in 1790 for the export of the local pottery clay and runs for just under two miles from Ventiford near Teigngrace to a point on the Teign near Newton Abbot. In 1820 the opening of the Haytor Granite Tramway, built to carry granite from the moorland quarries down to Teigngrace, gave the canal a fresh impetus. Not until 1938 did it go out of use, and it was finally closed in 1943. The little-known Hackney Canal opened in 1843 for the easier transport of clay on Lord Clifford's lands. It was only five furlongs long and had a short life. The lock, wharf, and basin are the most substantial remains of this minute waterway.*

Railways have their own archaeology. Brunel's most disastrous failure, the atmospheric railway which he tried out in South Devon in 1847–8, has its battered memorials in the pumping-houses at Starcross (now a youth club) and Torre. In Exeter the suburban station of St Thomas is the original building of 1846; and certain country stations (such as Bow, opened in 1865) have their own appeal. As the smaller lines are closed,

---

* For fuller details of the Stover and Hackney Canals, see M. C. Ewans, *The Haytor Granite Tramway and Stover Canal* (1964).

these delightful Victorian railway stations should be photographed and recorded before they fall into unrecognizable ruin.
The Lynton & Barnstaple Railway, opened in 1898 and closed
in 1935, was dismantled thirty years ago; but the fine Chelf-
ham viaduct remains standing as its memorial 400 ft long and
70 ft above the roadway, and has its devoted pilgrims from
time to time.

The Haytor Granite Tramway has already been mentioned
in passing. Opened in 1820, it had a life of less than forty years,
being disused by 1858. It was a horse-railway of 4 ft 3 in
gauge, with rails of granite slabs about 15 inches wide. Ul-
timately it ran to a total length of nine miles, ten miles with the
sidings. The topmost moorland section, from the Manaton road
to Holwell Quarry, has rightly been scheduled as an ancient
monument: so much for those blinkered purists who refuse to
recognize anything later than the Anglo-Saxon. Full details of
the tramway, and how to explore it, will be found in Ewans's
book already referred to.

The woollen industry, established in Devon since medieval
times, has left behind a number of early nineteenth-century
mills, notably perhaps those at Ottery St Mary and North
Tawton; but there are others, particularly in the Ashburton-
Buckfastleigh district, that need seeking out. Indeed, I suspect
that these two little towns contain enough industrial archaeology to justify a special survey. And not far away is Harbertonford, which once had two mills, a woollen mill and an
edge-tool mill, now both closed. This again was a small industrial settlement which would repay a more detailed inspection.

The paper-making industry has long been established in
Devon. The earliest mill was in or near Exeter and was set up
in the 1630s or slightly sooner. By the closing years of the
seventeenth century, and more especially the first half of the
eighteenth, the number of paper mills had greatly increased in
the Culm valley and the adjacent parts of the Exe valley. Some
of these possibly contain traces of their ancestral origin. At
Exeter the paper mill at Trews Weir (still active) contains a

good building bearing the date 1780. This was an abortive cotton mill, built in the hope that a new industry could be established in Exeter as the woollen trade fell off.

Warehouses are very much a subject for industrial archaeology. Up-river from Trews Weir paper mills, on the old quay in Exeter, stand two of the noblest warehouse buildings in South-Western England. They were erected in 1835, just before the coming of the railway which ruined Exeter as a port. Exeter indeed contains a greater number of old warehouses than might be supposed. Just north of these monumental warehouses, also facing the old quay, is a building of great archaeological interest. Now occupied by Do It Yourself Supplies Ltd, it appears to be a complete building of about 1600 behind its deceptive rebuilt front. On the upper floor, occupied by C. H. Quaintance & Son, the original roof structure survives almost intact. The whole building was in origin a late Elizabethan warehouse, belonging to the days when Exeter was one of the busiest outports in the kingdom.

Devon has sunk – if sunk is the right word – from being one of the greatest industrial and commercial regions of Britain to being a pleasant backwater, but all around the coasts and along the estuaries will be found the visible remains of former days – scores of disused lime-kilns, small abandoned harbours once the centre of great hopes, factories, and warehouses; and above all there is the remarkable complex of eighteenth- and nineteenth-century mining archaeology on Dartmoor. It is usual to associate Dartmoor with prehistoric remains. Few people yet realize that it is a wonderful treasure-house for vernacular building from the twelfth century to the nineteenth, for the study of deserted medieval villages, field-systems, and tin-workings, and in more recent times of mining of various kinds. The 2½-inch map will give the explorer a good start in looking for abandoned mines. Better still, he should consult the first edition of the 6-inch map, which dates from the 1880s and shows a good deal of detail which has disappeared from recent maps. Best of all, the first edition of the 25-inch maps (of the same date) should be used, but these can only be consulted in the

Map Room of the British Museum. To the best of my knowledge these maps cannot be seen anywhere in Devon.

A whole book is waiting to be written on the mining history and archaeology of Dartmoor. There was even a gunpowder factory on the moor, which has recently been made the subject of a model essay in this new field of industrial archaeology.* The placid county of Devon furnishes enough material for three or four volumes on the archaeology of its industrial past.

* *The Western Morning News*, August 6th, 1965, by Helen Harris.

CHAPTER THREE

Some Old Devon Bartons

SCATTERED all over the 1-inch map of Devon are countless farms, usually lying all alone, well away from any village, with the suffix of Barton. Though the word is not peculiar to Devon, it is far commoner in this county than in any other, and it signifies a farm much larger than the average. Occasionally the title has been added in recent years to a farm which never had it before – just as sometimes the even more pretentious title of Manor has been added to farms which have never enjoyed that ancient dignity – but nine times out of ten the word Barton on the map indicates a farm with a long and interesting history, a history that can be traced in many instances back to the Norman Conquest, and in exceptional cases to some time before that. Thus, Ruxford Barton, now an attractive early seventeenth-century farmhouse in the parish of Sandford, is first mentioned as *hroces ford* – 'rooks' ford' – in an Anglo-Saxon charter dated 930.

Even where a barton is not mentioned in a pre-Conquest charter, we can generally be pretty sure, if it is recorded in Domesday Book, that it existed at least a century or two before that. One can sometimes arrive at the approximate date of such farms from a detailed study of the topography of the parish in which they lie.

I have spent a good deal of time tracking down these ancient farms in Devon, for they present a number of features of great interest. Nor is this only an antiquarian interest – though this would be good enough in itself. A study of such farms throws much light on the local history of South-Western England, much of it not otherwise recorded. If we examine their precise site in relation to old roads, and to streams and other natural features of the landscape, the layout of their buildings in relation to each other, and the actual architecture of the surviving buildings, we can learn something new from nearly every one we come across, some fresh detail that illuminates the almost unrecorded process of the colonization of the English countryside in the dark centuries before the Norman Conquest and just after it.

Nor is their interest by any means exhausted with this remote period. They throw light in various ways upon the history of English farming and the families who have farmed their land for so many centuries up to recent times. Many of these old bartons, rebuilt more than once in their long history, have been the cradle of great families, the nest in which they slowly grew from the twelfth century onwards, until they became too large for the ancestral home and migrated to mansions and parks elsewhere.

Such a farm is Acland Barton, in the parish of Landkey and only two miles in a straight line from the town of Barnstaple. Though so near a busy town, Acland seems remote enough on its little tree-fringed plateau, high above the valley in which the church reposes. It lies at the end of a narrow lane, which is its only approach and which leads nowhere but to this farmyard. This lane was known in the twelfth century as Acca's Lane. Acca was a neighbouring landowner, two or three miles away, who gave his name also to the isolated farm of Accott, above West Buckland; and his lane in turn gave its name to the farm at the end of it. In an assize roll dated 1238 the farm is referred to as *Akkelane*, and we find the Aclands at home there in that year.

The original charter which settled them here does not survive, but later records tell us that they held Acland in free socage under the great manor of Bishop's Tawton, which belonged to the see of Exeter, by a chief rent of 10s a year. A number of estates were carved out on the frontiers of this large manor during the twelfth century, of which Acland was one. All were held in socage or by a fraction of a knight's fee, and a small annual quit-rent.

Nothing remains of the earliest house at Acland, but the present farmhouse is nevertheless of exceptional interest. It consists of a western block of late fifteenth-century date, and a main block running at right angles to it, built of coursed rubble masonry and apparently altered some time in the eighteenth century. But a closer inspection reveals that this later work is the least important. Over the front doorway is the date 1591. This in turn only commemorates the alteration of an older building which still survives in great part. Despite its outward appearance, the main block of the house is contemporary with the west wing. The whole house was probably rebuilt about 1470–80 by John Acland, or his father Baldwin Acland, both of whom married heiresses to substantial local estates. It may be said perhaps that the Aclands showed an uncommon propensity for marrying heiresses, and their rapid rise in the fifteenth and sixteenth centuries was due more to this nice judgement than to anything else. Many of these old Devon freeholders rose by a series of successful marriages, like the Aclands; others, like the Pollards, the Carys, and the Wadhams, made their fortunes in the law as early as the fourteenth and fifteenth centuries. The Devonians have always been notable lawyers, from the great Henry de Bracton onwards.

The Aclands signalized their rise by rebuilding the old farm-house in a manner more worthy of their new position. Their fifteenth-century chapel, over the kitchen in the west wing, still survives, with its carved wagon roof and oak-mullioned windows. After the Reformation, probably in 1591 when the house was remodelled internally, the chapel was converted into a parlour; and among the debris that now lies piled high in this room one can see a decorated plaster frieze around the walls and the Acland arms in plaster at each end. A fireplace and a chimney were put in at the same date.

The original fifteenth-century hall remains in the main block. Five pairs of moulded and arched principals (couples) rise through the bedrooms and meet in the loft above. The bedroom floor was probably put in in 1591, so cutting the original open-roofed hall into two levels more convenient for modern living. The original fifteenth-century door is still in use, studded with nails and covered with initials.

Acland Barton is therefore a late fifteenth-century house, remodelled internally in 1591 and altered again slightly in the eighteenth century. It may once have had an eastern wing, corresponding with that on the west side and containing the parlours suitable for a sixteenth-century gentleman; but the Aclands, still marrying profitably, left their old home early in the seventeenth century for a larger house in East Devon (Culm John, not far from their present house of Killerton) and Acland sank again to the level of a farmhouse. The east wing, if it existed, may have been demolished as a consequence. The Monks' house at Great Potheridge, over beyond the Torridge, similarly expanded from a farmhouse into a ducal mansion and then contracted again into a farmhouse, as we see it today.

About eight miles south-east of Acland Barton is Honiton Barton, a very attractive farmhouse rebuilt in 1676 by Anthony and Elizabeth Pawl. It is an E-shaped building, with projecting wings at either end of a central block, and a central porch, the whole plastered white. It seems to be of one date, outside and inside. Behind the house is the chapel, now derelict. This was built in 1730 by the Rev Lewis Southcomb, to whom the property had come, and was handsomely fitted up by him. He and his father were both buried here. The Southcombs were rectors of Rose Ash, a parish not far away, without a break from 1675 until 1941.

Although Honiton Barton is recorded in Domesday Book as Hunitona or 'honey farm', and has been a farm since Saxon times, its history is almost a complete blank. It was only a small manor in 1086, worth 5s a year, and like many other small Domesday estates in Devon it became attached to some larger manor and got all but swallowed up in it. It would, however, still have retained its separate identity as a freehold of the manor and its history could be retraced with sufficient patience and some luck.

Moving east and south from Honiton Barton we enter a wide upland district of lonely farms and hamlets, with few villages, and with much moory ground seven or eight hundred feet above sea level where the curlew is heard all day long in the spring.

Here, in the parish of Knowstone, we find the remote farm of
Wadham, and a couple of miles farther on, Shapcott Barton.
Wadham today is a pleasant but undistinguished farmhouse,
probably rebuilt in the eighteenth century. It is now notable
merely as the original home of the Wadhams, whose descendant
Nicholas founded Wadham College, Oxford, in 1612.

Wadham, too, has been occupied since before the Norman
Conquest. It was 'Wada's *hamm*' or enclosure, a small farm
lying all by itself from the beginning. In 1066 it belonged to the
Saxon Ulf, who was allowed to retain it in the general upheaval
that followed the Conquest. The Wadhams appear there early
in the thirteenth century, and it is not improbable that they
were descended from Ulf himself, with a good pre-Conquest
ancestry, though we cannot prove it. They had moved across
the county, however, before 1327, from the cold unrewarding
clays of the Exmoor foothills to the warm fertility of Edge
Barton in the parish of Branscombe, on the south coast. Here
they prospered. Sir John Wadham, one of Richard II's judges,
raised the family fortunes, adding greatly to their estates and
social position. His contemporary, Sir John Cary, Chief Baron
of the Exchequer, was also a Devonian and was similarly
making his name and fortune on the judicial bench. He had
been born at Cary Barton, in the far west of Devon, now a
rebuilt farmhouse and only interesting as the original home of
the Carys. By the fifteenth century the Cary estates stretched
from the north coast at Clovelly across to the south coast at
Cockington, and much of this came from the judge's pur-
chases.

But to return to Knowstone: Shapcott Barton is even lonelier
than Wadham, lost among the buzzard-haunted trees at the end
of an almost impossible lane. Although not recorded in Domesday under that name, Shapcott was in fact one of the four
small estates called Knowstone in that record. Later it took the
distinctive name of 'sheep cote', and it is interesting to see in the
Domesday record that sheep were even then the most numerous
of the livestock on the estate. Algar held Shapcote in 1066 and,
like Ulf up at Wadham, was allowed to keep it after the

Conquest. Here, too, we may have a family with a Saxon ancestry, for the Shapcotes were here in the thirteenth century, when the more detailed records begin. The last of them died at Exeter about the year 1770, but his Elizabethan home still survives in the backwoods. Indeed, it may be older than this in part. One enters it by the Elizabethan door, and on the right, leading into the hall, are the carved screens. The hall, with its great open fireplace, is just as it was left after the sixteenth-century reconstruction. At Shapcott (to give it its modern spelling) the dwelling-house and barns are all under one long roof, an unusual arrangement for an important farm.

Rashleigh Barton, on the hills above the Taw, has been described in *Country Life* (August 28th, 1915). It is recorded in Domesday, and was the home of the family of that name until Thomas Clotworthy married the heiress about the middle of the sixteenth century. It was his son Thomas who rebuilt the house about 1600–10 and put in the superb plaster ceilings for which the house is well known. The ceiling in the upper room, the so-called Cromwell room, is the finest, and is still in almost perfect condition. The interior of the house is still very much as Thomas Clotworthy knew it, though a person from Birmingham has removed a piece of the carved oak coat of arms over the mantelpiece as a souvenir. Apart from the house itself, there is much of interest in the layout of the farm buildings round a great open courtyard that is typical of large farms everywhere in Western Europe where cattle are more important than corn; and in the long, picturesque, and dilapidated shippons all down one side of the yard, and the tracks leading into the yard from all points of the compass. Most of the farm buildings seem to be of the same date as the house (Illus. 2). The stable has a good oak-framed doorway and oak-mullioned windows.

Rashleigh belonged until recently to the Tremaynes, who acquired it by marriage with the Clotworthy heiress in 1708. It had, until a few years ago, changed hands only twice (and never by purchase) since the thirteenth century, when the Rashleighs had it, and perhaps only three times since Domesday. It is comforting to come across such solidity and resistance to change in the modern world.

Only five miles to the south-east of Rashleigh, on a steep hill above the valley of the Yeo, stands Bury Barton, with a detached medieval chapel beside the roadside, now used as an implement-shed. The farmstead itself is a good example of a large barton arranged around a courtyard, with the dwelling-house along the side farthest from the road and massive farm buildings around the other three sides of the yard. The entrance from the road lies through a gateway in the side facing the house.

Bury takes its name from some earthwork (*burh*) which must formerly have occupied the summit of the ridge on which the farmstead now stands, commanding the two valleys of the Yeo and the Dalch and a wide stretch of country to the east. No trace remains of this earthwork today. It was presumably a small hill-top camp of the type usually found in the late Iron Age, immediately preceding the Roman conquest. When the first Saxon settlers re-occupied the old site – most probably in the eighth century or possibly the ninth – this earthwork gave its name to the new farm. It is called *Beria* in Domesday Book and was then a small manor belonging to the bishop of Exeter, having been given to the monastery at Exeter by Athelstan early in the tenth century. In 1086 it seems to have consisted of three or four small farms, covering about three hundred acres in all and worth 7*s* 6*d* a year.

At some unknown date this small manor was granted by the bishop to the ancestor of the Burys, who subsequently took their name from their estate. No record of the Burys has yet come to light before the early part of the fifteenth century, when they had already acquired Colleton Barton, farther down the Taw valley, also on a steep hillside like Bury. They seem to have made Colleton their chief residence from then onwards, and to have largely rebuilt the house, as it now stands, in the early seventeenth century. The gatehouse, with the chapel above, is however early fifteenth century in date, probably built about 1402 when Bishop Stafford licensed a chapel at Colleton.

To return to Bury, however, we are safe in assuming that the
Burys began here in the thirteenth century, if not somewhat
sooner, and like so many of these ancient freeholders expanded
their estates by judicious marriages. By the end of the fifteenth
century we know that they held the manor of Colleton and
some thirty-seven other farms in sixteen or seventeen parishes
in this part of Devon. In their origin as small freeholders on an
episcopal manor, and their rise into the ranks of the squirearchy
by the late fifteenth century by means of successful marriages,
they closely resemble the Aclands, who have already been mentioned.

The chapel now standing by the roadside near the farm is
pretty certainly that dedicated to St James the Apostle, in the
parish of Lapford, which was licensed by the bishop in 1434.
It is built of rubble masonry, in the dark local dunstone so
commonly found in this part of Devon, and is substantially a
fifteenth-century building in fairly good order. The east
window retains its original tracery, the south doorway is also
original, and so, too, is the arched brace roof. Although it has
lost some of its features as a chapel, it is still one of the best-
preserved examples of its kind in the county.

The barton itself is partly of early sixteenth-century date
and partly of a hundred years later. The reconstruction of the
early seventeenth century is probably the work of John Bury
who married Mary, the daughter of Arthur Arscott of Tetcott,
about 1620. Their arms and initials appear on the plaster coat
of arms over the mantelpiece in what was the hall of the Tudor
and Jacobean house. John's father – Humphrey Bury
(1584–1631) – had rebuilt Colleton about 1612 and was living
there. Bury was evidently regarded as their second house, the
residence of the eldest son and his wife before they succeeded to
the estates. Colleton is still a much finer house with its beautiful Jacobean plaster ceilings in the hall, dining-room, and
drawing-room; and its drawing-room panelled with carved oak
and adorned with the coats of arms of the Burys and their allied
families.

Although Bury starts in recorded history as a Domesday

manor, it became attached soon afterwards, like so many small
Domesday estates in Devon, to a larger manor under the same
lord, and was treated thereafter as a free tenement of the latter
– just like Honiton Barton, and the manor of South Molton.
Colleton, on the other hand, seems to have begun as a post-
Conquest tenement held in socage of the manor of Chulmleigh
for a rent of 20s a year. It was on these terms that Roger Cole
held it in 1242, when its existence is first recorded. It took its
name from one Cole or Cola (*Cola's farm*) who was in all probability the father or grandfather of this Roger. Roger got his
surname as Roger (son of) Cole. If this Cole was the first man
to settle and colonize the farm on the edge of the manor of
Chulmleigh, as is implied by his name being attached to the
farm, then Colleton must have originated in the closing years of
the twelfth century, or the early years of the thirteenth. By the
late fifteenth century, however, when Colleton had become the
chief residence of the Burys, the centre of their considerable and
widespread estates, it acquired the title of manor (just as
Traymill did for the same reason) and appears in the inquisition
of 1502 on William Bury's lands as the manor of Colleton, held
of Edward, earl of Devon, by knight service. The last of the
Burys died here in 1804, and his widow left the estates to Captain Richard Incledon, who took the name of Bury. He died in
1825 leaving two daughters, one of whom (Penelope) married
in 1830 the notorious hunting parson, Jack Russell. Russell was
notorious even in a diocese where it was reckoned that twenty
parsons kept packs of hounds. He ran through £50,000 of his
wife's money, beggared and sold off the estates, and Colleton
reverted to a farmhouse and went down rapidly. It is recorded,
among many tales of Russell, that upon one occasion when he
was trying out a possible new curate by testing his abilities with
a hunter, the curate remarked how bare of trees Russell's lands
were. 'Ah!' said Russell, 'the hounds eat 'em'. The day of such
sporting ruffians is fortunately over for good; and Colleton has
been rescued and restored to its former dignity.

Upcott Barton, in the little-known country between the Exe
and the Taw, is in some ways a more interesting house than

either Bury or Colleton, both as a building and for its historical associations. It lies in the parish of Cheriton Fitzpaine, getting on for two miles north of the village, on a hillside rising sharply from a deep and narrow combe in which the Holly Water flows rapidly down to join the Creedy. It is approached up a very steep lane turning off yet another lane, the whole setting very remote and beautiful, and then one comes upon the stone walls of the outer courtyard, mottled grey and green with lichens, with the roofs of the barton rising behind, beyond an inner gateway flanked by brick piers of Queen Anne's time.

The cypresses that used to grow here are now gone, all but one, the gardens are a wilderness, and the bowling-green on the hill behind the house is a haunt for rabbits, but the house still keeps much of its ancient character and dignity though it has long been a farmhouse. It stands on a small plateau below the summit of the hill, sheltered on the north by higher ground (where the bowling-green lies) and by a large clump of chestnuts planted as a windbreak. It faces south down a precipitous slope, the other three sides of the farmstead being formed by continuous high walls or farm buildings. One enters the outer courtyard between high stone walls of rubble masonry, and then passes through another gateway to the inner yard in front of the house. Though the house at first sight has all the appearance of a late sixteenth-century building, with its oak-mullioned windows and its fine porch carried on oak timbers elaborately carved, it turns out upon closer inspection to be substantially a medieval house (probably early fifteenth century) which was modernized, as so often in Devon, late in the sixteenth or early in the seventeenth century. The façade may well be entirely late Elizabethan in date, but according to the present farmer there are two thick walls at the front of the house with a cavity some 18 ins wide between them which may represent the original medieval wall and an Elizabethan one constructed in front of it.

Internally, there are two late Elizabethan staircases and an elaborately decorated plaster ceiling in the room at the west end of the house, now a parlour and probably so originally.

Among the motifs of the ceiling are the three moorcocks from the arms of the Moores, who acquired Upcott by marriage about 1620. There are rabbits, fishes, bunches of grapes and vine-leaves, strawberries, tulips, and peas in pods all represented in this ceiling. Over the fireplace is a sporting picture painted in oils on a wooden panel, showing sportsmen with guns and pheasants, probably of the same date as the ceiling (*c* 1610–20). There are two other decorated ceilings upstairs, one with a Tudor rose in the centre, both rather poor and dilapidated now.

At the east end of the dwelling-house, above the kitchen, is a largish room, entered through a fifteenth-century oak doorway, which has its original wagon roof thinly disguised under a later ceiling. Here again mullioned windows of late sixteenth-century date have been inserted. A small closet opens off this room, in the north wall, probably a garderobe. The whole north wall of the house seems to be of fifteenth-century rubble masonry with two contemporary chimney-stacks.

This fifteenth-century room at the east end of the house one might have suspected to have been the chapel, which we know was here in 1455 when Nicholas Radford lived here, but for two pieces of evidence which tell against it. One is that according to Polwhele, quoting from 'an old MS', John Moore converted the chapel into a cider-house upon taking up his residence at Upcott. If this is so, the chapel must have been in a separate building as it was at Bury and Ayshford and other bartons in the county. The other piece of evidence is that the room seems to have been a bedroom throughout the sixteenth century, with a mullioned window in its east wall and a garderobe in the north wall. One might have hazarded the guess that the medieval chapel had been converted into a bedroom after the Reformation, when most of these private chapels were desecrated (compare that at Acland, for example) but for the fact that the Courtenays, who lived here from Henry VIII's time up to the end of James I's and perhaps a few years after that, remained true to the Catholic faith during all that time and almost certainly continued to make use of their chapel.

Certainly they would not have turned it into a bedroom. We must therefore look upon the room as perhaps the best bedroom of the fifteenth-century house, and the garderobe as an original feature.

Upcott was a free man's estate before the Norman Conquest and has remained so through all its history. It belongs today to the farmer, though it has been shorn of some 90 of its original 300 acres. In Domesday Book it was part of an estate called *Estocheleia*, which may be identified beyond doubt as South Stockleigh *alias* Sutton Satchvill in Cheriton Fitzpaine together with Upcott. It was then held by Alured the Cup-bearer under the count of Mortain, but in 1066 had been held by Orgar who, we are told, 'was the man of Edmeratorius, but could go with that land to what lord he liked'.

By the early thirteenth century Upcott had become sep-arately distinguished by name and had given its name to its owners. We find Gervas de Upcote installed here in 1242. In the time of Henry VI – probably in the 1430s – it was purchased by the lawyer Nicholas Radford, who was murdered here in 1455, as we shall see, and thence passed to a younger branch of the Courtenays of Powderham. The first of this line was James, a younger son of Sir William Courtenay, who took up his resi-dence at Upcott in the time of Henry VIII according to Pole. The Courtenays held the estate for about a hundred years until the 1620s or 30s, and from them it passed to the Moores by marriage with their heiress. The Courtenays had also thrown out a new branch at West Molland in the late fifteenth century. All three branches of this great family – at Powderham, West Molland, and Upcott – remained true to the old faith after the Elizabethan settlement. Those at Powderham were certainly Catholics until towards the middle of the seventeenth century; at West Molland they remained Catholics until the end of the family in 1732; and so they remained at Upcott also, until their end there. The Recusant Roll for 1592–3 (published by the Catholic Record Society, vol XVIII) records James Courtenay of Cheriton Fitzpaine as owing the staggering sum of £1,360 in fines for his recusancy. Under the Act of 1581 a fine of £20 a month had been laid down for refusal to attend the service prescribed by the Act of Uniformity. James Courtenay's fines had accumulated over a period of sixty-eight months at that rate. Such ferocious fines were intended to cripple the Catholic families and to bring them to submission through financial distress, for it was agreed that imprisonment 'by sparing their housekeeping greatly enricheth them'. James Courtenay persisted in his recusancy and apparently kept his private chapel intact: it was left for his Protestant son-in-law to turn it into a cider-house.

The Courtenays had been associated (if that is the word) with Upcott some forty or fifty years before they came to own it. Nicholas Radford, who then owned the estate and lived at the house, was an important legal figure in Devon during the second quarter of the fifteenth century. In 1422, during the minority of the then earl of Devon, he had been appointed as one of the stewards of the earl's lands; later he became godfather to the earl's second son, Henry. He was thus closely associated with the Courtenays, who had one of their principal residences at Tiverton castle, only a few miles away. In some way, however, he incurred their powerful enmity: William of Worcester says that he acted for the Bonvilles in some dispute with the Courtenays. This alone would have been sufficient cause, for the feud of the Bonvilles and the Courtenays in Devon was the most long-standing and bitter political feud in the county, between its two greatest families. Whatever the precise cause of the Courtenays' rancour against Radford, it was enough to lead to his brutal murder in the lane just below his own gates.

On Thursday October 23rd, in the year 1455, Sir Thomas Courtenay, the eldest son of the earl of Devon, rode out from Tiverton with a large party, some ninety-four armed men, and reached Upcott at midnight. Radford and his wife, and all their servants, were in bed, and the great outer gates were shut and barred. The invaders surrounded the place, and set the gates on fire. Radford, hearing the loud noise and tumult, awoke and opened the window of his chamber, whereupon Courtenay told him to come down and speak with him, promising Radford no harm to himself or his property. Radford thereupon came down and opened the gates, the whole mob pressed into the courtyard, but Courtenay assured him once again that he would come to no harm. Courtenay and Radford then ate and drank wine together, but in the meanwhile Courtenay's men were pillaging the rest of the house and the chapel and loading their horses with the spoil.

Radford was then persuaded to go with the party, being told that the earl wished to speak with him at Tiverton. A stone's throw from his own gateway Sir Thomas Courtenay bade him farewell and rode on down the lane into the night. Immediately Radford was murdered with the greatest brutality by several of Courtenay's men and left mangled in the lane. On the following Monday, Henry Courtenay, his own godson, rode out from Tiverton castle with another party, compelled Radford's servants to carry their master's body to Cheriton Fitzpaine church to the accompaniment of derisory songs, and there took his body out of the chest it was in, tumbled it naked into the open grave and hurled down upon it the stones which Radford had previously purchased for his own tomb, with no more compassion, says the record, than if he had been a Jew or a pagan. The detailed story may be read in the indictment in the Public Record Office, and has been told also in the *Transactions* of the Devonshire Association for 1903. The news of the murder is also referred to at some length in the Paston Letters. The farmstead of Upcott looks substantially as it did on that October night: not much has changed, especially if one sees it in a sombre autumn twilight. And the farmer, late one night some years ago, heard a great clattering of horses in the outer yard which came nearer and eventually reached the inner court. There were no voices, only the sound of many horses moving about. But his own horses the next morning were exactly where he had locked them up the night before.

Miles away across Devon is Westcott Barton, on the borders of Marwood parish, another Domesday estate and one of the old homes of the ubiquitous Chichester family, whose mem-

orials and houses are to be found all over North Devon. Ayshford Barton, near the Somerset border, was the home of the
Ayshfords from Henry I's time until 1688. The monument to
the last of the Ayshfords is on the wall of the little fifteenth-
century chapel that stands in the meadows near the house. And
so one could go on all over Devon, for every parish has at least
one such farmhouse, and some have three or four, each with its
own peculiar history. A whole book could be written about
them. They, and the men and women they nourished, are a
most distinctive part of the social history of England; from
them have sprung the great majority of the historic families of
Devon.

CHAPTER FOUR

A Sheaf of Modern Documents

An East Devon Yeoman

THE GREATEST disaster in the world of English archives in recent times was the destruction of the probate registry in Exeter in World War II. In one night in May 1942 the entire contents of the registry in Bedford Circus perished for ever: probably a hundred thousand wills and perhaps half that number of inventories. The loss of the wills was an irreparable disaster for genealogists, for only a small fraction had ever been copied; and the destruction of the inventories was a major blow to the writing of the social history of Devon as a whole.

Even now too few people, in compiling the history of an ordinary family, for which private records rarely exist in any number, know of the inventories of personal estate that were drawn up for the purpose of proving a man's will in the ecclesiastical courts. These inventories were usually attached to the appropriate wills, though at certain dates, and in some registries, they appear to have been bundled separately under their respective years. They represent the valuation of a man's personal estate or movable goods, at prices current at the time, assessed usually by neighbours and relatives of the dead person.

The detail given varies considerably. Generally speaking, the poorer a man's possessions the fuller the information; every item of a man's clothes, eating and cooking utensils, and furniture, will be carefully noted and priced. In larger and more opulent houses there is often less detail – the deceased's clothes are valued as a whole, for example, and we do not get each different item catalogued – but there is still enough in most cases to

enable us to reconstruct a picture of the house of three or four
centuries ago, the layout of the rooms, the furniture, domestic
utensils, farm gear, livestock, crops, and all the paraphernalia
of past life. Generally speaking, too, my own experience is that
the earlier inventories are often more detailed than the later
ones. They are good from Henry VIII's reign (when the series
usually begins) up to the early eighteenth century; after that
they tend to be rather perfunctory and we miss many of the
lively little details of earlier generations; and after about 1760
they tend to disappear altogether in favour of a bare and colour-
less statement that the deceased's effects were worth so many
hundred or thousand pounds.

Neither the family historian nor the historian of town or
village can present a real picture of the past without the aid of
these records, which yield all sorts of oddments of social and
domestic history that we find nowhere else at all. We can, for
example, follow changes in farming practice by reading the
inventories of one district over a period of, say, two hundred
years; we observe the introduction and spread of new im-
plements, and changes in clothes, furniture, and fashions generally; we observe the rise of some families to opulence as the
generations succeed one another, from husbandman to yeoman,
and on to gentleman and esquire; and we perceive gentility
creeping into a farming family when the inventory mentions
'chamber pots' where once an outside wall had been good
enough. We see other families slowly sinking over several generations; and we can trace through the inventories changes in
the local building style and plan, when kitchens first became
common in farmhouse and cottage, when two-floored houses
began to replace those with only one floor and people began to
sleep upstairs and to keep the parlour for a sitting-room rather
than a bedroom; all these things and many more can be un-
earthed from these interesting documents if one reads a
sufficient number of them to form general impressions. They
provide an inexhaustible store of information on matters of
social and domestic history, whether of a family or a village,
and this note upon an ancestor of mine is intended mainly to

illustrate in a modest and limited way the sort of picture one may reconstruct of the domestic arrangements of three centuries ago on an East Devon farm. I was fortunate in that I discovered the inventory and copied it just before the war began, or I would never afterwards have known of its existence.

George Hoskyns, of whom I write, was baptized at Stoke Abbott in Dorset on March 25th, 1563. He was a son of Thomas Hoskyns, born about 1524 at Beaminster, a little market-town about two miles away, where the family had been settled since the days of Henry V, if not somewhat earlier. They had come to Beaminster from just over the Wiltshire border, from Ebblesbourne, a village between Shaftesbury and Salisbury. Thomas Hoskyns was a parishioner of this place and a juror at an inquisition here in 1341.

The Beaminster branch of the family prospered exceedingly during the fifteenth and sixteenth centuries, some becoming bailiffs of the manor, others constables of the town. In the subsidy list of 1524 the eight members of the family then living in Beaminster were assessed to pay practically a third of the tax demanded from the entire town. In 1538 Henry Hoskyns took a long lease of the manor of Beaminster Secunda, and in 1598 his son John acquired the lease of the other Beaminster manor. Both acquired much other property also, attaining the social status of esquire and a coat of arms, and rising in the early seventeenth century to the dignity of refusing a knighthood.

George Hoskyns came of a younger branch of this family. He was therefore fairly well-to-do and enjoyed a standard of living and education well beyond that of most Devonshire yeoman farmers. He could read and write, play the treble viol, and he drank wine instead of the ale or cider consumed by all around him.

On February 9th, 1548, when he was barely 21 years of age, he married Margaret, the daughter of John Pulman, a yeoman of Luppitt in East Devon. They were married in George's own church of Stoke Abbott and the first-born of the marriage was christened George in the same church on November 27th of the same year. After that there are no more children christened at

Stoke Abbott until 1594 (though many were born) and it seems
clear from other evidence that George Hoskyns moved to Luppitt in 1585 and began farming there. His farm was probably
Overday, high up on the hill behind Luppitt church, which the
family possessed in 1702 (church rate). The inventory of his
personal estate speaks of crops in the ground and in the barns at
Luppitt in 1626, and it seems likely that this refers to Overday
Farm, which the family continued to own until 1828. It is
possible that George's father had set him up in this farm in
1585. In the subsidy of 1628 Robert Hoskins, probably the
second son of George, was assessed 'on lands', indicating ownership and not merely the occupation of a farm.

In the autumn of 1593 George's father died at Stoke Abbott,
and he was obliged to return to his native village for a time.
Upon his return to Devon, however, probably about 1596–7,
he settled at Axmouth and later left his Luppitt farm to his son
Robert. On December 1st, 1614, as his will informs us, he took
a lease of another farm for the usual term of ninety-nine years
or three lives from John Drake of Ashe, esquire. This farm, of
which unfortunately I do not know the name, was probably in
the adjacent parish of Musbury, where his son George, to
whom he left it in his will, was rated in the 1640s.

It is clear from George Hoskyns's inventory that he was a
sheep-farmer on a large scale by Devonshire standards, and the
chalky downland behind Axmouth and Musbury must have
been admirably suited to this kind of farming. Indeed, it is very
likely that his Dorset ancestors had risen to affluence in the
same way during the fifteenth century, and especially during
the first half of the sixteenth century, when wool prices were
rising rapidly all the time. Sheep were the most profitable thing
for a farmer, and the downland that almost encircles the little
town of Beaminster produced some of the best Dorset
fleeces.

At the time of his death, in the last days of December 1625,
George Hoskyns was the most well-to-do farmer in the district.
The inventory of his personal estate amounts to £704 19s 10d,
or about £7,000 or £8,000 in modern money, and is, indeed,

the largest total I have come across for a yeoman. The average yeoman at this time left between £100 and £200 in personal estate, many left only £50 to £100.

He was what Westcote, who wrote about this time, called 'a yeoman of the better sort' who kept a good house and a man-servant, who did not push the plough himself but directed operations. According to Westcote, this sort of yeoman 'speaketh to his servants as a prince to his subjects, in the plural number, we will do this, or, let us do that; we will set forward such a business . . .'

He made his will on December 20th, 1625, and died within a few days at the age of 62, being buried at Axmouth on January 1st, 1626. On the following day, as was customary, an inventory was made of his worldly goods, and this was exhibited at Honiton with the will when the latter was proved on April 12th, 1626. To his eldest son, George, was left the lease of the Musbury farm, out of which he had to pay an annuity of £20 to his mother Margaret. The four unmarried children were left £100 each, to be paid on the occasion of their marriage – about £1,000 each in modern values; and the three married daughters were left smaller sums and a trifle for each of their children. After the death of Margaret, the widow, the two unmarried sons, to whom George Hoskyns could leave no farm, were to receive £10 apiece of the annuity, with a further sum of £5 upon the birth of each child after their marriage. Finally he left 10s to the poor of Axmouth, a similar sum to the poor of Musbury and Stoke Abbott, 7s to the poor of Luppitt and 3s to the poor of Combpyne. This last bequest suggests that he was farming a certain amount of land in Combpyne also.

An Inventory of all the goods Chattells and Debts of George Hoskenes yeoman late of Axmouth deceased taken and praysed the second daye of January anno 1625 by Thomas Serle, Gawen Ford, Francys Pulman, Symon Hoskyns & Richard Cox as followeth –

Imprimis his wearing Apparell   v^{li}
Itm one tablebord one Cubbord w_{th}
    Chayres stooles and formes in the hall   i^{ll}   vj^s   viij^d

Itm five flitches & halfe of Bacon   ij^{li}.   x^s

Itm a dozen and halfe of pewter
    dishes   i^{li}

Itm a bible wth other little Bookes   vj^s viij^d

Itm one silver spoone   iiij^s

Itm a treble viall   iiij^s

Itm wooll & Loakes   xxvj^{li}

Itm butter & Cheese   vij^{li}

Itm tallowe & grease   xiiij^s

Itm two standing bedsteeds wth
    feather beds belonginge to the
    same furnished   vij^{li}

Itm seaven other bedsteeds wth dust
    beds belonging unto them fur-
    nished   v^{li}

Itm fower payre of Sheets   i^{li} vj^s viij^d

Itm three boardclothes & halfe a
    dozen of Napkins   x^s

Itm a Spruce Chest   ij^{li}

Itm fower other small Coffers   x^s

Itm two Cheeseracks   xviij^s

Itm Leather   vj^s viij^d

Itm a garner   x^s

Itm in salt beefe & porke   i^{li} x^s

Itm two payre of Wayne wheeles
    one wayne wth all manner of
    plough stuffe   x^{li}

Itm Shovells, mattacks, peckaxes,
    Hatchetts hookes wth all other
    husbandry tooles   i^{li} v^s

Itm one Hackney saddle on side
    saddle tenn pack saddles wth all
    manner furniture to them be-
    longing   ij^{li} x^s

Itm a Silver wring   iij^{li}

Itm tenn brasse panns   iij^{li}

Itm two brasse Crocks & one
    Cauldron   i^{li} x^s

Itm brewing tubbs, Bucketts, payles,
    wth other such vessells   ij^{li}

Itm five hogsheads wyne barrells wth

all manner of wooden vessells	ij^{li}		
Itm a Gridiron a Chaferdishe Andirons two spitts & potthookes		x^s	
Itm a fornace	i^{li}		
Itm five oxen & one steere	xxvj^{li}		
Itm seaventeene kine	li^{li}		
Itm a fatt Cowe & one fatt steere	viij^{li}		
Itm eight yearlings	viij^{li}		
Itm nyne beast of two yere old	xviij^{li}		
Itm six others of three yeers old	xviij^{li}		
Itm eleven horses and one mare	xxx^{li}		
Itm fortie eight fatt weders	xxvj^{li}		
Itm 100 sheepe of one yeere old	xx^{li}		
Itm three hundred fortie five other sheepe	cx^{li}		
Itm six piggs & one sowe	v^{li}		
Itm powltrie		iiij^s	
Itm Wheate threshed & in mowes	xxx^{li}		
Itm Wheate in ground newly sowen 24 acres	xx^{li}		
Itm barlie threshed & in mowes	xxxvij^{li}		
Itm oats & peese in mowes & in the barne	xxvj^{li}		
Itm Corne in the barne & in mowes at Luppitt	xxxvj^{li}		
Itm Wheate in ground at Luppitt 7 acres	iij^{li}		
Itm hay & fodder	xvj^{li}		
Itm Tymber wood & furse	xx^{li}		
Itm Chattle lease	c^{li}		
Itm in Debts and reddy money	x^{li}		
Itm Armour	i^{li}		
Itm in small trifles & thinges forgotten	i^{li}		
Sum total	vij^{c}iiij^{li}	xix^s	x^d

(exhibited at Honiton April 12th, 1626)

This inventory gives us a good picture of a large farmer with land in three or four parishes, and nearly five hundred sheep, forty-eight cattle of all sorts, and a dozen horses. He also grew much corn (wheat, barley, and oats) and a considerable acreage of peas, which were a staple article of diet in those days. In other items of the list we catch a glimpse of Elizabethan times through most of which George had lived: the Bible in English, the treble viol, the armour of his younger days (perhaps used in 1588), and the wine barrels.

As was usual at the time, the great bulk of George's personal estate was composed of his farm goods, the implements, live-stock, crops, and the lease; in all these amounted to just over £650, leaving about £50 for the total value of his household goods, the furniture, linen, brass and pewter ware, and kitchen stuff.

The livestock and their produce accounted for just a half of the total value of the inventory – £353 in all. Of this the sheep were worth £146, cattle £129, horses £30, and pigs £5. In addition, the wool was worth £26 and the butter and cheese another £7. The crops in barns and ricks and newly sown am-ounted to £152, with another £16 for hay and fodder. Timber and furze amounted to the large sum of £20, and finally there was the value of the lease, £100. The farm gear and im-plements were worth in all £11 5s 0d.

The inventory does not, as such documents often do, proceed from room to room in the farmhouse, listing the furniture and other goods in each and so giving us an idea of the plan and size of the house. But the inventory of Margaret, George Hoskyns's widow, who died in March 1630, supplies the missing infor-mation. In the hall, which was the principal living-room en-tered directly from the porch, stood the long table at which all fed together, some seated on chairs, others on stools, and the farm-servants and children on the forms. In one corner of the hall stood the cupboard which is specially mentioned in the in-ventory, probably a kind of dresser on which stood the dozen and a half pewter dishes. The spruce chest also stood in the hall, and probably contained the linen – the tablecloths, napkins, sheets, and so forth – while on a shelf were the Bible and the other books that George read by the fire in the long winter evenings.

Behind the hall, in all probability, lay the kitchen, which seems to have been of about equal length, for over both rooms were an eastern and a western chamber, ie, bedroom. The 'little chamber over the enterie' was also used as a bedroom; that is, a room over the porch by which one entered most Devon farm-houses. In the kitchen stood the fine array of brassware, the ten pans, the crocks, and the cauldron, while around and in the fireplace were the spits, the gridiron, the andirons (on which the spits rested), the pot-hooks in the chimney, and a chafing-dish. The house was lighted by candles, as witness the large amount of tallow and grease in the inventory, for these were all made at home by the women of the household. Beyond the kitchen lay the farm offices – the buttery, which actually contained butter in large quantities in Margaret's day, and not bottles. Her inventory mentions a barrel and a half of butter, worth the considerable sum of £1 6s 8d. Then there were the milk-house, the larder-house, the old kitchen, and the brewhouse. Most farms of any size brewed their own beer, the malt-house or the brew-house figures in most yeoman inventories in these centuries. Beyond this again were the cheese-chamber, the bacon-chamber, and the apple-chamber, and lastly the stable, the stalls, and the barn. The latter were all grouped around a large yard, with the house forming the fourth side, probably on the north. Such was a typical Devon farmhouse of the larger sort in the early seventeenth century.

George Hoskyns's fairly substantial estate was divided up among his numerous children (five sons and five daughters), none of whom appears to have left as much at death as he had done. Indeed, after leaving Dorset, where they had been energetic and acquisitive, the family never exerted itself to any conspicuous extent in the enervating climate of Devon, but generation after generation were content to get a modest competence from farming and nothing beyond. Then came the long and severe depression in agriculture following the boom of the Napoleonic Wars and nothing remained but to come to the town and start again; and so about the year 1825 my great-grandfather arrived in Exeter to seek a living as a baker. He started on his own account in 1834, and the business ended only in 1945 when my father retired.

Devon Ports in the Early Eighteenth Century

A paper at the Public Record Office (CO 390/8) gives an account of the number and tonnage of ships cleared from English ports in the foreign trade only, between Christmas 1714 and Christmas 1717. A summary table for the Devonshire ports alone is as follows:

Port	Ships cleared (1714–17)	Tonnage cleared	Average tonnage per ship
Exeter	277	14,552	52½
Plymouth	242	12,497	51½
Bideford	218	9,723	44½
Dartmouth	132	4,927	37
Barnstaple	73	3,667	50
Ilfracombe	29	1,167	40

Exeter is first among the ports of Devon, though fourteenth in the list for the whole kingdom. This contrasts remarkably with the position in 1702, when, according to a return given in Macpherson, *Annals of Commerce* (II, p 719), Exeter was the fourth largest port in the country in point of ships registered in the port, surpassed only by London, Bristol, and Yarmouth. Within a dozen or fifteen years of this date Exeter was already losing ground rapidly; the reign of Anne was the most prosperous time in the history of the port. Bideford, too, as we shall see, lost much trade after 1714.

In 1714–17 Exeter, Plymouth, and Bideford were the only ports of any consequence in the county. The small average tonnage at all ports will be noticed, especially that of Dartmouth, a quarter of whose outward trade was with Jersey and Guernsey, just across the Channel. Another quarter of Dartmouth's trade was accounted for by Newfoundland and Rotterdam; the remainder was with a score of ports in North America and Europe.

The chief outlets for the trade of Exeter were Rotterdam (45 ships, 2,089 tons), Lisbon (23 ships, 1,672 tons), Oporto (28 ships, 1,118 tons) – all markets for Exeter woollens – and Newfoundland (22 ships, 1,469 tons) and New England (26 ships, 1,567 tons). Other important woollen markets for Exeter goods were Ostend, Hamburg, and Bilbao.

The South-Western ports were the stronghold of the Newfoundland trade. Of the 186 vessels sent out to Newfoundland in 1698–1700, 92 sailed from South-Western ports, Topsham alone (in the port of Exeter), sending 34 vessels. Even later in the century, when the trade had fallen away, Exeter (or more particularly the havens of Topsham and Teignmouth) remained the most important centre in the South West. An Act passed in 1778, fixing the quantities of wheat-flour, peas, and biscuits allowed to be exported 'for the use of the fisheries at Newfoundland, Nova Scotia, and Labrador', probably indicates also the proportion of the fishing trade of these ports. Poole in Dorset was allowed to export 5,900 quarters and tuns, Topsham and Teignmouth 4,700, Dartmouth 4,400, and London 3,150. The collapse of the Newfoundland trade in the North Devon ports is shown by Barnstaple's meagre quota of 700 quarters and tuns.

Plymouth's trade was to a very large extent with North America, from New England down to the Barbados. The New England trade accounted for 1,784 tons; the Plantations trade (Virginia, Maryland, etc) for 1,130 tons; the West Indian trade for 1,680 tons. Altogether, nearly 40 per cent of Plymouth's outward foreign trade was with North America, unlike that of Exeter, which was predominantly in the direction of Europe.

Plymouth had, too, a considerable cross-Channel trade with Jersey and Guernsey, though the average cargo was very small, barely twenty tons. She had also an appreciable connexion with Spanish ports (Bilbao and Alicante) and with Leghorn in Italy.

Bideford, long the rival of Barnstaple in North Devon, was in the early eighteenth century incomparably the more important. Inwards, Bideford's most flourishing trade was that in tobacco from Virginia and Maryland, begun a century earlier.

Sir Richard Grenville, lord of the manor of Bideford, had made expeditions to Carolina and Virginia, in which Bideford had had some share, chiefly in providing the mariners. When the Plantations trade began to open up in the time of James I, Bideford took a leading part and some of her merchants acquired 'extensive possessions' in those parts. The Newfoundland trade also attracted Bideford ships in the seventeenth century, and by 1714–17 fully one-third of the trade of the port was with Newfoundland.

Bideford had suffered greatly, however, from the attempts of the French during the reign of Anne to share the Newfoundland fishery. Her merchants sustained great losses for which, as Watkins records, they got no compensation from the government. This, together with French privateering in 'the Golden Bay' beyond Appledore Bar, gave such a shock to the trade of both Barnstaple and Bideford that it was 'never afterwards thoroughly repaired'. The Newfoundland trade had greatly diminished by 1720, that to Maryland and Virginia ceased about 1760, and to every part of America by 1772–4.

In 1714–17, however, the Plantations trade accounted for a quarter of Bideford's trade, the greater part being the tobacco trade from Virginia. Thus about 60 per cent of her outward foreign trade was with North America. Most of the remainder was with Ireland (Waterford, Cork, and Dublin), amounting to 2,215 tons. This was mostly return cargoes for the Irish wool and yarn imported at Bideford and sent by pack-horse to the inland manufacturing towns of Devonshire, as far as Exeter.

Magna Britannia (1720) calls Bideford 'one of the best trading towns in England' and tells us that she had 'almost drawn away the trade of Barnstaple', chiefly because of the silting up of the Taw at Barnstaple. The return for 1714–17 shows indeed that Barnstaple's outward foreign trade was hardly more than one-third that of Bideford, and was much the same in character, except that she had no considerable trade with the Plantations.

A Treasury paper at the Public Record Office (T 1/278 shows that Barnstaple's tobacco trade rose suddenly after 1726, and where before it had been but a tenth of that of Bideford it now greatly exceeded it in some years. Of the 20¾ million lb imported at all Devonshire ports between Christmas 1721 and Christmas 1731, Bideford and Barnstaple took between them some 13½ million lb, of which the latter received rather more than 5 million lb. The bulk of this great import was re-exported to Holland and France.

Barnstaple's outward trade was highly specialized: in 1714–17 nearly 60 per cent of the tonnage went to Newfoundland. No other trade was of any outstanding importance, except perhaps that with Ireland (especially with Cork), while the New England trade was an appreciable trifle.

Ilfracombe's foreign trade was insignificant; hardly one ship a month left for foreign parts, and of those practically half went to Ireland, a hundred miles beyond the dim blue tableland of Lundy. Most Ilfracombe ships went to Cork; a few to Barbados. All the North Devon ports had a considerable coal trade from Milford, Tenby, Swansea, and Neath, across the Bristol Channel. Most of the coal was used, not in domestic fires, but in the lime-kilns that by this date were dotted along the broad estuaries of the Taw and Torridge, for lime was now the widely used, and often misused, fertilizer for the fields of Devon.

The Lysons Correspondence

When the brothers Samuel Lysons and the Rev Daniel Lysons were gathering material for their history of Devon – a work which appeared in two parts in the year 1822 and is still by far the most useful history of the county – they corresponded for some years with the gentry and parsons all over Devon.* The letters of this regiment of correspondents are now preserved in

* Devon was the ninth and last county to be published by the Lysons, whose great project began with Bedfordshire (1806) and proceeded county by county in alphabetical order. It was to have covered the whole country under the general title of *Magna Britannia*. Samuel Lysons died, however, in 1819 at the age of fifty-five. The correspondence makes it clear that for a time his brother thought of abandoning the Devonshire history as a result of this blow. He completed it, but no other counties appeared.

five bulky volumes in the British Museum (Additional Manu-
scripts nos 9426–30) and contain a considerable amount of information about most of the parishes in the county which
could not be used in the published history, besides often being
entertaining in themselves. Occasionally, there are scandals
which the Lysons thought it wiser not to print, but mostly the
tales are harmless enough, and there is a good deal of social
history for the parish historian.

A correspondent at Silverton, a large village about seven
miles north of Exeter, writing on June 5th, 1820, said that four-
fifths of the population lived in 'the Town', which is denomi-
nated 'the Borough'. We do, indeed, find Silverton called a
borough in 1321, probably on the strength of having a weekly
market and a fair. The market had been discontinued about
thirty-five years ago, wrote the Silverton correspondent – 'the
period when a butcher first settled in the place'. This is a nice
little piece of social history. Two cattle fairs were still held,
however – on the first Thursday in March and July. The fair in
September was now held 'solely for the amusement of the
poorer class of people', but it was merely the ghost of former
times.

Another letter, this time from Nicholas Carlisle, the topo-
grapher and antiquary, warned the Rev Daniel Lysons that he
would get little help for his history at Exeter. 'As to the
Chamber of Exeter you will find them jealous and illiberal in
all their measures – and their Town Clerk knows *nothing* of
their documents. Our Commissioners [the Charity Com-
missioners] have not yet been there, but I hope they will go this
Summer, when I understand there will be a fine harvest for
them.'

From Bridford, a parish in wild hilly country to the west of
Exeter, the parson wrote voluminously and helpfully. He was
the Rev R. P. Carrington, who was compiling his *Parochiales
Bridfordii* during these years, a valuable notebook of parish
memoranda which has never been printed in full, though ex-
tracts from it have appeared. 'A small Cluster of Cottages and a
Poor House constitutes the *Hamlet* of Bridford (commonly

called Bridford Town).' There was no endowed school, 'and the part of the Poor House which I succeeded in having fitted up for a School has been given up to accommodate the recoil of our population after the war: there not being a sufficient number of Cottages in the Parish'.

Carrington records in his *Parochiales Bridfordii* that when during the Napoleonic Wars a French invasion seemed likely (and the South West had good reason to think it would fall there) at least one well-to-do family in Exeter made plans for retiring to Bridford which, though only six or seven miles from Exeter, seemed remote enough to elude any invader. Partly as a result of this 'the last 25 years have considerably increased the intercourse of this retired and picturesque Parish with Exeter and the other more populous places'.

There are anecdotes also about the Civil Wars.

> The extreme part of the wing of Ireton's army, whose Headquarters were at Bovey Tracy, rested on Bridford, and the intermediate ground between this and Canonteign (a defended post of the Cavaliers) was tilting ground ... A party from hence threw themselves into the Orchards surrounding some part of the village (of Christow, adjacent to Bridford) which is detached and commanding the Church Yard, and shot the Clerke of the Parish at the entrance of the Church Porch where he had run for shelter and lies buried under the stone on which he fell.

From East Worlington, a remote parish in mid-Devon where Daniel and Mrs Lysons had stayed in the summer of 1818 to prosecute their researches, the parson wrote on February 19th, 1819: 'Your Letter of ye 2nd inst. found me confined to my Bed by a severe Fit of the Gout in both my Feet and Ancles ... [but] I am happy to tell you that I have laid aside my Crutches and was able to hobble to Church yesterday and do my own duty'.

At Chulmleigh, not far away, there were signs of the gathering gloom in English farming: the great slump that was to force thousands of farmers off their farms was on the way. 'Many of the little Freeholds in this neighbourhood being mortgaged for nearly as much as they are worth, their Title deeds are in other hands than those of the owners,' so that Lysons's correspondent could not give any information about the descent of the estates.

Squire Mallock wrote on the same melancholy theme from Cockington Court on April 16th, 1822: 'How do you feel in this time of dismay, Peace and plenty will ruin us all, there must be something radically amiss when two of the greatest blessings man can have shall cause his ruin.'

There is a very characteristic letter from old Mr Pine-Coffin, the squire of East Down, near Barnstaple. He writes from Bath on January 22nd, 1822:

>...The manufactory of Ochre and Umber was carried on for a few years by me at East Downe about 1785; the Ochre was dug in East Downe, the Umber in Berrynarbor; the latter not inferior to the Turkish: Reeves the colorman (who had a shop at the back of the new Church in the Strand), declared he never was able to form a complete series of shades of colors 'till he had *that*; I was unfortunately unable to procure an honest and able man to manufacture it, as the art of preparing it was confined to very few, and kept a profound secret. The person to whose care it was consigned in London likewise gave me great reason to be dissatisfied with his conduct, and I found so many difficulties to encounter, and that it would require a greater capital to carry it on than I chose to embark in it, and involve me in trade (of which I was entirely ignorant) that I resolved to put a stop to it . . .

Then there is an amusing and scandalous letter about the great merchant family of Davie at Bideford, who made a fortune in the Virginia and Newfoundland trades towards the end of the seventeenth century and early in the eighteenth.

A Widow Davie was the last Merchant – I think she pur-

chased Orleigh and Watermouth. Halsbury was purchased of
Benson, expelled the House of Commons for Malpractices –
his Estates were sold under an extent from the Crown. This
Widow Davie lived to a great age & conducted a very extensive concern with so much acumen & constant good luck that
she acquired the character of a Witch – a character of no
inconsiderable advantage to her with the Sailors employed in
her Shipping who believed she had knowledge of whatever
they did in Virginia or Newfoundland – Her son emerged
from the Warehouse & was Sheriff of the County.

The notorious Benson crops up again in another letter:

Halsbury was purchased of the Giffords by Benson, a merchant of Appledore – not Auditor Benson. Thomas Benson
was the representative of Barnstaple in the House of
Commons & at one time possessed a very considerable
property – but sustaining heavy losses by sea he sought to
retrieve his fortune by fraudulently sinking a ship or ships –
he was detected & expelled the House of Commons but had
the good luck to escape to Viana in Portugal – his Agent was
convicted and hanged. Halsbury, under an extent from the
Crown, was then purchased by Davie of Orleigh.

All this countryside gossip and scandal remained fresh after
generations. This letter was written in 1822, nearly seventy
years after Benson had fled the country and fifty after he had
died, an exile in Oporto.

The last letter I shall quote introduced a curious, almost
fantastic, character – Sir Manasseh Masseh Lopes. In a letter
dated from Exeter, June 22nd, 1820, he informs the Rev
Daniel Lysons about his large estate in South West Devon,
near Plymouth. He had bought the estate of the late James
Modyford Heywood, through the latter's executors, in 1798.
This comprised the manors of Maristow, Buckland Mona-
chorum, Walkhampton, Shaugh Prior, and Bickleigh; and in
1808 he had rounded this off with the manor of Meavy, bought
from Hugh Malet, esquire. 'I calculate,' he goes on, 'I have

about 32,000 acres belonging to me altogether in a ring fence (including Commons, waste lands, & c.).'

This letter is almost certainly written from the Devon County prison at Exeter where Lopes was serving the sentence of two years' imprisonment passed upon him in the King's Bench division on November 13th, 1819, for outrageous electoral bribery both at Grampound in Cornwall and at Barnstaple. A brief outline of his career is given in the *Dictionary of National Biography* but much remains unknown. He was born in Jamaica in 1755, the descendant of an old Jamaican family of Spanish Jews. His father – Mordecai Rodriguez Lopes – who is said to have made a fortune from his sugar-plantations, came to England and settled at Clapham, just outside London.

Manasseh, an only son, inherited his father's large fortune, and descended upon Devon in 1798 where the Heywood estates were in the market – including the beautifully sited house of Maristow, which he made his principal seat – and bought the entire estate. In 1802 he abandoned Judaism, conformed to the Church of England, and was elected for the pocket borough of New Romney in the same year. In 1805 he acquired a baronetcy. From 1812 to 1818 he represented the borough of Barnstaple, and was returned again for Barnstaple in 1818. But here retribution overtook him. His return was petitioned against on the ground of widespread bribery of the electors and he was unseated.

Worse was to come, however. It was revealed that he had arranged with a voter in the rotten Cornish borough of Grampound to procure his return for that place by dividing £2,000 among the sixty freeholders of the borough. He had also distributed £3,000 in bribes in the Barnstaple election of 1818. He was tried and found guilty at the Bodmin assizes for the Grampound affair, and again tried and found guilty at Exeter for the Barnstaple business. Sentence was postponed until the autumn sitting of the King's Bench. On November. 13th the King's Bench sentenced him to two years' imprisonment and fined him £10,000. The imprisonment of a baronet and a member of the House of Commons for bribery and corruption at this date was a notable victory in the slow campaign for electoral purity. Lopes had also been sheriff of Devon in 1810 and Lt-Col Commandant Roborough Volunteers. He had certainly lost no time since his sudden arrival in the county only a dozen years earlier.

His political career was not ended, however, by this setback. In 1823, free once more, he was returned to the House for his pocket borough of Westbury in Wiltshire, of which he had presumably bought the patronage and had also made himself Recorder. Though he was very unpopular there, he was returned again in 1826.

Three years later a mysterious transaction occurred at Westbury which has never yet been explained. Lopes suddenly resigned his seat – in his own pocket borough – to Sir Robert Peel, then Home Secretary and leader of the House of Commons, who had been rejected only three days earlier at Oxford. Peel had changed sides over the issue of Catholic emancipation, and consequently applied for the Chiltern Hundreds and offered himself again to his old constituency of the University of Oxford for re-election on this issue. The Protestants of Oxford rallied around their champion and Peel was defeated on Friday, February 27th, 1829, by 146 votes. It was urgently necessary to find him a seat, and Sir Manasseh Masseh Lopes was the victim. The *Dictionary of National Biography* says that Lopes made way for Peel for an unknown consideration. It is not known what bargain was struck, or how, but the proceedings at Westbury were pretty scandalous even by the standards of the time. When one reads what meagre facts are to be discovered about this transaction, one feels that if there is any moral distinction between Lopes's simple bribery at Grampound and Barnstaple, and Peel's shameless intrusion into Westbury, it is so small as to be imperceptible to the twentieth-century eye. But Lopes was that ever-unpopular figure, a monied Jew who could not help displaying his wealth – and Peel was an Englishman, a minister of the Crown, and leader of the House.

Peel's account in his *Memoirs* of this affair at Westbury is disingenuous in the extreme, even for a politician.

> After my rejection by the University, [he says] there being a convenient vacancy at Westbury I became a candidate (a very unpopular one I must admit) for that borough. The Protestant feeling was much excited even among the quiet population of a small country town; and notwithstanding all the assistance which Sir Manasseh Lopez (the patron of the borough) could render me, my return was not effected without considerable difficulty.
>
> Sir Manasseh himself suffered in his person from one of the many missiles with which the Town-Hall was assailed during the ceremony of the election. It was fortunate for me that the ceremony was not unduly protracted. Very shortly after my return had been declared by the proper officer, the arrival of a Protestant candidate in a chaise and four from London was announced. If he had entered the town a few hours earlier, it is highly probable that I should have fared no better in Westbury than I had done at Oxford.

There are two or three letters among the Peel Papers in the British Museum which add a few details to this account. Peel had been defeated at Oxford on Friday evening after a two days' contest. By the following Monday morning he had been returned for Westbury. Somehow Lopes was persuaded to resign his seat as soon as the Oxford result was known, and an 'election' was hurried through at Westbury before any opposition could dispatch a candidate to the scene. William Holmes, MP for Bishop's Castle in Shropshire, 'for thirty years the adroit and dexterous whip of the tory party' and their powerful political manager, had arrived at Westbury on the Sunday morning, March 1st. By the following morning Lopes had resigned and Peel had been elected. Lopes wrote to Joseph Planta, Secretary to the Treasury, the same morning:

> Westbury 2 March 1829 – My dear Sir, I have written

by this post to announce to Mr. Peel that he has this morning
been unanimously elected as a member to serve in Parliament for this Borough – and I assure you that I feel great
pleasure and satisfaction in this event – Mr. Holmes has been
with us since yesterday morning and will inform you of all
our proceedings here. I have felt in an awkward situation to
take the steps I have after what has occurred at Oxford as it
has occasioned a prejudice among my friends here.*

By the same post Holmes also wrote to Planta:

My dear Planta, Peel has just been returned for this place.
Mr. Franco the Mayor, his brother in law Mr. Radcliff from
Devonshire, and Sir M. Lopes signed the return, every other
member of the Corporation and voter declined taking any
part in the proceedings ... I am writing this at Mr. Lopes
House where the Windows have been broken and am very
cold. I must wait for Dinner which is a cursed bore to
me ...

Holmes left Westbury the same evening, with no further use for
Sir Manasseh Lopes, and Lopes departed for his Devonshire
house at Maristow the following day. Peel had not shown up in
the place at all. There can be little doubt that the presence of
Holmes at Westbury on that Sunday morning was for the purpose of getting Lopes to make way forthwith for Peel, but of
the nature of the pressure or the inducement not a clue remains.
Certainly Lopes seems to have got nothing out of it. He was
already a rich man; and no further political honour came his
way.

A little later in the year we find him writing to Peel, remind-
ing him that he had promised to intercede with Lord Aberdeen,
the Foreign Secretary, for a consulship for his nephew, Mr
Henry Cowper – but this is too trivial to have been the consideration for the ending of Lopes's political career in an odour

* This letter, and the others subsequently quoted, will be found in
the Peel Papers now housed in the British Museum (Add Mss 40399).

of even greater unpopularity than he had been accustomed to in his own borough. Lopes pointed out that the consulships of Madeira and Bahia had both been vacant for some time but nothing had been done to find a place for his nephew. He begged Peel to intercede with the Foreign Secretary for the post in Madeira. Peel wrote an exasperated note to Planta: 'My dear Planta, What a torment this Jew is! I thought that Lord Aberdeen had appointed or was about to appoint his Nephew. What shall I say in reply?' To Lopes he wrote curtly that he had already made three or four applications to Lord Aberdeen in the last few months on the subject, that Lord Aberdeen had assured him of his disposition to do something about Mr Henry Cowper's employment soon, and that no good purpose would be served by his interceding again. But a few days later, on October 30th, 1829, he wrote again to Lopes with exceeding curtness that Lord Aberdeen had signified to him his intention of appointing Mr Cowper to the consulship of Pernambuco at a salary of £1,000 a year, ending his letter with contemptuous impatience 'I have &c Robert Peel'.

Sir Manasseh Lopes died at Maristow on March 26th, 1831, leaving a great fortune, estimated at £800,000, chiefly in government and East India stock and in land. His baronetcy devolved upon his nephew Ralph Franco, the son of his sister Esther who had married Abraham Franco, of London, merchant. Presumably it was this Ralph Franco who was mayor of Westbury – while Manasseh was its recorder – when the shameless election of Peel took place. One begins by disliking Lopes, such little as one knows about him from the published facts, but it is hard not to feel some pity for him at the end of his career in English politics: struck by Protestant missiles which would have been more fairly directed at Sir Robert Peel, his windows broken, jockeyed out of his seat by the dexterous political manager of the party (for there is no evidence that he ever gained anything by it personally), an unpopular figure to the electors, a scapegoat for Peel's change of views which the latter had not the time or perhaps the inclination to defend in person. He was used by the party, and they rewarded him with contempt. To William Holmes, who had engineered the triumph, it was a cursed bore that he should be cold because of the broken windows, and that he was kept waiting for his dinner before he set off back to town as fast as he could.

The hard-faced, solid governing class of England – the Peels, the Plantas, and the Holmeses – had used the outsider for their own ends and then thought no more of it – 'there being a convenient vacancy at Westbury'. Peel took his seat in the House on March 3rd, and two days later, on the evening of the 5th, he made one of his greatest speeches, introducing the Catholic Emancipation bill in a crowded House. One wonders what Sir Manasseh Lopes thought as he sat in his library at Maristow, an old man nearing 75, looking across his sloping lawns down to the broadening reaches of the lovely Tavy; the Tavy shining in the soft western light of a March evening, with the dark, hanging woods of Whittacliffe and Blindwell rising on the far side towards Bere Alston and the hills beyond; and the only sound in the intense quiet of that spring twilight the faraway whistle of the curlews coming up from the estuary flats by Gnatham Point, as the evening tide ebbed away to the sea.

CHAPTER FIVE

The Elizabethan Merchants of Exeter

THE FIRST meeting of the Chamber, the governing body of Exeter, after the accession of Queen Elizabeth I, took place as usual in the ancient Guildhall that still stands in the High Street of the city, though it lacked in the autumn of 1558 its now-familiar Renaissance portico. Of this assembly of twenty-four men, including the mayor, all but one were merchants. The single exception was Robert Chafe, an ecclesiastical official connected with the cathedral, a skilful and learned lawyer, 'a man of very good condition being of great modesty and gravity, very friendly and loving to all men', who was twice to be chosen mayor of the city – in 1568 and again in 1576.*

John Buller, as mayor, presided over this first Elizabethan assembly, but the father of the house was old William Hurst, now in his seventy-sixth year. He had been mayor as far back as 1524 and three times since, and three times had represented Exeter in parliament. He had come to the thriving city, the son of a South Devon yeoman, as long ago as 1497 and so could look back over sixty years in its streets, and to more than forty years of service on its governing body. Around this venerable figure on the benches of the Guildhall sat not a few prosperous men who had been his apprentices in their youth. Even at that great age, his fifth mayoralty – in 1561 – had yet to come and he had another ten years of life ahead of him.

The city governed by this assembly was one of the largest and wealthiest in Elizabethan England. It was the social and

* Exeter city records, Book 55 (known as John Hooker's Commonplace Book), which contains a number of biographies of mayors written by Hooker from his personal knowledge. He was chamberlain of the city from 1556 until his death in 1601.

cultural capital of a large province, a cathedral city, an industrial town, and a busy port. In wealth and population, among the provincial towns, it ranked after Norwich, Newcastle and Bristol, and was the most important city between London and Land's End. Yet it was very small in extent. A man could walk comfortably around the entire circuit of its walls in twenty minutes or so, for it was less than a mile and a half around. The entire area enclosed by these walls was but ninety-three acres, though to that one must add, by the year 1558, small suburbs outside all four gates which carried houses along the road in a ribbon development for possibly a couple of hundred yards in each direction. The extra-mural suburbs consisted almost entirely of working-class houses, except for a few merchant houses outside the West Gate in the principal industrial and commercial quarter. But the great majority of the merchant class lived within the walls, in one of half a dozen small, rich, central parishes, and in one or other of only half a dozen streets.

The merchant class was similarly small, compact, and closely interrelated by marriage. We can get a rough idea of its total size in a given generation from the number of admissions to the freedom of the city, a necessary qualification for all who practised as merchants whether they had been apprenticed in boyhood to an Exeter freeman or had come to the city from elsewhere as grown men. In the last quarter of the sixteenth century the number of merchants and mercers admitted to the freedom amounted to 104. We may reasonably assume that the average business-life of a merchant was not much above twenty-five to thirty years, so that at any given time there may have been about a hundred merchants in the city. Such a figure is clearly only approximate, but it will not be far wrong: at its worst it serves to give us an order of magnitude.

The total population of the city in this generation was between nine and ten thousand – about two thousand families at the most. Of these, then, one family in every twenty was a merchant family and belonged potentially to the governing class. From these alone, with very few exceptions, were chosen the mayors, sheriffs, and members of parliament for the city.

The choice, indeed, was even finer, for within this small class there were closely knit dynasties of the wealthiest merchants related to each other, often more than once over, by marriage. The fifty Elizabethan mayors – there were two mayors in some years because of early deaths – were chosen from twenty-six different families. But in this narrower field, too, marriages had united Hursts, Martins, and Peters, or Periams and Blackallers. In this way we are reduced to perhaps a score of ruling families in the Elizabethan city and this oligarchic rule carried over well into the seventeenth century.

In the smaller town of Leicester, the Elizabethan mayors were also drawn from twenty-six different families: but Leicester had just about one-third of the number of families at Exeter, so to that extent its choice of mayor was far less oligarchic. At Norwich, by far the largest and richest of provincial cities, the forty-seven Elizabethan mayors were drawn from twenty-nine different families. Here, with a total population of well over three thousand families, the field of choice was even narrower than at Exeter. The larger the town, the more oligarchic was its government likely to be in the sixteenth century. Yet there was a wider choice at Norwich as between occupations. Whereas at Exeter only four of the fifty mayors were chosen from outside the ranks of the merchants, at Norwich the non-merchant groups provided thirteen out of forty-seven mayors, drawing upon worsted and dornix weavers, a butcher, a baker, a saddler, a scrivener, and a goldsmith.

At Bristol, the second richest provincial city, the choice of mayor was more widely made. Of the eighteen mayors between 1558 and 1576, eight were not merchants, tanners and brewers being conspicuous in the list. After 1576, however, the merchants predominated heavily. Out of the next twenty-eight mayors only three were not merchants, and Mr McGrath has shown that in the seventeenth century the key positions of mayor, sheriff, and chamberlain were all held by merchants. Mayors were chosen also from a much wider range of families than at Norwich or Exeter. No fewer than thirty-eight different families are represented in the mayoral list from 1558 to 1603.

Bristol was, for some local reason, the least oligarchical of the large provincial cities, though it was becoming more so in the last quarter of the century.

The merchant class at Exeter, as in all the larger provincial towns, was recruited to a considerable extent from outside – not only from the surrounding countryside but from such distant parts as Wales, Cheshire, Worcestershire, or Suffolk. Younger sons of ability for whom there were no bright prospects at home would naturally tend to move to a thriving commercial city like Exeter; but their biographies by John Hooker make it clear that their destinies often depended upon some human accident and not upon any inhuman calculation of economic prospects. 'The girl at the door of an inn' is as important in this respect as the account-book, perhaps more so.

So it was that Thomas Prestwood the elder, who died in the autumn of 1558, had come to Exeter from his native city of Worcester exactly thirty years earlier. His father, 'conceiving a good hope of him by reason of his pregnant wit and forwardness sent him to London, where he bound him apprentice unto a rich and wealthy merchant under whom he prospered and did very well. And upon occasion, being a traveller for his master and in his affairs, he came to this city [Exeter] and in course of time he became acquainted with the widow of one John Bodley of this city. She ... having found favour in his sight, he made his master acquainted therewith and with his good favour he followed his former suit to the widow and obtained and married her. And then, leaving his master, he remained and dwelled in this city, and followed the trade of merchandise wherein he had been brought up, and did prosper very well and increased unto good wealth and riches ...'

Thomas Prestwood followed a familiar pattern in marrying a rich widow. So did Thomas Bodley, the grandson of John Bodley, when he married the widow of a wealthy Totnes merchant in the summer of 1586, within four months of her husband's death. Nicholas Ball of Totnes, then one of the richest little towns in England, had made a fortune in a short space of time 'specially by trading for pilchers', and much of this fortune passed by the marriage of his widow to Bodley. The Bodleian Library is founded in part at least upon the humble pilchard.

The marriages of Prestwood and Bodley illustrate a general thesis: the influence of rich widows upon economic progress. In an age when men generally died young, the supply of active and wealthy widows was a noticeable feature of society. Many an enterprising young man in the sixteenth century owed his ultimate success to this simple biological fact.

Thomas Richardson, a merchant dealing principally in wines, mayor in 1566–7, had come to Exeter from Cheshire, through some personal relationship which is not made clear by Hooker. 'By means of one Michael Lymett of this city, apothecary, he was brought to this city and served under the said Lymett. When he came to ripe years and was married, he kept a wine tavern and was a merchant adventurer for wines, and following that trade in good order and diligently he attained to good wealth and nobility, and did not only serve this city by retail but also all the gentlemen in the shire of Devon by the tuns and hogsheads, with whom he was in great credit and favour. He was of very good conditions and qualities, given to all good exercises and a good companion for any gentleman or honest man, whether it were shooting, bowling, or any other pastime. And albeit he were very honest, friendly, and courteous to all men, so would he not receive wrong at any man's hands, neither would he give his beard for the washing. He had passed and borne all the offices of the city, in every of which he used and behaved himself very well ... for which he was well respected both in town and country.'

Simon Knight, mayor in 1570 and again in 1579, was Somerset born, of good parentage.

His father having many other children brought him to this city and bound him apprentice unto a merchant named John Morgan, after whose death he served under Mr William Hurst, who, having a good liking of the towardness of the young man did employ him both at his side and beyond the

seas, and he did so well follow his business that he prospered
very well and was of good wealth and hability, and was at
length twice mayor of this city. [He] did very well in the
first, but in the latter he was so encumbered in litigious and
troublesome matters that in following of them he was the
more remiss in public matters . . . [But] well thinking of himself and standing in his own conceit to be wiser than others,
and also for his too much jesting of other men, he was much
blamed and the less liked.

Though the Elizabethan merchant class was liberally recruited from outside, more often than not from the younger sons
of good families, it contained also a solid core of second-gener-
ation mercantile families. Such were the Periams, the Mid-
winters, Blackalls (or Blackallers), Martins, and Spicers. Some
successful merchants failed to find successors in trade: their
eldest sons either moved out to a country estate or withdrew
their money from trade to use it in other ways: we shall return
to this point later. But a few merchant families continued into
the second and occasionally into the third generation. Of these,
the Periams were perhaps the most notable. The first of them in
the city, William Periam, was the son of a franklin in the
nearby parish of Broad Clyst. He had been admitted to the freedom of the city as a capper in the same year as William Hurst
(1504–5) and had flourished exceedingly, making most of his
early fortune at least in the tin trade and dying a rich man. He
was followed in business by his second son, John Periam, who
was chosen mayor in 1563 and again in 1572. He was a zealous
Protestant and had assisted Lord Russell during the Catholic
rebellion of 1549 in the West 'with money and other necessaries
to his great comfort'. As a consequence of this, he was obliged to
spend several years abroad during Mary's reign, by which he
lost nothing, for he became the chief governor of the company
of English Merchants in Antwerp. He was apparently an un-
likeable man, for Hooker, though a good Protestant and therefore well disposed to Periam on religious grounds, speaks of
him with modified approval as 'a very worthy man in many

respects, and had many good parts in him'. Nevertheless, he made a good mayor of the city.

His government was upright. A great favourer of the poor man's cause, an upright judge in all causes of law depending before him, severe against the wicked and lewd persons who received at his hands according to their deserts, and friendly and loving to the good and honest, and them he defended against all enemies ... As he lived, so he died virtuously, godly, and in years, whose memory deserves not to be forgotten.

The Periams were perhaps a quick-tempered lot. Hooker tells us of William Periam, mayor in 1532, that 'he was but a plain dealing man, but rough and soon offended if he was abused and with wrongs he would not lightly lay up ...' He remained a peasant for all his business acumen and wealth. And the temper of his son is revealed to us in his will. He had left 'to Jasper Horsey to fynde at one of the Universities £30'. In a codicil a few months later he tightened his bequest: 'Jasper Horsey only to have his legacy if he stand bound to be at one of the Universities there to study Divinity and so to be of the ministry'. A few days later, there was a row. Young Jasper was evidently not amenable to the dictates of old Periam. To the will was added:

This I write 22 May 1573. Forasmuch as Jasper Horsey went from the house on Whitsunday morning very ungratefully and uncourteously not saying farewell to me or any of all the household, whereas he had been sufficiently brought up as I take it v or vi years, I having in remembrance this his ungratefulness give him only 40 shillings with his apparel and his books and nothing else, so god bless him.

John Periam was a great believer in education. His own father, rough as he was, had caused him 'to be brought up in knowledge and learning', later putting him as apprentice to a merchant. His own eldest son, William, he sent to the High

School in Exeter and thence on to Oxford, where he became a fellow of Exeter College, apparently at the age of seventeen, in 1551. William Periam turned to the law, in which (surprisingly) Devonians had always shown unnatural abilities, and eventually became a judge (1581) and sat on the commission for the trial of Mary Queen of Scots. Down in Devon he had his country seat at Fulford, a few miles outside Exeter, not far from his younger brother, John, who had ceased also to have any interests as a merchant and lived, for the latter part of his life, as a country gentleman.

Once admitted to the freedom of the city, by apprenticeship or by fine, the merchant set up in business for himself. No Exeter merchant was substantial enough to own a whole ship, or even half a ship. The great majority joined with half a dozen others to fill a ship with cargoes. Harry Maunder (died 1564) owned 'half a quarter of a barke called the Dragon, of Topsham', valued at £8. George Hunt (died 1565) owned half a ship called the *George*, valued at £30. And the ships of the late sixteenth century were generally very small. Of the 123 ships that entered the port of Exeter in the year 1597–8 no fewer than 96 were of less than thirty tons. The average ship belonging to the port of Exeter was one of twenty to thirty tons. The largest in that year were the *Dolphin* of Exmouth (100 tons), the *Endeavour* of Topsham (80 tons), and the *Rose* of Exmouth (70 tons). A typical sort of ship was the *Robert* of Topsham, of only twenty tons, which came in from St Malo in Brittany with a cargo shared among eleven Exeter merchants; or the *True Meaning* of Kenton, of thirty tons, which came in from Bordeaux with a cargo of twenty-four tuns of Gascon wine shared between two Exeter merchants and one from Tiverton.

Even at the end of the century, too, the range of the Exeter merchants' trading activities was not great. Of the ships entering the port in 1597–8, nearly one-half were engaged in the coasting trade, mainly from Wales with coal, from London with mixed cargoes, and from other Devon ports. Of the fifty ships coming in from foreign ports, Brittany sent the most (eighteen), and the 'salt ports' of Western France were second

with sixteen. Other French ports (Rouen and Bordeaux) accounted for four more. So three ships out of every four in
Exeter's foreign trade came from or went to France. Of the
rest, five ships entered from Newfoundland (mainly with salt
fish), four came in from Middelburg or Danzig, and three from
Madeira or Portugal. The merchants of Exeter were certainly
not as adventurous and wide-ranging as those of Plymouth.
Their trade with France was a long-established one and they
felt little desire, apart from Newfoundland, to open up new
lines of country. What they could not get from France, and to a
limited degree from a few other foreign ports, they relied upon
getting through the re-export trade from London. There was, at
the end of the sixteenth century, the beginning of wider
interests. By about 1600 a small trade with Ireland and with
the Baltic had been developed, and we can detect the beginnings of the trade with Holland which was to become the
greatest of all the Exeter trades during the latter half of the
seventeenth century. There was, indeed, a more considerable
trade with Spain than might appear from casual references in
the port books. This trade was stopped for years by war, but it
is significant that in 1580, for example, the biggest 'adventure'
that William Chappell was engaged in was in Spain, where he
had £322 owing to him. From Spain, when political conditions
permitted it, came Spanish wool and Bilbao iron.

The inventories of Exeter merchants' personal estates tell us
a good deal more about their trading activities than we could
gather from the port books or custom accounts. Nearly every
merchant at this period carried on a retail business through a
shop on his premises. The list of people who owed money to
Harry Maunder at his death in 1564 is probably typical of most
merchants' businesses. There were 112 debtors, of whom no
fewer than 75 owed small sums ranging from 1d to 20s. These,
and probably others, are clearly retail customers. Other debtors
owed several pounds and are identifiable as wholesale buyers.
Such are Thomas Richardson, the vintner, who owed £18 9s
8d, and Philip Yard of Exeter, also a vintner, who owed £9 6s
8d for sack.

Harry Maunder had an extensive business in Spanish iron, supplying numerous smiths in the city and for a dozen miles around. But besides wine and iron, he dealt in an extraordinary miscellany of commodities: the 'shop book' speaks of canvas, calico, figs, coal, tin, linen cloth, hops, grindstones, mustard mills, vinegar, raisins, dowlas, saffron, alum, playing cards, shirts, and woollen cards, while in the shop and warehouse we find many other commodities, such as brass, brown paper, soap, wax, kerseys, yarn, thread, silk, nails, buttons, parchment, lead, pepper, ratsbane, and heaven knows what else.

Much went to other shopkeepers and to country gentry. The Elizabethan merchant covered the whole range of trading, rather indiscriminately, from direct import from overseas or London and the coastal ports, down to pennyworths of things sold in the shop. There is some indication, however, that by the early seventeenth century the keeping of a shop was regarded as beneath the dignity of a big merchant, and he was beginning to leave that to others. When John Periam, in the third generation of the family (1616), left £1,000 to be lent to five Merchant Adventurers of the city, trading beyond the seas, he stipulated that they should not be shopkeepers by retail.

The only inventories of personal estate to survive are those in the court of orphans records among the city muniments. This court was set up in 1563 to safeguard the interests of widows and orphaned children where a citizen died leaving children under age. Hence the value of many estates is less than it would have been had the head of the family lived to his full term of years. On the other hand, it may well be argued that death in the forties or fifties was a common feature of sixteenth-century life and to that extent these records are more truly representative of the economic facts of merchant life than those drawn from men who all died of old age. A table of twenty-seven merchants' estates for the period 1564 to 1618 is therefore as instructive as any (Table 1).

The average merchant estate was one of £1,913 gross (that of John Aplyn, 1594). This compares very closely, as we might expect, with the average personal estate of a Bristol merchant

TABLE I
Exeter Merchants' Estates, 1564–1618

Name	Date	Gross Personal Estate £	Net Personal Estate £
Harry Maunder	1564	556	360
Edmond Whetcombe	1565	791	710
Edward Lymett	1571	509	382
John Bodley	1572	156	146
Thomas Prestwood	1576	905	662
William Chappell	1580	2,378	2,265
Thomas Chappell	1590	3,266	3,225
Richard Swete	1591	1,485	708
John Follett	1591	255	135
Richard Mawdytt	1592	356	277
Richard Reynolds	1592	2,086	1,473
John Aplyn	1594	1,913	1,592
John Spurway	1595	1,074	862
Walter Horsey	1597	2,670	2,464
Richard Beavis	1603	3,492	3,063
William Spicer	1604	3,825	2,916
David Bagwell*	1604	675	—102
John Trosse	1605	236	166
Thomas Cooke	1606	3,000	1,716
Alexander Germyn	1608	986	551
Robert Parr	1608	3,976	2,223
John Plea	1609	827	713
Thomas Snowe	1609	2,032	1,818
William Newcombe	1609	2,174	2,037
William Martyn	1609	6,381	4,401
Thomas Mogridge	1617	5,189	4,343
John Lant	1618	7,317	4,664

* David Bagwell died young at St Malo. His debts amounted to £777, exceeding his assets at that time.

(over a somewhat wider period) which Professor Jordan puts at £1,921. In the same period, the average (median) personal estate of a London merchant was £7,780, about four times that of Exeter or Bristol men. About one-third of the Exeter merchants left personal estate valued at £3,000 or more.

It will be observed from the table opposite that there is often a considerable gap between the gross personal estate and the net estate. This gap is accounted for in two ways: by the money owing at the time of death by the dead man, and by the debts due to him which the executors write off as 'doubtful', or more usually, 'desperate'. The proportion of 'desperate debts' to the whole debt owing to the merchant's estate is often remarkably high. In some instances they were greater than the 'good debts'. An outstanding example is that of the rich merchant William Martyn, who died in 1609. The good debts amounted to nearly £1,542, and the desperate debts to over £2,633. William Spicer (1604) was owed £300 in good debts, but a further £662 of debts were written off as 'desperate'. No uniformity is observable in this respect. Sometimes the desperate debts are less than one-tenth of the whole; in other cases they are as much as two-thirds of the whole debt due to the dead man's estate. Much must have depended upon whether England was

TABLE II

Good Debts and Desperate Debts, 1565–1617

Name	Date	Good Debts	Desperate Debts	Total Debts Due
		£	£	£
Edmond Whetcombe	1565	230	81	311
William Chappell	1580	902	113	1,015
Thomas Chappell	1590	957	21	978
Richard Beavis	1603	256	193	449
William Spicer	1604	300	662	962
Alexander Germyn	1608	257	270	527
Robert Parr	1608	1,958	1,310	3,268
John Plea	1609	350	38	388
Thomas Snowe	1609	696	52	748
William Martyn	1609	1,542	2,634	4,176
William Tothill	1609	201	95	296
Thomas Mogridge	1617	1,186	410	1,596

at war with the country where the debtors lay; but it is also clear from many inventories that a high proportion of 'desperate debts' were purely local.

The variation from one inventory to another is so great, and must so often arise from accidental circumstances at the time, that an average proportion of bad debts to good is probably rather meaningless. All we can note is that the Elizabethan merchant had to reckon with the serious possibility that a considerable proportion of the money owing to him at any given time was going to be difficult to collect, and that a considerable residue might have to be written off as beyond hope of realization. The estimate of 'desperate debts' was probably a rather subjective one also, and might be considerably amended before the estate was finally wound up. We see this in the case of Richard Swete (1591), where the original estimate at the making of the inventory was of £295 3s 11d in desperate debts. In what seems to be the final reckoning, the figure had been reduced to £46 8s 5d. Executors probably tended to take an extremely conservative view of debts outstanding as a precaution against arousing optimistic hopes in the widow, but hoped for better things eventually.

We also notice the great variation in the sums of ready money kept in merchants' houses at any particular time. This is largely a reflection of the opportunities for investment and also perhaps of the enterprise, or lack of it, manifested by different men of wealth.

The second smallest sum of ready money was left by one of the wealthiest merchants in the city. This was Thomas Prestwood, the son of the Thomas Prestwood already referred to. The inventory of his personal estate does not reveal his true wealth, for he had put a great deal of money into real estate – both farms in the countryside and houses in the city. His total personal estate was therefore comparatively small – only £905, less than half the average. In such cases as this the inventories can be quite misleading about a man's true wealth.

TABLE III
Ready Money in Merchants' Houses

		(*nearest* £)
Harry Maunder	1564	69
John Bodley	1572	20
Thomas Prestwood	1576	25
William Chappell	1580	192
Thomas Chappell	1590	1,303
Richard Swete	1591	566
Richard Beavis	1603	410
Thomas Mogridge	1617	914

Thomas Prestwood senior had built up a substantial merchanting business, but then, Hooker tells us,

in his later age by little and little he gave over his trade of merchandise and employed his wealth in purchasing of lands and in building of houses, especially within the city, which do yet remain as goodly ornaments to beautify the same. He died in good age and left his lands and possessions to his only son Thomas Prestwood ... who, beginning where his father left, did not much follow the trade of merchandise in which also he was trained up, but lived rather as a gentleman by his lands ...

This is why there was so little ready money in the house at his death in 1576, and why also his shop – for he still continued to live in a merchant's house in the High Street – contained nothing but a few oddments worth less than £4 in all. When Thomas Prestwood the elder died in 1558 he possessed the manors of Butterford, Tynacre, and Venny Tedburn, and farms in a dozen other parishes, besides a tin-blowing mill and a fulling mill, and eight large houses in the city of Exeter. His son Thomas inherited this estate, was styled gentleman, and divided his time between a large town-house in the High Street of Exeter and his 'mansion house' of Butterford, some thirty miles away in the South Hams.

William Chappell, who died in the early months of 1580, 'was brought up in the trade of merchandise and by the same he grew to good wealth, and giving himself to purchasing of lands he in a manner gave over his trade'. Hooker here gives a slightly false impression, for there is a very marked difference between the financial affairs of Thomas Prestwood (1576) and William Chappell (1580). Prestwood's inventory shows very little ready money, the shop abandoned to the storage of junk, and very small debts due to the estate. William Chappell's inventory also shows a shop containing nothing but oddments, but a larger sum of ready money (nearly £200), and very considerable trading interests. More than 40 per cent of his large personal estate took the form of trading debts due to him, and another 20 per cent was wrapped up in 'adventures abroad', most of it 'in the Isles' and in Spain.

Merchants' wills and inventories tell us little or nothing about their real estate, which in some instances was substantial. At least half a dozen Elizabethan merchants at Exeter founded landed families, as for example the Hursts, the Martins, the Periams, the Davys, and the Prestwoods. The real estate of old William Hurst, who died in 1568, was exceptionally large. It included six manors, farms in more than a score of parishes, and a certain amount of house-property. John Periam had probably inherited some lands from his father William, but of these we know nothing. By 1572, when he made his will, he was able to set up his elder son William (the future judge and baron of the exchequer) with the manor of Pancrasweek and lands in Pyworthy, Ottery St Mary, and Pinhoe, while to his younger son he left houses in Exeter and lands in half a dozen other parishes. This was not a large accumulation by comparison with the Hurst estate, but that was quite untypical. The successful Exeter merchant could probably hope for the lordship of one or two manors, and to possess farms in perhaps half a dozen parishes. Many big merchants achieved less than this.

The majority of merchants in the Elizabethan period had begun their careers as apprentices to Exeter merchants, though there was, as we have seen, always a small but important influx of men who had been apprenticed elsewhere and who had come to the city as mature men. These are usually distinguishable in the city records by the fact that they obtain the freedom of the city, without which they could not trade within its bounds, by fine and not by apprenticeship. Those born in Exeter received their education at the High School, the only grammar school in the city. From this they passed on to a seven-year apprenticeship and then set up in business on their own account, unless, as in a few cases, they remained in the family business, like John Periam, or Thomas Prestwood, or Thomas Chappell.

Marriage was the next important step, and it was most likely to be to the daughter of a fellow-merchant. The close relationships by marriage among the leading Exeter merchant families at least (perhaps there was a slightly wider choice of partner among the lesser men) have been worked out by Professor MacCaffrey, and could certainly be paralleled in other commercial cities. By his marriage, then, the Exeter merchant became related to a more or less numerous group of leading families, and his social standing was henceforth assured. Sometimes the merchant married into a small landed family. Thomas Prestwood the elder married the widow of another Exeter merchant who had been the daughter of a Kingswear gentleman; and his son married the daughter of William Strode of Newnham near Plymouth.

As time went by his family grew. Nothing could be further from the truth than that sixteenth-century children died like flies, or that the average family of survivors was a small one. Certainly it is not true of the latter half of the sixteenth century and of the first generation of the seventeenth. At Exeter the court of orphans records give us a good picture of the typical family. Out of thirty-three merchant households in the Elizabethan period, in which the father had died before his time, about one in seven (15 per cent) had seven, eight, or nine children. At the other end of the scale, one-third had only one, two or three children. The average number of children for the thirty-three households was 4.7; but against this we must set the fact that many men in the sample had died relatively young and before they could produce a 'normal' family. The largest single group (40 per cent of the total) had five or six children, and this must be regarded as the 'normal' family in this social class. Of all the children in the sample, 55 per cent were male, 45 per cent female.

A very small sample of merchant-wills from Totnes, the wills moreover of men who lived (as far as we can discover) their normal term of life, shows forty-one living children in five well-to-do families, an average of eight per family. A fuller sample, were it obtainable, would unquestionably lower this remarkable figure; but it serves to indicate that our 'normal' figure for Exeter of five or six children is a very credible one. To this typical family of seven or eight, including the parents, we have to add probably two apprentices at any given time and at least a couple of maidservants, giving us a household of some dozen people.

With such a high figure in mind, we need not be surprised at the number of rooms in the Elizabethan merchant's house as we find it described in the Exeter inventories. A sample of twenty houses described between 1564 and 1609 shows that only six were smaller than ten rooms, eleven contained ten to fifteen rooms, and three more than fifteen rooms.* The largest houses were those of Henry James (22 rooms) in 1578, and Robert Parr (20 rooms) in 1608. Seven of the eighteen houses had fourteen or fifteen rooms and may be regarded as the typical dwelling of the wealthier merchant.

There is good evidence for saying that houses became larger and grander during the Elizabethan period, either by additions to an existing house or through a complete rebuilding. Thus the inventory of Richard Beavis in 1603 shows a fifteen-room house of which at least two rooms are described as 'new'. More often, however, a completely new house was built on the site at some date in the Elizabethan period or in the early seventeenth century. In particular there seems to have been some considerable

* In counting rooms I have excluded the shop, cellar, warehouse, stables, and any 'domestic offices' such as a brewhouse.

rebuilding in the 1550s and 1560s. We have already seen that Thomas Prestwood the elder built some good houses before he died in 1558, and there are dated houses (1564, 1567) still surviving in the High Street as well as others of exactly the same design which no longer exist but which can be recovered in old drawings and photographs (Illus. 7 and 8).

The fact that larger and more ostentatious houses were being built in increasing numbers is suggested by a civic by-law, made in 1563.

> For avoidance of sundry inconveniences which daily do grow by the excessive buildings in sailing (sealinge) themselves further out than it appurtaineth or should be used: it is ordered that no manner of person or persons shall build nor attempt to build any house or houses within this city outwards towards any of the streets whereby the same shall have any sailing into the streets without the view and assent of the mayor, aldermen, and of the chamberlain be first had therein.

On the same day (August 21st, 1563), Robert Hunte was ordered to pull down forthwith a room and a projecting window in it which exceeded the limits of an earlier regulation. This regulation permitted a room to be built outwards to a depth of 4 ft beyond the principal of the house, and a window to project not more than 16 ins farther, giving a maximum total projection of 5 ft 4 ins beyond the principal. The new regulation, made the same day, fixed no maximum measurements for oversailing, but required each building to be inspected and approved by the mayor and others.

We learn a great deal from the inventories about the houses of Elizabethan merchants, though we cannot always be sure of their exact plan in default of surviving buildings. Several such buildings survive, but most have been altered internally to meet later needs and do not therefore help us as much as we could hope over the original Elizabethan plan. Indeed it is unrealistic to assume that there was a single type of house inhabited by merchants at this period. For one thing, the merchant class covered a wide range of worldly wealth. Table 1 shows that even in the limited period between 1590 and 1603 the richest merchant was worth ten times as much as the smallest merchant and their houses would have been correspondingly different. And further, in any given generation (especially before the early seventeenth century), some merchants would have been living in houses that were survivors (slightly modernized perhaps) of the Middle Ages, while others were living in pure Elizabethan 'mansions' – for so they are repeatedly called in the records of the time – which were the result of a complete rebuilding on the old site.

To illustrate the variety of merchants' houses therefore we may take two or three examples in detail from the inventories. The house of Edmond Whetcombe, who died in 1565 worth just under £800, was one of only six rooms, or seven if we count the 'spence' separately. Apart from the shop, it had a hall, a parlour, kitchen and spence, and three bedrooms, called respectively, 'the Fore-chamber', the 'high chamber', and 'an other chamber'. It is difficult to be certain about the plan of this house and the disposition of the various rooms, but it may well have been a medieval hall-house of which a few (somewhat battered) still remain in the street where Edmond Whetcombe lived. The simple plan of shop, hall, parlour, and kitchen, with some chambers over, suggests a medieval house with a large open-roofed hall.

Nor was the six-roomed house of Richard Mawdytt very different at his death in 1592. He, too, was a small merchant worth only £356 gross. His house is described as consisting of a shop, a hall, parlour, and kitchen, and of three chambers (bedrooms) above – one over the kitchen, another over the parlour, and 'the maidens chamber'. Here there was pretty certainly no chamber over the hall, for the maidservants' chamber would have been a small one tucked away somewhere. It was still the open-roofed medieval hall, dating in all probability from the fifteenth century, like so many surviving examples in the city.

As against these smaller and older houses, occupied by the lesser merchants, we have the new-built grander houses of what may be called the civic merchants, that is those belonging or related to the governing oligarchy of the city and likely to fill the office of mayor, sheriff, or receiver. The house of Thomas Prestwood the younger (1576) is a fine example of this type, possibly one of the beautiful houses built by his father before 1558. Such houses, with fifteen or more rooms, are best described by means of conventional plans of each floor, which, while not accurate in every detail, give the essential disposition of the rooms beyond much doubt (see next page).

The Prestwood house, like all the larger town houses of the time, occupied a long narrow site, fronting on to the main street and running back to a smaller street which acted as what we would call a service-road. A side passage, running the length of the house and generally known as 'the entry' or occasionally as 'tween doors', gave access to the ground-floor rooms and finally emerged at the back gate. The total depth of the house and all its appurtenances was considerable – in all probability about 140 ft. The frontage, on the other hand, was probably no more than 20 to 24 ft. The Prestwood house stood in St Stephen's parish, on the High Street and pretty certainly near St Stephen's church, and has long ago been destroyed. Since the site is known, however, it is possible to give these measurements.

On the ground floor the almost invariable plan of the larger house from the middle of the sixteenth century onwards was that of two blocks of building separated by a small courtyard. The front block contained the shop with a parlour behind, and possibly a spence or small buttery. The back block contained the kitchen, larder, main buttery, and any other domestic offices such as the brewhouse. Access between front and back blocks in bad weather was provided by a covered way, formed by the first-floor gallery being carried on a short colonnade.

Behind the kitchen block of the Prestwood house lay a much larger court, called the Great Court in the inventory, on the other side of which was the warehouse. Behind that again was a little court containing the stable with hay-loft over, which abutted directly on to the back street and so completed the property. Above the warehouse in all probability was the granary. Stable and hay-loft, warehouse and granary, could be serviced (in or out) by way of the back street. The problem of handling

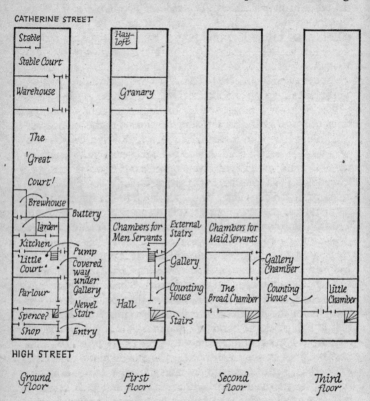

Conjectural plan of the Prestwood house in 1576
(Not drawn to scale)

heavy or bulky loads on such a narrow urban site was easily solved. It is an arrangement we find all along the main streets of Exeter. Back streets run parallel to the High Street and Fore

Street on both sides, and all the largest properties extended right through from the main street to the back street. Many do so to this day.

Access to the first floor of the front block was by means of a newel stair which carried on indeed up to the top of the house. In the Prestwood house, the hall, which was of course the principal living-room, overlooking the main street with a handsome oriel window, occupied the whole of this floor except for a small room where the stairs came up. This little room was used in the Prestwood house as 'the counting house by the hall'. A covered gallery connected the hall with the rooms over the kitchen block. These rooms probably comprised the men's bedroom and small service rooms. Food could be carried under cover from the kitchen along the gallery into the hall.

On the second floor we find the two principal bedrooms over the hall, called the fore-chamber and the broad (ie great) chamber. The stairs did not open directly into the great chamber but were shut off in some way. The fore-chamber overlooked the street by means of a handsome mullioned window (see Illus. 8 for a typical example) and the great chamber overlooked the inner courtyard. A higher gallery connected the great chamber with the back block, probably with 'the maidens chamber'. Finally, the front block rose to a gabled attic floor, which in the Prestwood house contained 'the higher chamber', the 'little chamber', and another little 'counting house'.

Thus the Prestwood house rose to a height of four floors (including the ground floor) on the street. It was not the largest house in Exeter. Illus. 8 shows an even more elaborate house (or rather pair of identical houses, for they are divided vertically all the way down) rising to five floors. This pair would have contained up to twenty rooms each, the additional rooms being chiefly bedrooms for servants and apprentices.

The inventories of the larger houses naturally show minor variations from the Prestwood house described above. Perhaps the most important variation was that on the first floor there were more usually two halls instead of one. That overlooking the street was called the fore-hall, while the hall proper over-looked the central courtyard by means of a mullioned window running the width of the room. The hall was generally the more important room, judging by its furnishings, but the fore-hall was nearly as comfortable. The fore-hall was probably more of a drawing-room (to use a later term), while the hall was the place where meals were taken by the family. Hall and fore-hall were separated by a small middle chamber where the stairs came up. The only other point worth noticing is that the Prest-wood house was exceptional in not having a cellar. Most of the houses along the four main streets of Exeter had cellars, in order to make the greatest possible use of restricted sites. These cellars were frequently excavated during the fifteenth century, when urban sites were becoming increasingly valuable; but some may be older.

The richer merchants of Exeter lived in considerable state, as the inventories show. Their plate 'napery', and apparel, as listed in the inventories, are all very considerable, indeed osten-tatious. It is not unusual to find plate worth £100 or more in a merchant house. The mayor of Exeter was an important man and was expected to entertain well, and to live well when not entertaining. Although he received a large allowance from the Chamber, his expenses were usually higher than this.* Only a rich merchant could afford the honour, and John Woolcot was passed over for many years because he was not considered rich enough to sustain the dignity of the office.

Woolcot in fact finally achieved the mayoralty in 1565. Of him Hooker says: 'this mayor had passed all the offices towards the mayoralty for about 22 years past and by reason of his age and his small wealth it was not thought nor meant that ever the office of the mayoralty should have fallen unto his lot. Never-theless, when the matter so fell out, and no means found how the same might be avoided, order was taken both that his house should be prepared and also he to be furnished with money for

* The mayor's allowance had been raised to £40 in 1551, to £60 13s 4d in 1564, to £80 in 1579, and to £120 before the end of the century.

his diet with liberality. The Chamber did consider he was in times past a great merchant and adventured very much, whereby he had great wealth, but in the end his losses were so great that he was very poor and lived in very mean a state.'

We know little that is personal of these merchants of Exeter beyond the brief glimpses Hooker gives us. John Woolcot was one of the old way of thinking.

He was a zealous man in the Romish religion and too much addicted unto papistry, and in the commotion time [the local description for several generations afterwards of the rebellion of 1549] when the Commons of Devon and Cornwall were up in rebellion for the same, and he was in the city the time of the besieging of the same: yet his affection was such towards them that upon a day, when he was captain of the ward for the charge of the West Gate of this city, he went out at the West Gate to the rebels without any commission and had conference with them, which was not after forgiven but turned him to displeasure.

Hooker was an old Protestant and doubtless remembered where others charitably forgot. Many of the leading merchants in that year had been Catholics – the city seems to have been pretty evenly divided at the top – but the older generation were dying one by one, and the younger men seem to have changed over easily enough. Indeed, it was not always a case of conforming to the established order of the new Settlement. John Periam had assisted Russell to crush the Catholics in 1549 while old William Periam, his father, kept his Catholic sympathies to the end. One would give much to know what passed between father and son in that bad year; but we do not even have William Periam's will to guide us. He was still a Catholic a year or two before his death, when he refused to give up a chalice and a pair of vestments to the Commissioners for Church Goods. He had given these to his parish church of St Olave about 1547 and had taken them back again when the Commissioners appeared.

The Elizabethan merchants were probably Protestants to a man. Of Thomas Prestwood the younger we have a more certain glimpse. A man's character is revealed by what he reads (above all when he has to buy his own books) and Prestwood's books are very revealing. The inventory of 1576 speaks of 'two bibles, one of Geneva making, and Calvin's book [presumably the *Christian Institutes* published definitively in 1559], Turner's *Herbal*, two books of service, one book of *The Fall of Princes*, a bridgement of the Statutes, Hall's *Chronicles*, with divers other books of Latin, French and English'. Prestwood read at 'a desk for a book' in the hall, looking out on to the teeming High Street below, though it was quiet enough in the evenings. Everybody was indoors by nine o'clock, and most were asleep.

Most merchants, apart from their business, lived private lives. The opportunities for public service were very few. There were only twenty-four places on the Chamber and once admitted a man stayed on for life. Vacancies occurred only at long intervals on the death or disablement of a sitting member. The great majority even of the merchant class could not expect to reach the Chamber, least of all the mayoralty. Members of parliament for the city, sheriffs, and receivers, all were chosen from the twenty-four. Beyond that, there were no opportunities for a man to make a public mark.

In the prime of his life, usually, the Exeter merchant made his will. By this he generally settled such real estate as he possessed – houses and other small properties in the city, farms, tithes, and even manors in the country if he were a successful man. He also distributed considerable sums of money among his wife and children. John Periam (*c* 1510–73) disposed of nearly £3,000 in money by his will, chiefly to his two sons (William got £1,400, John £800, and an unmarried daughter £300). Some of the sons' money may have been reinvested in the family business. But it is evident that in many families, especially where a merchant died young and the court of orphans administered his estate, the distribution of his personal wealth must have involved the end of the business, rather like the savagery of death duties today. Of Alexander Germyn's net estate of £550 11s 5d (1608), his widow got about £367 (two-thirds of the whole) and the five children got £36 14s 1d each. Robert Parr's nine children (1608) got £82 6s 10d each, the widow just over £740. Harry Maunder apparently left £360 net estate in 1564, with no surviving widow but nine children, each of whom got £40. So the Maunder business dissolved at once. Thomas Chappell left a widow and ten children in 1590, and even his large business (worth over £3,224 net) is heard of no more. Where the legacy was a large one, it may, as suggested above, have been reinvested in the business; or an elder son may have used his small inheritance to build up another business almost from scratch. But the general tendency was for a business to dissolve in every generation, mainly because its assets had to be realized and distributed among a considerable number of children. A large number of daughters was a particular misfortune from this point of view; the average merchant had to provide for the marriage of three or four daughters. Even here, a dowry might go to fertilize the son-in-law's own business. Only the really large businesses, however, could stand the effect of the merchant's death, and only these therefore survived into a second generation and, more rarely still, into a third.

In every generation, some merchants had left money for charities according to their means. Professor Jordan has recently traced the tremendous flow of charitable bequests in the sixteenth and seventeenth centuries, above all from the merchant class in the leading towns. How do the Exeter merchants stand up to this scrutiny?

A number of merchants took a special interest in the welfare of poor and friendless prisoners. Griffith Ameredith, who died in 1558, had been appalled in his lifetime by the way in which the bodies of those hanged were treated. They were brought back from the gallows, a mile or so outside the city, slung on a staff between two men, and having been brought to Exeter they were then flung into a grave in their clothes. Ameredith left a piece of property in East Devon, yielding 38s a year, to provide a shroud and a coffin for each body. William Tryvett, mayor in 1573, bequeathed 'one great Brass Crock, to boil meat therein, for the Use of the Prisoners in the Southgate Prison'. The main flow of bequests was, however, for the relief of the poor, more especially those who were old, and for the encouragement by timely loans of young artificers. The largest single benefaction was that of William Hurst in 1567, when he founded an almshouse for twelve poor men and endowed it with lands to the value of £12 4s 0d per annum. Both Thomas Prestwood (1576) and John Davy (1599) left money also for the foundation of smaller almshouses.

In 1572 John Periam left £100, to be lent to two young merchants freely for four years in order to set them on their feet. And from 1599 onwards there was a steady flow of bequests designed to provide free loans for young artificers or tradesmen for a period of years. The main flow of benefactions at Exeter came, however, a generation or two later, well into the seventeenth century, and even then Exeter saw nothing to match the noble foundation of Peter Blundell, of a school at Tiverton (1599). But Blundell had accumulated a fortune as a cloth merchant at Tiverton, fourteen miles to the north, far beyond that of the richest merchant in Exeter at this time.

The rich merchant's funeral was usually a costly affair. For some of the lesser men a sum of £10 to £20 sufficed to cover all the charges; but Thomas Chappell's funeral in 1590 cost as much as £120, and Walter Horsey's £100 in 1597. The funeral charges of Thomas Prestwood in January 1577 amounted to a modest £12 7s 2d. This included the cost of ten yards of black cloth 'for the children's gowns and coats' £4; 'to a tailor for making the boys' coats, 3s'; 6s to a joiner 'for the chest', 'for a tombstone 13s 4d' and 'for engraving the Tombstone, 9s'. At William Newcombe's funeral in 1609 the mourning clothes cost £42, the actual burial in the cathedral £20, and finally – the closing scene in the life and death of the merchant – the funeral dinner, in the hall of his dwelling-house, costing £13 6s 8d. But it is, perhaps, more fitting to say farewell to the

Exeter merchant as he is lowered into the grave, in the nave of his own little red-sandstone parish church to the mournful singing of the Vicars Choral and amid the darkening light of a cold January afternoon.

CHAPTER SIX

Three Devon Families

Cholwich

CHOLWICH TOWN (Illus. 3) lies nearly seven hundred
feet above the sea, eight or nine miles north-east of Plymouth, on the south-western flanks of Dartmoor. It is almost at
the boundary of the large parish of Cornwood, whose 10,117
acres run northwards for six miles into the depths of the moor,
as far as the boggy wastes of Erme Head. More than six thousand of Cornwood's acres are still common and wood.

Cholwich Town consists only of a large farmstead, the word
town being used, as it is so often in Devon and Cornwall, in its
Old English sense of *tun*, 'a farm'. It is a fine example of the
solid moorstone buildings one sees in all the parishes on the
fringes of Dartmoor, many of them dating from the sixteenth
and seventeenth centuries, some even older. They were the
homes of ancient freeholders whose pedigree goes two or three
centuries further back, and, one suspects, as far back as the
twelfth century in most cases, if one could only know. There
are, indeed, instances where we do know, and this essay is concerned with three such ancient families who were never important enough to have their pedigrees recorded by the heralds. –
Cholwich, Galsworthy, and Sokespitch.

The beginnings of the Cholwich family, and of their estate at
Cholwich Town, are made known to us in a charter, one of
a number in the British Museum relating to the parish of
Cornwood. This charter, endorsed in a seventeenth-century
hand 'The Anntient deed for Cholleswich granted by Guy of
Bryttavilla lord of Cornwood unto Edryke Syward with the
common ther', is in an early thirteenth-century hand but is
otherwise undated. It may be ascribed with some confidence to

a date between about 1200 and 1230, possibly from shortly after the great charter of disafforestation in 1204. It is a grant of the estate to Benedict son of Edric Siward, setting out the bounds so precisely that one can follow them on the 2½-inch or 6-inch map today, drawing upon it the exact limits of that ancient grant; and it takes the pedigree of this peasant family back into the mists of the twelfth century.

By this charter Guy de Brittevilla, lord of Cornwood, grants to Benedict son of Edric Siward:

> all my land of Cholleswyht in free, pure, and perpetual socage, namely, from the ford in the paved road [*via ferrata*] over that water which comes from Bromwiht [Broomage today] and falls into Pial. And thence from that ford along the paved highway above Torizhete and so westwards as far as the water of Toriz [Tory Brook]. And then up the Toriz as far as the stream by the north of Blacaorde [Blachford today] and so along the aforesaid stream as far as the spring which is at Pial head. And so along Piall, descending as far as the water of Bromwiht, and thence up to the aforesaid ford.

Benedict was to hold 'all the said land of Cholleswiche' with all its appurtenances to his heirs and assigns by right of inheritance in pure, free, and perpetual socage for ever, paying annually 4*s* at two terms of the year.

> And I grant to the said Benedict, his heirs and assigns, common pasture in all my moor and waste belonging to my demesne of Cornwood beginning at the north at the headwater of the Toriz in a line eastwards as far as *yalumphauede* [Yealm Head today] in woodland, open land, ways, and paths, and all other easements, freely to the said land of Cholleswiht in dry and wet, and to take there hay, turves, coal [peat], furze, and all other necessary commodities.

Benedict was not to do suit of court, except twice a year at *La More* in Cornwood and not elsewhere. Relief was limited to 4*s*.

The witnesses to this charter are Walter of Furthedele [Fardel],
Robert Eustaz, Randulph of Colland, William of Mewi
[Meavy], Edward le Danais, Walter of la Holamede, Roger of
Olleville, Richard Curteis, 'and many others'.

The estate delimited in this charter is roughly triangular in
shape, bounded on the south-west by the paved way from Cornwood to Cadover Bridge, on the north-west by the Tory
Brook, and on the east by the Piall river as it flows down
Cholwich Town Bottom. The base of the triangle along the
Piall is about a mile and a third long, and the other two sides
about a mile each, and the area so enclosed amounts to about
200–220 acres as near as one can estimate. At the time of the
Cornwood tithe award of 1842 Cholwich Town amounted to
just over 334 acres, but the map shows that a considerable tract
of waste to the east of the Piall river had been taken in by that
date. This probably formerly belonged to Parkland farm, judging from the way the boundaries run, and indeed the inquisition
post-mortem on Andrew Cholwich's lands in 1612 reveals
that he had bought more land round here from the lord of the
manor, some of which we are told lay in *Parkeland*. Thus the
eastern boundary of Cholwich had been considerably altered by
the nineteenth century. At the southern tip of the triangle also it
had lost two fields to another farm, amounting to about twenty
acres in all (fields nos 969 and 981 on the tithe map). We cannot
use the tithe maps of the 1840s, valuable as they are, as evidence
of the original shape and size of farms in any parish without
corroborative evidence.

The farmstead of Cholwich Town lies within a few yards of
its orginal eastern boundary, on the lee side of a ridge which
rises about 150 ft above it and affords some shelter against the
bitter north-western wind off the moor. A spring which bubbles
out into the yard today probably fixed the exact site for the first
farmstead, for there can be no doubt that the present site of the
farmstead is close to the granite-rubble buildings built by the
first settler, Benedict, out of the surface stone on his upland
farm. Other stones, as they were laboriously cleared in a widen-
ing circle around the house, went to the building of the dry-

walling around the first small fields. Cholwich lies half a mile along a rough lane off the old paved way mentioned in the first charter, a characteristic site for an early farm in Devon, a lane which ends in the cul-de-sac of the farmyard. For the whole of its length it is lined on either side with massive hedgebanks composed of granite boulders, many of which weigh several hundredweight, a monumental construction which must have accounted for several hundred tons of stone, all of it picked off the surface of the moorland waste in the early days and used in this effective way. There cannot be much doubt that this granite-lined lane leading in to Cholwich Town dates back at least to the early thirteenth century.

The foundation charter of Cholwich takes the pedigree of the Cholwiches – for they took the name of their new estate in the first generation of their ownership – well back into the twelfth century. Benedict, who was dead by 1249 (as we learn from a later record), was the son of Edric, who was the son of Siward. The name Edric Siward in the charter is almost certainly to be interpreted as Edric (son of) Siward, judging by similar instances in midland charters where our information is fuller; and Siward must have been alive in the middle decades of the twelfth century. The second half of the twelfth century is indeed a period which sees the emergence from total obscurity of many well-known Devonshire landed families – Kelly, Cruwys, Coffin, Fortescue, and Monk, to name only a few, mostly holding their lands by knight service. It also saw the emergence of a considerable class of lesser freeholders, most of whom held their lands in socage and by a very small annual rent. These would have been called *sokemen* in the midlands, but were never so called in Devon. By the end of the thirteenth century they form a numerous class in many parts of the county, particularly in the districts which were not settled at an early date but were left for clearance until after the Norman Conquest. For the origin of some at least of these lesser freeholders we must look back to the latter half of the twelfth century. It may well be that some come through from pre-Conquest times, as they undoubtedly do in the midland

Danelaw, though in Devon their ancestors are disguised as *villani* in the Domesday record.

It is in this setting that we observe the emergence of the Cholwiches as a distinct family towards the close of the twelfth century. Their socage estate at Cholwich was burdened from the first with a rent of 4s a year. In 1249, however, this rent was reduced to ½d yearly by John de Raddon, lord of Cornwood, by an exchange with Thomas, son of Benedict de Caldeswich. Thomas gave up all right and claim in two ferlings of land which he already possessed in *la Mora*, elsewhere in the parish. One is tempted to see in this the ancestral farm of Siward and Edric, before Benedict had been granted Cholwich.

The subsequent history of the family is one of long periods of darkness punctuated by flashes of light from such documents as have survived by chance. The process of clearing the fields of Cholwich Town was going on all the time, but we have no record of it. Like many other peasant freeholders, not only in Devon but all over England, the family was able in the course of time to put a younger son into the Church. William de Col-wiche, clerk, was instituted at Huntshaw, a North Devon parish, by bishop Grandisson in 1328. Towards the end of the fourteenth century we find the family being called Powne or Poune, possibly after another farm called Pound in Tamerton Foliot – not many miles away – where an elder son may have lived for a time before stepping into Cholwich. Fortunately, we are saved from any confusion arising from this change of name by the explicitness of a charter (Add Charter, no 26159) in which Isobel Choldeswych, widow of Ralph Powne, grants to John Choldeswych alias Powne, her younger son, and Beatrice his wife, her messuage and lands in Choldeswych, with common pasture on the moor between Yealm and Plym. This charter is dated from Cholwich in the year 1411. Here we have the ancestral estate being handed on during life from the older generation to the next, as was the custom.

Slowly, too, the peasant hand of the Cholwiches was closing over other little farms in their neighbourhood. In 1402 they took over some land in Cornwood, not specified in the charter,

which William Dunstone had held. In 1416 they got hold of
farms at Nether Bromwich and Rokmore. By the end of the
fifteenth century, or the beginning of the sixteenth, they were
also holding two other farms in Cholwich Town itself by copy
of court roll. On December 20th, 1528, at the court of Henry,
marquess of Exeter, Walter Chollesweche took from the lord
through Humphrey Colles, esquire (probably the steward of the
manor), two tenements with their appurtenances in Chollesweche, containing forty acres of land, which the same Walter
had held before and which was formerly in the tenure of
William Chollesweche (probably his father, now dead) – 'to
have and to hold for the term of his life according to the
custom of the manor. Walter paid an entry fine of 10s and
was admitted as the tenant of the two farms.

Ten years later, on July 20th, 1538, William and John
Cholwich took the reversion of the same two farms after the
death or surrender of Walter, for which they paid a fine of £16.
Henry, marquess of Exeter, had been attainted by this date and
his lands were in the hands of the Crown. The manor of Cornwood was being administered by Anthony Harvy, gent., who
was apparently administering many of the marquess's lands in
Devon on behalf of the Crown. This may account in great part
for the marked rise in the entry fine, but part is also due to the
fact that the term is for two lives and not one as in 1528. Thirty
years later the entry fine had risen to £40 for three lives, with a
reserved rent of two capons or 4s yearly. On this occasion
Walter Cholleswech senior, and his sons Andrew and Walter,
were admitted to the two farms as copyholders by Elizabeth
Pollard, then lady of the manor. They had in addition to do
suit of mill at Slade, in the manor of Cornwood. This form of
copyhold is hardly distinguishable from the lease for three lives
which was to become the universal form of tenure in Devon
from the late sixteenth century until the late eighteenth, coup-
led with a definite term of ninety-nine years. Here, in 1568, we
have what is virtually a lease for three lives, with a high fine
upon entry (almost equivalent to the purchase of the freehold)
and a small reserved rent.

The appearance of these copyhold tenements at Cholwich Town at this comparatively late date calls for some comment, for it introduces an element of confusion into the history of the farm and the Cholwich estate. The boundaries set forth in the foundation charter in the first quarter of the thirteenth century clearly enclosed a compact estate of some 200–220 acres, as we have seen, albeit the greater part of it was moorland waste and could never be anything else; and equally clearly it was a grant of the complete estate as a free tenement. The confusion is not lessened by the discovery, in the inquisition's post-mortem on the lands of William Cholwich (1561) and Andrew Cholwich (1612), that the ancestral estate of Cholwich is described as a messuage, thirty acres of land, three acres of meadow, two acres of wood, and ten acres of furze and heath. It is true that the interpretation of acreages in fines is always a matter of difficulty, but at least we know that the fines never under-estimated the true acreage whatever else they did. Their general tendency was to over-estimate acreages greatly so as to ensure that everything was safely included within the scope of the fine. As a general rule, too, it is the acreage attached to the word 'land' in these fines that is the most significant figure, which gives an area of only thirty acres for the Cholwich free-hold. Even if we include the other figures, we get only forty-five acres all told. It looks very much as though by the sixteenth century the ancestral estate of the Cholwiches had become a mere thirty-acre holding, in other words the typical ferling tenement that one finds all over Devon during the medieval period.

Moreover, the inquisition of 1612 reveals that outside this ancient freehold at Cholwich, but still in Cholwich Town, there were not two copyhold farms but four. These are described as four messuages and four gardens, two orchards, eighty acres of land, twenty acres of meadow, twenty acres of pasture, forty acres of wood, 200 acres of furze and heath, and 200 acres of moor, with common pasture on Pen Moor belonging to them. The acreages given for furze, heath, and moor may be ignored for our purposes. We shall be safe in assuming that the four

copyhold farms comprised eighty acres, especially as we know
that two of them were stated to cover forty acres in the record of
1528 already cited. With meadow, pasture, and wood they
amount to 160 acres. In the same inquisition the acreage of the
Cholwich freehold farm adds up to thirty-five acres, ignoring
the furze and heath once more, giving us a total for all five
farms at Cholwich Town of 195 acres. This looks very like the
whole of the land originally included in the first Cholwich
grant. But why this original grant of some 200 acres should
appear in the sixteenth century in the form of five small farms,
four of them copyhold and only one freehold, is something we
cannot explain. There must have been some transaction of
which we now have no knowledge. One can only state the facts
as one finds them.

The inquisition of 1612 further tells us that by that date
Andrew Cholwich had bought the four copyhold farms from
the lord of the manor, Richard Cole esquire, and added them to
his growing estate. The record of his purchase of two of them
survives among the enrolled deeds for the year 1603, and from
this we learn that they were probably the same two copyhold
farms his ancestors had held a hundred years earlier. Andrew
still had an estate in them by copy of court roll from Elizabeth
Pollard, but he had in fact leased out both farms to other and
smaller men, as so many big copyholders were doing in Devon
during these years, investing in copyholds and re-letting them
at an annual rent to show a profit on the original investment.

We have anticipated a little in following these copyhold
farms through the sixteenth century. Walter Cholwich, who
had taken the farms in 1528, died in 1557. His will, which
survives in the British Museum with all the other Cornwood
documents, describes him as yeoman but tells us nothing about
his farming. It is unfortunate that the inventory of his personal
estate has not survived as it would have given us a picture of a
Devon moorland farmer in the mid-sixteenth century. As it is,
his will gives only a few details about some of the household
treasures at Cholwich. He directs his son and heir, William, to
leave after his own death to his own son Walter 'a folyng tabell

& a Coborde, a brasen Crocke of the best, a short leged Crocke,
& the best brasen panne, too flanders pannys of brasse, halff a
dosen of pewter vessells performed, a dosen of sylver spones, a
bounden weyn & all the plowgere of the same'. If Walter the
younger should die without heirs, then these heirlooms should
go to his brother Edward.

William Cholwich, who succeeded to his father's farms, died
only three years later – on October 10th, 1560. For him we
have neither will nor inventory, but something better – an inquisition post-mortem on his lands. This document enables us
to see how far the Cholwiches had gone in their accumulation
of lands, to sum up their career, as it were, from the standpoint
of their material advancement. Besides Cholwich itself, which
they had owned since the first years of the thirteenth century,
there was Nether Bromwich and the meadow on Rook Moor
which they had acquired in 1416. Then there were three small
pieces of land in the parishes of Brixton and Newton Ferrers
amounting to about twenty-six acres at the most, all held in free
socage at small annual rents; there was a house and garden in
Plymouth held by fealty of William Trelawnye alias Hawkyns
as of his manor of Sutton Vautort; and there was a biggish farm
called Stiddeston (Stidston today) in the parish of South Brent,
about 100–115 acres. It is a typical yeoman estate – three farms
of some size, some smaller parcels of land elsewhere, a house in
the nearest market-town, and (as we know from the other
records) two copyhold farms as well. The Cholwiches were
beginning to emerge from the ruck of village farmers by the
middle of the sixteenth century.

Walter Cholwich is named in the inquisition as son and heir.
He and his brother Andrew were named in the court roll of
1568, already cited, when with their father they had paid a fine
of £40 for entry into the two copyhold farms at Cholwich.
Walter must have died young, for in 1587 we find Andrew
Cholwich ruling at Cholwich and buying another small property in the adjacent manor of Lutton. By the time he bought
two of the Cholwich copyholds in 1603 he is described as
gentleman in the records; and in 1605 he set the seal on his new

status by acquiring the manor of Down Thomas in the parish of Wembury. Finally, he married the heiress of a gentle family called Rich, by whom he acquired a not inconsiderable property in two or three parishes in the South Hams, including the estate and mansion of Oldstone in Blackawton parish, a few miles west of Dartmouth. He abandoned the moorland farm of his ancestors, leaving it to the occupation of his son William, and took up his residence in the more genial house of Oldstone, where he lived on his rents like a country gentleman and farmed some of his land round about. The Cholwiches, with this move, left behind them their long descent as medieval peasant-farmers and Tudor yeomen. They had now entered the lower ranks of the seventeenth-century gentry.

A rental of Andrew Cholwich's lands, drawn up in 1605, survives in the British Museum. It is a modest document and not as informative as we should like, but it shows that he had a considerable number of farms and other properties in the five parishes of Cornwood, Brixton, South Brent, Ugborough, and Wembury, besides the house in Plymouth. His total rents amounted to £24 17s 11d, eleven capons, and one ploughing day or 2d for the same. Out of this he paid out five chief rents, amounting to 9s a year in all, on his socage estates. His net rental was therefore £24 8s 11d a year. But the great tracts of rough pasture on the moor above Cholwich Town, granted to his forebears so long before, were also valuable. They brought him in £27 6s 8d a year in seven 'Justment Rents' of varying amounts.*

These agistment rents probably represented the full annual value of the land, but the rents of his farms, scattered over the fertile South Hams for the most part, were only the small reserved rents and take no account of the more or less substantial entry fines which had been paid on each property. Probably all his farms – except Oldstone, which he would have kept in hand, and Cholwich, where his son farmed – were let on leases for three lives at this time, and we have no idea of the sum total of

---

* Justment = agistment, the right to graze cattle over land.

the fines in these leases. Andrew Cholwich was much better off
than his modest rental would suggest; but for all that he was
only one among the numerous class of minor gentry with
whom the county of Devon swarmed in the seventeenth century. The inscription to his memory in Blackawton church calls
him 'esquire', another step upwards in the social hierarchy, but
the heralds passed the family by in their visitation of 1620. It
was understandable that the visitation of 1564 should have ignored them, for they were then only moorland yeomen, but
even in the second generation of their gentility they could not
achieve recognition. And when William Cholwich, son of
Andrew, obtained a grant of arms in 1657, this was shortly
afterwards disowned.

The Cholwiches continued to live obscurely. They took no
discoverable part in the Civil Wars, though the fighting wan-
dered up and down Devon and there were great doings at Dartmouth, only a few miles away. They might even have heard the
thud of the cannon on their fields at Oldstone on an easterly
wind; but they took no sides. Perhaps they were not yet far
enough removed from the peasant mentality to have any strong
passion for either side, or at least to take any chances with
either. And so the wars left them, so far as we know, undis-
turbed. William succeeded Andrew at Oldstone, then another
Andrew and another William; and Thomas succeeded
William in the placid middle years of the eighteenth
century. Thomas died unmarried and with him the elder
branch of the family died out. For generations they lived useful
and obscure lives on their own estate, unknown to all but a
small circle in their own countryside, and their monuments
went up one by one on the walls of the parish church at Blackawton, or their names were incised in slate on the church
floor as the years went by – 1646, 1673, 1726, 1764, 1768,
1775.

The historical interest of the family shifts now from the
house at Oldstone to the teeming streets of Restoration Exeter,
rising fast among the cities and trading centres of England, a
place where able and well-favoured men could make fortunes

1. Bellever Farm, c 1890

2. Rashleigh Barton: seventeenth-century farm buildings

3. Cholwich Town, Cornwood

4. Morwellham, *c* 1870

5. Water-wheel at Blanchdown, Devon Great Consols

6. Exeter Quay. The seventeenth-century Custom House is in the centre, with nineteenth-century warehouses on the right

7. Elizabethan merchants' houses, High Street, Exeter

8. Elizabethan houses, Fore Street, Exeter

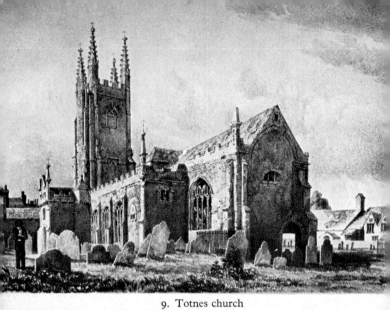

9. Totnes church

10. Harberton church

11. Broad Clyst church

12. Christow church

13. Lower Tor, Widecombe-in-the-Moor

and careers in a single generation. Ships from Holland, Spain, Portugal, Italy, Flanders, and Germany crowded at the quays and wharves on the Exe. Most of the flourishing woollen industry of South-Western England centred upon the city, which was an industrial town and a large port, the political and social capital for the South West, and the seat of a bishopric. Into this town, on the rising tide of its fortunes, came John Cholwich, a younger son of Andrew Cholwich of Oldstone, who could not succeed to the family estate and who therefore sought, as did scores of younger sons of Devonshire squires and gentry, a career as a merchant. He married the daughter of another successful Exeter merchant – John Cooke, who had bought the estate of Kenbury about five miles south of the city in 1668 and whose handsome coloured monument to his wife decorates the walls of Exminster church (1690). John Cholwich in turn had prospered sufficiently by 1677 to purchase the manor of Farringdon, some five miles east of the city, and there he founded a new branch of his ancient family, more opulent than the old.

He became an alderman of Exeter, though never mayor, and his attempt in 1701 to sit for Exeter in parliament as a Whig failed, two Tories being elected. The tide was already turning against the merchant-aldermen and ex-mayors, who had sat so often for the city in the seventeenth century and earlier, in favour of members chosen from the leading landed families of the county, especially those who lived near the city. John Cholwich never stood again but seems to have preferred to cultivate the county henceforward. He became a justice for the county, and a deputy lieutenant in 1701. In 1704, however, he was suddenly removed from the commission of the peace, together with a number of other county justices – all 'outed without any cause assigned'. A letter from Richard Duke of Otterton, who was himself removed, to Robert Harley in London, gives a list of these justices and their incomes. Cholwich was reckoned to be worth £600 a year in lands, besides £5,000 in money. He became a trustee of the Rolles, then the richest family in Devon, and exchequer commissioner in 1718, the year before his brother William at Oldstone became sheriff of Devon.

The way now lay open, with this foundation of mercantile wealth and a country-house near the city, into new fields which touched the local society of Devon at many points. John Cholwich, the eldest son of the merchant, was brought up to the law and became recorder of Exeter, an office which he held from 1751 until his death in 1764. He, too, married the daughter of a successful Exeter merchant and left three sons. John, the eldest, married the daughter of Samuel Burridge, one of the wealthiest woollen merchants in Tiverton, and seems to have exercised no profession except that of a country gentleman on his Farringdon estate. The second son, William, married and produced a daughter who in turn married Sir John Duntze, an eminent merchant and banker in Exeter, member of parliament for Tiverton (1768–95), and the great rival of John Baring in the commercial and political fields. Samuel, the third son, became the Rev Samuel Cholwich, DD, rector and vicar of Ermington, and vicar of Holbeton, who married the daughter of his kinsman at Oldstone. Of the daughters of the recorder, one married Edward Drewe, a barrister of Exeter who came from the Drewe family of Grange in Broadhembury (founded by another Devonshire lawyer in Elizabethan days) and the other became the wife of the archdeacon of Cornwall, who was also a canon of Exeter Cathedral and rector of Farringdon.

John Burridge Cholwich, the son of the Cholwich-Burridge marriage, seems to have lived for many years at Tiverton, though he contested Exeter unsuccessfully as a Whig at the by-election of 1776. He was then a young man of 23, and his formidable opponent was John Baring (1730–1816), the second generation of the great merchant house in Exeter, and a man of exactly twice his age. Baring got in by 659 votes to 558. There was said to have been much bribery at this election – John Baring himself said it had been expensive – but Cholwich's petition was unsuccessful.

Cholwich had married a daughter of Sir John Duntze, now a squire at Rockbeare, just outside Exeter, so doubly cementing

the alliance between the two families. Duntze had defeated
Baring at Tiverton in 1768, after a bitter struggle, and the two
men who had been friends remained enemies thereafter. Eight
years later Baring had his revenge on Duntze, by keeping his
son-in-law out of the House.

In the general election of 1780 the Chamber of Exeter
adopted Baring and Cholwich as their candidates, to the ex-
clusion of Sir Charles Warwick Bampfylde of Poltimore, a
Whig like Cholwich. But Cholwich did not go to the poll, and
Baring and Bampfylde were returned without a contest. In the
following year Cholwich was chosen sheriff of Devon, at the
age of 28, but he nourished no more parliamentary ambitions.
He contented himself with supporting his father-in-law's political interest at Tiverton (for which he sat until his death in
1795) and in taking part in Tiverton town affairs. In 1800 he
was mayor of the town when his uncle at Oldstone died and left
him his South Devon estate. 'Mr Cholwich, the Mayor, has
been left by his uncle an estate of about £800 or £1000 a year,'
wrote the indefatigable Beavis Wood to Lord Harrowby on
April 19th, 1800.* By then the mayor was a power in Tiverton.
Wood adds that 'the Mayor has told Mr Worth that he expects
to have the next vacancy in parliament reserved for the Duntze
family'. Cholwich seems to have retired to Farringdon shortly
after this. His fortune must have been substantial for he now
enjoyed all the family estates, the old and the new, and his
mother also must have been well-to-do.

The genealogical details of the Cholwich alliances, tedious
perhaps in themselves, paint a good picture of the compact
upper-class society of eighteenth-century Exeter and of the
country around it. The plain grey homespun of those early centuries on the edge of Dartmoor had been transformed by the
passage of time into a rich and many-coloured tapestry of local
life in and around the provincial capital of Georgian Exeter – a
tapestry peopled with lawyers, parsons, archdeacons and

* Beavis Wood was town clerk of Tiverton and political manager
to the Ryders (Lord Harrowby) who controlled the borough at this
time.

canons, merchants, bankers, members of parliament, and country squires.

But it all ended quickly after this, as if this exuberant flowering in the eighteenth century had exhausted the sturdy plant at last. The quiet country life among the woods and gardens of Oldstone was all very well, but this was too much. When Lysons wrote in 1822 John Burridge Cholwich was living on his estate at Farringdon, in a spacious house set in a park, with much fine timber and flourishing plantations. And here, on May 14th, 1835, he died, the last of his race. Down at Blackawton the widow of the last Cholwich to live at Oldstone lived on to the great age of 97, dying at Larcombe House in that parish in 1857. But both Farringdon and Oldstone had been sold to others by that date, and the estates broken up.

In 1873, when the Return of the Owners of Land was made, not an acre of land was entered under the name of Cholwich, and the very name itself is now unknown in the county. But how far they had travelled while they lasted! From the peasants Siward and Edric and Benedict, groping in the cold moorland mists of the twelfth century, hauling at the granite boulders with their bare hands, clearing their little fields, building the first farmstead to house themselves and their cattle under one roof and the massive granite walls we see today as we pick our way up the long rough lane to the ancestral farmstead; from all this to the Georgian squire in his mansion and his park, with his silver and his maidservants, all set down among the luxuriant and softer landscape of eastern Devon, among the tall elms and the cornfields of that warm red soil. The Tudor moorstone farmstead of Cholwich Town still stands like a primeval monument and farming goes on there still; but Farringdon House – rebuilt in Victorian days – is an approved school under the new social order, and Oldstone is a dark and melancholy ruin among the chestnuts, the nettles, and the elder.

Galsworthy

Towards the end of John Galsworthy's *Swan Song*, Soames Forsyte travels far down to the South West, to Dorset, to visit the original home of his ancestors. He visits the little grey church close to the sea and stumbles in the churchyard over the worn and lichened stone that marked the grave of his great-great-grandfather who had died in 1777 – Jolyon Forsyte. Then, after a call at the vicarage, he finds his way round the Coombe to the lonely field called Great Forsyte, where only a stone or two of the ancestral farmhouse remains among the grass, and there he sits and muses nostalgically.

It had been the old England, when they lived down here – the England of pack-horses and very little smoke, of peat and wood fires ... A static England, that dug and wove, where your parish was your world, and you were a churchwarden if you didn't take care. His own grandfather – begotten and born one hundred and fifty-six years ago, in the best bed, not two dozen paces from where he was sitting ... In the old time here, without newspapers, with nothing from the outer world, you'd grow up without any sense of the State or that sort of thing. There'd be the church and your bible, he supposed, and the market some miles away, and you'd work and eat and sleep and breathe the air and drink your cider and embrace your wife and watch your children from June to June; and a good thing too! What more did you do now that brought you any satisfaction? 'Change, it's all on the surface,' thought Soames; 'the roots are the same. You can't get beyond them – try as you will!'

Such a pilgrimage was made by Galsworthy himself in the autumn of 1912, not to the coast of Dorset but to that of Devon, at Wembury not far from Plymouth, for he was intensely interested in his own origins and descent through a long line of Devon farmers. The Forsyte family tree bears a striking resemblance to his own in each generation of the nineteenth century: headed by Jolyon Forsyte the Dorset farmer, then Jolyon his son, the builder, and then 'Old Jolyon', the director of companies, and James the solicitor; and then Soames Forsyte, the solicitor and connoisseur.

Galsworthy spent some thirty years pondering over the history of his family. As long ago as 1903 he addressed a query to *Devon Notes and Queries* which shows that he was even then giving thought to the problem of his Devonian ancestry, for he knew that his grandfather had left Devon for London in the 1830s. He knew too that Devon was his native heath, for in the north-west of the county there is a remote farm called Galsworthy. No other of the thousands of farms in the county bears this name: clearly, this was the very origin of his family. And clearly, too, this interest in his ancestry and in the generations of his family, was one of the main impulses towards the creation of the Forsyte saga. He began to write *The Man of Property*, which was the first of the great Forsyte sequence, in 1902, and with its publication in 1906 his name was made. In 1908 he made his country home in Devon – at Wingstone, in the Parish of Manaton – and here he lived for some years, completely at home. 'He could never forget', says his biographer, 'that he was of Devon origin, and to him Devon was home as no other part of the world could quite be.'*

Galsworthy's inquiries into his family's past history were apparently confined, so far at least as the earlier generations went, to research into the parish registers of Wembury and Plymstock, parishes to the east and south-east of Plymouth. But the surviving Plymstock registers do not begin until 1591, and those of Wembury not until 1611, so that the earliest ancestor known to him was Edmund Galsworthy, farmer, who died at Plymstock in 1598. For the next eight or nine generations the Galsworthys farmed in Plymstock and Wembury, down to John Galsworthy – great-grandfather of the novelist – who died in 1811 and whose prone and broken tombstone may be found in Plymstock churchyard. But let us begin at the beginning and turn back to the eleventh century.

The ultimate origin of the Galsworthy family is to be sought in a remote farm in north-western Devon, in the parish of Buckland Brewer and about seven miles south-west of the town

* Marrot, *The Life and Letters of John Galsworthy*, p 403.

of Bideford. Much of the country to the west and south-west of
Bideford lies high, six or seven hundred feet above the sea, on
stiff and waterlogged clays. It is a landscape mostly of thin and
stunted trees, unlike the normal luxuriant growth of Devon, of
poor pasture and cold, unrewarding ploughland. A good deal of
it is moorland, where the bubbling note of the curlew is the
only natural sound except that of the soft, rustling rain. It is in
this country that we find the first Galsworthys, and once again,
like the Cholwiches across the other side of Devon, their ancestry goes back into the dim period towards the middle of the
twelfth century; and once more – but with a very different
history from the deep-rooted Cholwiches – we can trace them
into modern times. We are far from being able to write a continuous history of any of these lesser families who have contributed so much to the making of Devonshire history, least of
all perhaps the Galsworthys, who moved around the county in
the sixteenth century and left it altogether in the nineteenth.
All we can do is to illuminate certain periods in their history
between the twelfth century and the twentieth, mainly the earliest phase and the most recent.

Galsworthy, now and for long divided into two farms –
North and South – was a small pre-Conquest estate which belonged to Ansger the Breton in 1086. One Edwi had held it in
1066, in the time of Edward the Confessor, 'and he could go to
what lord he liked'. He was a free man, but he was dispossessed
at the Conquest and he disappears forthwith from history. The
full Exon Domesday entry relating to Galsworthy is as
follows:

> To this manor [ie, Buckland Brewer] has been added a
> manor called *Galeshora* which Edwi held in the time of king
> Edward and he could go to what lord he liked and it paid
> geld for half a virgate. This one plough can till. Ansger [the
> Breton] holds it of the count [of Mortain]. There Ansger has
> three *villani* who have one plough and twenty acres of pas-
> ture. It is worth ten shillings and was worth the same when
> the count received it.

The meaning of the name Galsworthy has been variously interpreted. It is not a *worthy* (an enclosed farmstead) by origin, but has assumed this suffix in a countryside which is closely sprinkled with *worthys*, both villages and farms. It was originally *Galeshora* (1086), or *Galshore* (1244, 1249), and *Galsore* (1330); the *worthy* creeps in during the sixteenth century, perhaps even in the fifteenth. *Ora* means a slope, which suits the position of the farm well enough, running down as it does to the small stream which forms its western boundary. *Gal-* has been interpreted as possibly the Celtic name of this stream, but Ekwall derives it more plausibly from the Old English *gagol*, 'bog myrtle' or 'sweet gale', a plant which would flourish in these waterlogged fields. Galsworthy was therefore 'the bank or slope where the bog myrtle grew', something, one feels, which would have pleased the novelist John Galsworthy had he known.

So far the Galsworthy family have not emerged in the records, but they do so in unmistakable fashion in an assize roll of 1249. The assize came to determine whether Walter Gerveys of Exeter, William de Bikeleg, and three others (named) 'disseised Gilbert de Galeshor of his free tenement in Galeshor', apparently a piece of ground of 5½ acres with its appurtenances. William de Bikeleg (Bickleigh) asserted that Gilbert could not be disseised of any free tenement because Gilbert was his villein (*villanus*); Gilbert replied that he was a free man and that all his ancestors were free men. The two sides then produce rival pedigrees going back another three generations, back into the twelfth century.

The pedigree put forward by William de Bikeleg is worth reproducing in full.

He says that one Kin was villein of Walter le Bret in his land of Galeshor' in the time of king Richard, uncle of the present king (1189–99). And afterwards Walter le Bret gave the said land, with all its appurtenances and with the aforesaid Kin his villein, and all his brood, to William Bruer the elder. And William Bruer the younger, son of the foregoing, gave the premises with all (&c. as before) to Huward de Bikele, father of the aforesaid William, whose heir William is. And the aforesaid Kin had four sons, viz. Robert, William, Curnell, and Aleuric. And from Robert issued one Elyas, and from Elyas Gilbert the present plaintiff. From William no issue. From Kernell (*sic*) one Estrilda. From Estrilda two daughters, Agnes and Emelota. From Agnes one Thomas, who is present and avows that he is a serf. From Emelota one Roger, who is also present and avows himself a serf. From Aleuric two daughters, Claricia and Ragenilda. From Claricia issued Jordan; and from Jordan issued Gilbert and Roger, who are present and avow that they are serfs. He also says that the aforesaid Kin, the ancestor, had a sister, by name Aluina [Ælfwynn], from whom issued Gunnilda. From Gunnilda issued Robert, and from Robert, John, who is present and avows himself a serf.

On the other hand,

Gilbert says he is a free man and all his ancestors were free men. And he says that one Dunewell his ancestor was a free man, and had three sons, Robert, Austin, and William, all alike free.

William de Bikeleg' then comes and offers the king 20s. to have enquiry made whether all the ancestors of Gilbert were serfs of Walter le Bret and the others named above, and whether Gilbert is his serf.

A jury chosen by consent of the parties declare on oath that the aforesaid Gilbert is a free man and his ancestors were free and held the aforesaid land freely. Therefore it is adjudged that G. shall recover his seisin by view of sworn men, and that he a free man, and quit against William and his heirs of all serfdom (*nativitas*) and earthly servitude. William, Walter, and all the other defendants are in mercy. Damages 2s.

The pedigree overleaf will make this somewhat complicated

record clearer, besides furnishing an interesting example of an early peasant descent:

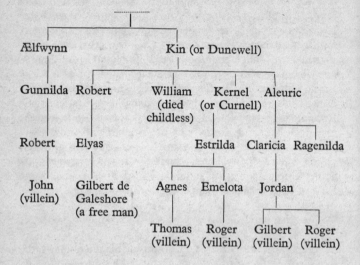

It appears from this record that Kin and Dunewell are one and the same man, and that Gilbert de Galeshore accepts the pedigree so far as William and Robert are concerned, but repudiates Kernel and Ælfric, to give them their English names. The contrast between the Old English and the French names is interesting; and there can be little doubt of the pure English ancestry of the founder of the Galsworthy family. What is also interesting is that while Gilbert is accepted as a free man, descended in the male line from Kin or Dunewell, his great-grandfather, all his kinsmen – John, Thomas, Roger, another Gilbert, and another Roger – are all agreed to be villeins, and all have descended through the female line. Clearly, the female Galsworthys, born into a free family, have all married villeins, and their offspring are therefore born villeins also.

Galsworthy, which had been a separate though small manor

in 1066, had been added to the great manor of Buckland Brewer twenty years later, no doubt because Ansger the Breton came into possession of both manors at the Conquest and there was no point in maintaining the separate identity of the smaller one. Under William Brewer, shortly after 1200, Buckland Brewer was divided into two moieties, one of which – the more valuable – he gave to his foundation of Ford Abbey on the eastern borders of the county. The other moiety, that which was given to Huward de Bikelegh, became known as the manor of Vielston after its capital estate of that name in the southern portion of Buckland Brewer parish, and Galsworthy went with this manor henceforward.

A survey of the manor of Vielston, made as late as 1609, throws a little more light upon the early history of the Galsworthy family in their remote outpost; but it also raises questions which we cannot answer for lack of information. The manor of Vielston then had four freeholders, of whom three (John Bray, John Westcott, and Philip Risdon, esquire) divided South Galsworthy between them equally. Each of them held in free socage, paying a third of the ancient socage rent of 8s a year, and holding a third of the acreage of the farm and 'a third part of half Galesore moor'. We are told that John Bray held his share as the heir of Agnes Bray, daughter and heiress of the last of the Galsworthys, and one assumes that John Westcott and Philip Risdon had acquired their shares by marriage with or descent from other daughters and co-heiresses. We are further told that the farm of South Galsworthy had originally been granted to Roger de Galsore by William de Alneto for ever, paying a rent of 8s a year for it in lieu of all services.

A William Daunay (de Alneto) had acquired the manor of Vielston some time before 1303, probably through an heiress of the Bykeleghs, so that the grant of South Galsworthy in socage to Roger de Galsworthy may be put back to the late thirteenth century or the early fourteenth. What is not clear is what had happened to North Galsworthy, a little farther along the lane, but one is tempted to say that this was probably the free tenement about which trouble had arisen in 1249 and which another branch of the family had held freely since the late twelfth century at least.

It is also possible that the Roger who was granted the farm of South Galsworthy to hold freely for ever may have been one of the two Rogers (de Galesore) who were alive in 1249 and were then described as villeins. Such grants to villeins of their freedom and of a free tenement in return for large sums of money can be found at this period elsewhere in Devon, and it is possible that here at Galsworthy we have the villein side of the family purchasing its freedom and with it a freehold estate, as we should say in modern language.

The Galsworthys, then, were free tenants by the fourteenth century, and we find them still farming at Galsworthy in Henry VIII's time. In the lay subsidy assessment of 1524 for Buckland Brewer there are named, representing three different households:

Thomas Gallysworthy in goods 60s		18d
Jane Gallysworthy executor of the will of John		
Gallysworthy in goods 40s		12d
John Gallysworthy in goods 40s		12d

We have already seen that Galsworthy had been divided into North and South, possibly when Roger de Galsworthy received his grant. But the division may be earlier than this as the Domesday entry reveals that there were three villeins on the estate in 1086, who were probably working two or three separate farms. However this may be, South Galsworthy contained, in 1609, some sixty acres of land (each of the three freeholders had just about twenty acres) and a half of Galsworthy moor. Presumably the whole estate of Galsworthy contained about 120 acres, which corresponds closely with the one ploughland mentioned in Domesday. In the Buckland Brewer tithe award of 1842, Galsworthy added up to 128 acres, plus 81½ acres in three fields on Galsworthy Common. There were then two farms, but they were not distinguished as North and South.

By the end of the sixteenth century the Galsworthys at South

Galsworthy had died out in the male line, leaving three co-heiresses who carried the ancestral farm by marriage into three other families; and it appears that all the Galsworthys had left the parish of Buckland Brewer by this time. The family had begun to disperse.

A John Galsworthy was assessed on goods (probably 'wages') to the value of 20s at Hartland in 1524. He is probably the John Galsworthy whose son Thomas was baptized at Hartland parish church on February 21st, 1558, the entry of which occurs on the first page of the parish register. In 1566 a John Galsworthy, possibly the same John (or his son) who had been assessed on his wages forty-two years earlier, turns up as the customary tenant of Moor Farm in Hartland parish, about ten miles west of Buckland Brewer and a mile and a half to the north of Hartland town. His descendants continued to farm Moor (a forty-six-acre farm in the survey of 1566) without a break for nearly three hundred years, until the last John Galsworthy died in 1848.

Moor Farm in Hartland is at the north-western extremity of Devon. Another branch of the Galsworthys turns up at the extreme south-western corner, just outside Plymouth, in the early sixteenth century; and it is from this branch that John Galsworthy the novelist was descended. Edmund Galsworthy died at Plymstock in 1598, as we have seen, but there were earlier Galsworthys at both Plymstock and Wembury. In the Plymstock assessment to the subsidy of 1524 William Galsworthy is named, paying 4d, and at Wembury in the same year Benett Galsworthy paid 2s, about the usual assessment of a small farmer at this date. One or the other of these is probably the father or grandfather of Edmund. In the absence of parish registers for this period, and the total destruction of all the wills at the Exeter Probate Registry in an air raid in 1942, the main hope of linking these two ends lies in other tax assessments in the Public Record Office, or in a lawsuit in Chancery, the Star Chamber, or the Court of Requests, for sixteenth-century Englishmen were passionately litigious.

At Wembury and Plymstock the Galsworthys farmed for

nearly three hundred years continuously, from the early sixteenth century until the early nineteenth. So far they had all been farmers – all the way back to that shadowy, primordial figure of Kin, the father of them all, on his lonely North Devon farm from which the family took its name.

The nineteenth century presented new opportunities to those who could take them, and it was now that the Galsworthy fortunes took an upward turn. Possibly, too, the great depression in English farming after the Napoleonic Wars, and especially in the early 1820s, helped to bring about the revolution in the Galsworthy fortunes. In these years, from about 1815 to 1840, thousands of English farmers were forced to give up farming, after centuries of it in the family, and to seek a new livelihood in the towns. In the North of England many entered the factories, or started small businesses of their own; in the South the ranks of the mid-Victorian shopkeepers contained many who had been born on a farm a few miles away. My own great-grandfather left the family farm in East Devon in the great slump of the 1820s and went to Exeter to learn the baking trade. By 1834 he had his own business, and was a Ten-pound Householder. He got on in a modest way, but he never made his fortune (nor have his descendants).

John Galsworthy, born a farmer's son at Plymstock in 1782, made a better choice when he left his father's farm. The Exeter of my great-grandfather's time was a respectable, somnolent cathedral city of about 20,000 people: its great days of industry and commerce were over. But the Plymouth to which John Galsworthy went was a booming war-town, especially its neighbour Dock, to the west, a roaring town of sailors and ships. Dock, created as a naval dockyard by William III out of empty fields and marshes, was in 1800 the largest town in Devon and one of the largest in the South of England. With its 24,000 people, it now overshadowed even its ancient and jealous neighbour Plymouth. Another ten years of war and Dock's population rose to 30,000. With the end of the war in 1815 this rate of growth slowed up immediately, but the new town had been consolidated. In 1821 it had more than 33,000

people, and three years later it was rechristened with the more
dignified name of Devonport. Foulston's fine Column was
erected to commemorate this event.

It was in this boom town, which trebled its population between 1780 and 1815 as a result of almost incessant wars, that
John Galsworthy II (1782–1855) made a comfortable fortune
as a merchant and ship-owner. A directory for Dock in 1823
names 'J. Galsworthy, dealer in marine stores' in Dock-wall
street. No man with a little capital and his head screwed on the
right way could fail to succeed in such a town. He retired from
business ten years after this (1833), migrated to London, and
settled down with his money invested in house-property, ad-
vised no doubt by his brother Silas, who was a builder in
London. And there he died, in March 1855, the man of property in the solid early Victorian age. His son, John Galsworthy
III (1817–1904), moved at a higher level, a solicitor and a
director of companies, another characteristically Victorian
figure. And to him, at the prudent age of 50, a son John was
born, on an August day in the year 1867, at his large and ugly
house at Kingston, just outside London. The Galsworthys now
owned not a single acre of farmland in Devon: their wealth lay,
not in crops and animals, but in the grey wilderness of the
streets of London.

Sokespitch

Hazlitt once asked James Northcote, the eminent Devonian
painter, why he did not come up to London, and why other
clever men born in Devon also stayed at home. To which
Northcote replied that Devon

is almost a peninsula, so that there is no thorough-fare, and
people are therefore more stationary in one spot. It is for this
reason they necessarily intermarry among themselves, and
you can trace the genealogies of families for centuries back
... There are country-squires and plain gentry down in that
part of the world, who have occupied the same estates long
before the Conquest (as the Suckbitches in particular, – not a

very sounding name) and who look down upon the Courtneys as upstarts.

Nor had this remarkable family of Suckbitch escaped attention before this, as Polwhele relates in his *History of Devonshire* at the close of the eighteenth century. He says:

> I have been informed by a gentleman, who knew much of what passed among the polite wits and eminent writers of his time, that Eustace Budgell, a Devonshire gentleman, who was honoured by an intimacy with Mr Addison, furnished that great man with the following hint from this family, in his first number of the Spectator, viz. 'I was born to a small hereditary estate, which according to the tradition of the village where it lies, was bounded by the same hedges and ditches in William the Conqueror's time that it is at present, and has been delivered down from father to son whole and entire, without the loss or acquisition of a single field or meadow during the space of six hundred years.'

Elsewhere in his *History*, Polwhele gives

a more particular account of this extraordinary family, which I shall extract from an authentic paper written by a gentleman who resided at Clyst St George in 1768. 'The family of *Sucpitch* was certainly settled here before the conquest, where they may remain unextinct for centuries to come, as the present sire has grandchildren of vigorous constitutions. Notwithstanding these *Sucpitchs* have possessed the same spot for such an immense succession of time, possibly as long before the conquest as since, not one of all their race has been conspicuous for any achievement or exploit, or celebrated in our annals for one heroic or famous action. What makes this yet the stranger is, that not a collateral branch hath thrown any lustre on them. Hence it is evident, that for so many ages it can only be said they have existed, and not that they have had the honour of living to their country, their neighbours, or

themselves. With supine indolence they have, in a manner,
slumbered over their little farm that is blessed with fertility,
and every natural advantage of land and water; inattentive
to those numberless improvements and embellishments, no
less in point of profit than beauty, of which it is capable.
Their sole dissipation was hunting and shooting, which they
(I speak of time immemorial) rather pursued as the business
than the amusements of life. The various rural scenes, and
numerous objects, with which this spot is finely diversified,
afford proper subjects for a landscape. From 70 l. per
annum, at which it was rated, (though occasionally for a
qualification, they could easily prove it worth 100 l.) an opulent gentleman, with taste and judgement, by erecting water-
mills, embanking the marshes, (improving the arable is impossible) might advance it to 500 l. In length of time the tide
has fretted, and made several channels and serpentine canals,
through three marshes; by which soals, and a variety of sea-
fish, daily make their way from the main river, up to the
garden-wall and orchard hedges. Duck, widgeon &c. may be
shot almost from their windows. Though they kept on hunting, till the neighbouring glebes were verdant with barley,
yet they never failed having the best crop. The first who
rouzed from his lethargy, and deviated for once into the right
path, was the old gentleman, *i.e.* the father of the present (the
oldest within memory) who planted in hedge-rows about 700
elms, which many years since, an experienced person told
me, annually gained sixpence a tree. This great grandfather
admitted me to a familiar acquaintance with him, which he
thought no small favour. He valued himself highly on his
extraction and honesty, though he had not a worthy action to
relate of any predecessor, nor a title to boast beyond that of a
head-constable or church-warden. He substituted age for
merit, and esteemed his eldest ancestor the best gentleman.
His narratives and fabulous stories, he told to others, till he
believed them himself. Often has he repeated to me, though
he thought it always new, that *Cyrus,* King of *Prussia,* [*sic*],
discovered their founder in the woods, *sucking a bitch.* He

looked down on his illustrious neighbours at Powderham-castle as his juniors, and would by no means allow the noble house of Courtenay, to be coeval with the family of Suck-pitch. The son (now the grandfather) has been one of the strongest men in the kingdom; one of exorbitant passions, which, uncultivated by education, he was never taught to regulate. The want of restraining the impetuosity of his temper, oftentimes involved him in troubles. Mr. Trosse, formerly lord of the manor, sued him for a trespass and assault, presenting his loaded piece, and threatening to shoot the 'squire. The defendant produced at the trial, by way of flourish, (being not very material to the issue) two small parchment grants or feoffments, which none present could read throughout, nor ascertain their æra, being without date or seal; however, the bar was satisfied of their being passed before the conqueror's time. These curious antique charters are their only archives, which may not be unworthy the notice of the virtuosi. From the conquest their progeny may not, however, have been numerous, by their longevity: the great-grandfather died fifteen years ago, was aged 90, and his son now about 80. I apprehend that, possibly, the present generation is not more than the seventh degree from that period.'

Polwhele adds some comments of his own about this curious family, who made so marked an impression on their entire neighbourhood despite their complete obscurity and the small-ness of their estate.

The whole series of these people, from the original down to the present descendant, seem to have been actuated by the one common disposition, to have adopted a narrow plan, and invariably adhered to it; that is, to preserve their estate entire without addition or diminution: and to transmit a posterity uninterrupted in the male line, was their highest ambition. They could never have engaged in commerce, because then their estate must have fluctuated: there is no

proof of any kind, not even a supposition, of their ever purchasing or selling any piece of land whatsoever: they ought,
therefore, to be allowed the little share of merit of steering
between the extremes of avidity, the *auri sacra fames*, on the
one hand, and of profusion and extravagance on the other . . .
It seems amazing that such a family, unknown a few miles
around them, never acquiring any fame, without alliance,
pedigree, or coat of arms, not an individual of improved
talents; in short, living almost in total obscurity within
themselves, no better than a race of unpolished peasants;
that notwithstanding all these circumstances, their antiquity
should from such remote ages, thro' the course of many centuries, be handed down to the present time.

The name of the family is variously spelt. Lysons renders it
as Sukespic or Sokespitch; Polwhele as Sucpitch, Sokespitch,
or Suckbitch. Risdon calls them Suckbitch, and so does his
contemporary Westcote. Sir William Pole preferred the form
Sokespitch. Contemporary records render the name in a wild
variety of ways; but we will fasten upon Sokespitch for our
purposes since that is how they generally spelt it themselves in
their latter days, except perhaps when they wished to lend
colour to their fabulous origin in the Persian woods.

The Sokespitches lived on their farm of Marsh Barton, in
Clyst St George, about four miles south-east of Exeter, a little
above the salt marshes and tidal flats of the river Clyst, and
close to the point where it enters the noble shining expanse of
the Exe estuary. One can see their farm well from the railway
line between Exeter and Exmouth as it crosses the mouth of the
Clyst by an iron viaduct. The legend that they had occupied
this farm since the Norman Conquest goes back at least to
Risdon's day, for he, writing in the early years of the seventeenth century, says: 'In this parish (Clyst St George) hath
dwelt a family called Suckbitch, even from the conquest to this
day, (as they affirm) never of any great eminency, yet worthy
memory, that it hath pleased God to continue one name
amongst a thousand, to enjoy a place so many ages.' By the

eighteenth century the legend of their antiquity had assumed a
more fabulous shape, as we have seen. Their neighbour of 1768
thought they might have dwelt at Marsh 'as long before the
conquest as since'; though the head of the family at the same
date took their pedigree back, in his story of their origin, to the
sixth century before Christ. No wonder they regarded the illustrious Courtenays, at Powderham, just down the river, as mere
parvenus and upstarts.

Who were the Sokespitches, and where did they really come
from? The truth about their origin is as interesting as any of
the fabulous legends told about it: more so, indeed, because it is
the truth. Once again, our inquiry takes us back to the middle
decades of the twelfth century: not to some untenanted moorland waste or cold clay farm, but this time to the ancient streets
of Exeter, dominated by the red and royal castle of Rougemont
and by the twin towers of the Norman cathedral, then just built,
their new Beer stone glowing in the sun.

By a fortunate chance, the 'two curious antique charters' of
the Sokespitches – those which had baffled the eighteenth-century lawyers when the old man had waved them in court – have
survived, at least in a later transcription, and they reveal the
beginning of the story of that farm beside the Clyst marshes,
though not the beginning of the family. One of these charters
was a confirmatory grant of Heathfield, another farm in the
manor of Clistwick or Clyst St George, about the year 1240,
which will be referred to later. The Sokespitches are not known
ever to have possessed this farm, and it is curious therefore to
find that they held an original charter relating to it. The other
charter is, however, the undated original grant by the lord of
the manor of the estate of Marsh to the first known member of
the Sokespitch family, a grant which it is possible to date at
somewhere between 1170 and 1180. Though this is far from a
pre-Conquest, not to mention a pre-Christian origin, it is a
respectable enough antiquity.

By this charter Henry de la Pomerei granted

  to William Sukespic of Exeter, and to his heirs for homage

and service, one ferling of land in my manor of Clistwic, together with the salt marsh which extends from the cold spring (*Chaldewilla*) as the great stream goes, as far as the channel (*alveum*) of Clist and beside Clist as far as the bounds of Woodbury and thence as far as the dry land, with all the gains he can win from the sea to his own improvement (*ad sui correctionem*) and with all other appurtenances, namely in fish, meadows, paths, waters, and other free customs . . .

For this estate, William Sukespic and his heirs were to pay a chief rent of 4s a year in lieu of all services and secular exactions; and as a recognition of the transaction William gave to Henry de la Pomerei a cask of wine, and to Henry, his son, an ivory bow. This charter is undated, and the preference of the Pomeray family for the name of Henry does not help.

One of the witnesses to the grant was William Howel, who was a provost of Exeter in 1159–60, again between 1160 and 1164, and again some time between 1170 and 1180. Another witness, John, son of Theobald, was provost between about 1165 and 1175. William Sukespic himself appears as a witness to Dean and Chapter charters at Exeter *c* 1160 and *c* 1180. We may date the Clistwick charter therefore as not likely to be later than 1170–80.

William Sukespic was probably a merchant in Exeter, exporting cloth and importing wine. The cloth manufacture of Exeter in the late twelfth century was a considerable one. In 1202 the city stood seventh in a list of payments made by the cloth towns, equal to Stamford, Newcastle, and Gloucester, and more important than Norwich or Coventry. There is evidence in the Pipe Rolls also that wine was being imported at Topsham and Exeter in the same period, and a gift of a cask of wine from William Sukespic to his new lord suggests that he may have been engaged in this trade. The rise of the wine trade in the South-Western ports is associated with the acquisition of the rich province of Aquitaine by the marriage of Henry II in

1152. The ports of Plymouth and Dartmouth owe their very
existence and early growth to the political and commercial relations established by this union. There can be no doubt that
the trade of the city of Exeter, already well established, received a considerable impetus from the same cause, though
with its less satisfactory harbour and greater distance from the
ports of South-West France the older town gained less than
Dartmouth or Plymouth.

Already, in the twelfth century, successful merchants in the
English towns had begun to buy lands in the surrounding
countryside. England developed no urban patrician class like
the great commercial centres on the Continent: its rich merchants tended from the beginning to leave the towns and estab-
lish themselves as lords of manors and to found landed families
rather than commercial dynasties.

William Sukespic contented himself with buying a farm on
the edge of the salt marshes, a few miles below the city. Some
years later, Hilary Blund, who was provost of Exeter on two or
three occasions in the second and third decades of the thirteenth century and mayor for several years in the 1220s and
1230s, bought the manor of Clistwick from the Pomerais, so
becoming the lord of Robert Sukespic, the son of William.
About the same time his kinsman Gilbert le Blund purchased
the adjacent manor of Clyst St Mary.

There is a hint from an early deed among the Exeter archives
that the Sukespics may have possessed land up at Whitestone,
in the hills to the west of the city, before they came down into
Exeter. In March 1221 Robert, son of William Sukespic,
granted to Jordan Bestelbise a rent of 6s arising out of property
in Exeter, which Robert had acquired in exchange for five ferlings of land in Whitestone. This may have been the family
property in the twelfth century, from which they, or one of
them, came down to the growing city to seek a living in trade.
The English towns drew largely upon the free peasantry of
their hinterlands for people and capital in the twelfth and thirteenth centuries, and Exeter was no exception. One may also
hazard the suggestion that, if this is what happened with the

Sukespics, they acquired a new name in Exeter, for it appears to mean 'Suck-spice'.*

Although William Sukespic had purchased the farm of one ferling at Clistwick (later known as Clyst St George) as early as 1170–80, the family continued to trade in Exeter for some considerable time after this, presumably leasing their farm to others. There is, indeed, one such lease among the Exeter archives, dated Michaelmas 1227, whereby Jordan Bestelbise took a moiety of Robert Sukespic's land in Clistwyk for a term of ten years at an annual rent of 2s. Jordan busied himself in reclaiming the salt marsh from the tidal waters of the river. Perhaps that is why the rent was so low: reclamation may have been a condition of the lease. Before this lease had expired, probably c 1234–5, Robert Sukespich granted to the hospital of St Mary Magdalen at Exeter a moiety of his marsh at Clistwyk 'which Jordan Bestelbise enclosed', together with four acres of arable land adjacent to the marsh on the east. Hilary Blund confirmed this grant as lord of Clistwick. Here we have an example of yet another kind of reclamation, this time of salt marsh that was normally flooded at high tide; and a later record suggests that the amount of land reclaimed was considerable. When in the 1420s John Sokespiche attempted to lay claim to the hospital land in Clistwick, which his ancestors had given to the hospital nearly two hundred years earlier and which he apparently leased from it, as it lay adjacent to his own farm, he had to be ejected after a lawsuit. The land is then described as four acres of arable and thirty acres of pasture. The thirty acres of pasture represent the moiety of the reclaimed marsh granted c 1234–5, which therefore amounted to about sixty acres altogether.

It has been said that the Sokespitches continued to live and trade in Exeter for a considerable time after they acquired

* Mr Cecil Spiegelhalter favours this suggested meaning if one takes the name to be of Norman origin. If one prefers an English origin, the meaning is 'Suck-bacon' (? equivalent to chaw-bacon). A writer in *Notes and Queries* for May 1852 thought 'Chaw-bacon' was the likeliest meaning of the name.

their Clistwick property. Robert Sukespic died before 1237, when we find Isabella, his widow, releasing her right of dower in the property which her husband had given to the hospital. This is described as four acres of land with marsh in Chaldewell, in Clistwick, and various houses in the High Street and South Street of Exeter. Her son Jordan assented to this release.

This is the last reference to the name of Sukespic among the Exeter archives, but one strongly suspects that a branch of the family goes on in Exeter under the modified surname of Spicer. In 1241–2 there is a grant by Jordan Speciarius to the dean and chapter of Exeter of a tenement in South Street, where we know the Sukespics had property. This grant is confirmed by Robert, son of Jordan Speciarius, in 1242–3. Further, we find Isabella, widow of Henry le Poter, granting a rent of 10s outside the West Gate of Exeter to Roger Speciarius, who re-granted it to the archdeacon of Exeter in 1240. And in 1246 there is a bond by Roger, son of Robert le Espicer, to pay a certain sum yearly to the Magdalen hospital. This combination of names – Isabella, Jordan, Robert – and the location of the property concerned in the deeds, taken together with the fact that the name Speciarius or le Espicer appears immediately after the name of Sukespic fades out, and the continuance of the trade of *spicer* – all these clues point to the possibility that the Sokespitch family, established on their farm at Clistwick, continued also in the city of Exeter, in another branch under the name of Spicer.

If this supposition be true we are presented with a wonderful contrast between the two sides of the family for the next five or six centuries. The Spicers were prominent throughout the four-teenth century as stewards, receivers, and mayors of the city; and in later centuries they go on with gathering strength, giving mayors and sheriffs to the city, and once – in 1766–8 – a member of parliament. For several generations they were im-portant merchants, especially in the sixteenth and seventeenth centuries, accumulating landed property all the while. William Spicer, esquire, bought the estate of Weare Park, just outside

Topsham, about the year 1760 and retired there to live the life
of a country gentleman. He represented his native city in parliament for two years, but did not stand at the election of 1768
as he believed the other members looked down upon him,
'though he had money'. In the nineteenth century the family
had much property in Heavitree, a suburb of Exeter,* but by
1873 they, too, had disappeared altogether from the list of
landowners in the county.

In contrast to these centuries of vigour and achievement by
the Spicers, the Sokespitches settled down as farmers at Marsh,
as their farm became called at an early date, and vanished into
almost total obscurity. They only become known to us at intervals through their tax assessments, as churchwardens occasionally, and in other trivial ways.

Jordan Suckespich witnessed an undated grant by Hilary
Blund to Thomas son of Durand of a farm called *Hetfelda* 'in
my manor of Clist Wiche', another free tenement to be held at a
rent of 4s per annum like that of the Sokespitches. This was a
piece of open heath ('heath field') which had already been reclaimed and brought under cultivation as the grant refers to the
previous tenant, Richard Basch, and the buildings on the tenement. Thus there were two free tenements in the manor of
Clistwick, or Clyst St George, each held at an annual rent of 4s,
one created about 1170–80, the other about the year 1240. The
inquisition post-mortem on the lands of William de Campo
Ernulphi in 1305 deals with the manor of Clistwick, which then
had two free tenants paying 8s a year and nine conventionary
tenants paying 42s 5d in assized rents. The subsidy of 1332
mentions both the free tenants by name, Hilary Darrant paying
12d, Thomas Soxspit 2s. In 1398 John Sokepych and Roger
Durant witnessed a charter at Clyst St George, but by 1524 the
Durrants had gone, probably replaced by the Beres. In the
subsidy of that year John Bere was assessed on lands and

---

* There is a Spicer Road on the Heavitree side of Exeter, presumably developed on part of their property here. William Francis Spicer
(1763–1853) is buried at Topsham. There is a mural tablet in Heavitree church.

tenements to the annual value of £4, and Thomas Sockysbyssh similarly to the annual value of £8.

Little remains to be said of the Sokespitches. It is not entirely true that they never added to their estate. According to Pole they acquired a small estate in Withycombe Raleigh at some date, and a Chancery suit towards the end of the fifteenth century reveals that for a time they had two farms, totalling about 200 acres. Thomas Sokespyk, son and heir of John Sokespyk, declared that he was seised in fee of two farms in Clyst St George and Kennford, which had descended to him as son and heir, but the deeds and evidences had come into the hands of William Pers who refused to give them up. The plaintiff prayed therefore, in the usual form, for a writ of subpoena to be served on the defendant to appear in the high court of Chancery and justify his action. There are no other documents in the case, and we do not learn what happened. This experience of extending their little estate from one farm to two perhaps taught the family a lesson and reinforced their native indolence, if such it was. And so they drifted peacefully on into the eighteenth century where we first encountered them, doing no more than planting trees in one generation, farming in a leisurely fashion, fishing in their own water, shooting over their own lands, content with complete obscurity.

Towards the end of the eighteenth century, when Polwhele was writing, Robert Sokespitch removed to a farm a few miles away at Littleham, though he still kept his hereditary estate in hand. He had two sons, and there seemed no reason why the family should not go on, as their neighbour had said, for as many centuries to come. But it all came to an end suddenly. One son was in the 'East Indies', says Lysons. He was the 'Capt. Suxpitch of Bombay' who died there in 1822 at the age of 44, as a headstone in Woodbury churchyard informs us. In 1803 they sold their ancient estate to Alexander Hamilton Hamilton, esquire, a neighbouring landowner, so ending a tenure which had lasted from the reign of Henry II to that of George III. Within a few more years the last of the family was buried in the churchyard at Woodbury: Thomas, the other son of Robert Sokespitch (or Suxpitch as the headstone has it), died November 1st, 1833, at the age of 65, the very last of that line.

The sudden end of the family at Marsh is curious. One wonders what lay behind the decision to sell an estate on which they had seemed so deeply entrenched fifty years earlier. The move to Littleham in the 1780s or early 90s was the first symptom of a desire for change that the family had shown for several centuries; and the son who left the farm to enter the service of the East India Company, and never came back – what was he thinking of? What restlessness seized upon the Sokespitches after 600 years in one small spot? At any rate, it was a fatal disturbance of the spirit, and within twenty years of making the first move they had ended their monumental life at Marsh in Clyst St George.

Like the Cholwiches, they had begun in the latter half of the twelfth century, full of energy, to create a farm out of what was largely waste land: for the one it was the granite-strewn moor, for the other a stretch of salt marsh over which the tides flowed twice a day. By embanking the river, and making ditches and drains, the Sokespiches had trebled the area of their farm during the early years of the thirteenth century, adding about sixty acres of good pasture to their ferling (about thirty acres) of arable on the slopes above the marsh. One can see all this so well on the map: how the farmstead stands today at one corner of the farm, on slightly higher ground, among its one-time arable, and how the rich and level pastures, interlaced with the blue veins of ditches in all directions, stretch away westwards to the edge of the river, where a long winding embankment on either side reduces its width to a few muddy yards. It is clear from the map that the Clyst, so small today, once flowed in a channel some 600 yards wide in its lower course. By the twelfth century, when the great colonization movement in the English countryside was gathering force again, the river had narrowed its own channel with broad stretches of mud and silt on either side, just as the Taw had done on a more massive scale in North Devon; rough grass had sown itself on these broad acres of silt, but the high tides still washed in and out and made it unusable.

The land was there for all to see at low tide, and so that Exeter merchant William Sukespic took it — *cum toto conquesto quod poterit ex parte maris perquirere ad sui correctionem*. He and his son recovered this land, made fine rich pasture of it, and the family settled down there. But it was too easy after that. While the Cholwiches toiled on unresting in the struggle against the Dartmoor climate, adding precious acre to acre to make certain of a living however hard Nature might fight against them, the Sokespitches basked in the warm Exe valley, with less than half the rainfall of Cholwich Town, short mild winters, early springs, a deep red arable soil on the slopes, and luxuriant pastures below. There was no basking for the Cholwiches while the sun ripened their barley; no tides brought their food up daily to their garden walls. They had to work hard, and they slowly expanded their estate through the centuries until they could safely blossom forth in the more genial climate of Restoration and Georgian Exeter. The Sokespitches spent two or three generations in making their farm, and then relaxed for most of the next fifteen or twenty. The achievements of the Cholwiches and lack of any achievement by the Sokespitches over the same long period arose from a difference of energies more than abilities; and energy in Devon is very much a matter of climate. Cholwich Town and Marsh Barton are worlds apart in this respect.

CHAPTER SEVEN

Epidemics in Tudor Devon

MANY PEOPLE have searched parish registers for their own genealogical purposes and are familiar with their contents. But few local historians have used them for a wider purpose such as the reconstruction of the public health of a parish or a wider region, by means of a detailed study of the burial registers week by week and year by year. Here is a new field of local history which has scarcely been scratched. Most of the major outbreaks of plague and other killing diseases are known and have been discussed, for example, in Creighton's two volumes on *The History of Epidemics in Britain,* published in 1891. But many local outbreaks, some of them on a large scale, remain to be identified in parish registers. Most of these were outbreaks of bubonic plague, but there were a number of other killing diseases at work, and a close study of the chronology of burials – the time of the year, the incidence within families, and within different age-groups – is required before we can claim to know all that we should about the health of our ancestors. I am writing here about the sixteenth century in particular, but a similar study could be made of every generation down to modern times, and I hope that some parish historians will be inspired to make a complete 'health survey' of their chosen territory.

Parish registers were ordered to be kept from the autumn of 1538, though few registers survive complete from that date. Even after that date, many registers were not well kept and are not a complete record of all baptisms, marriages, and burials. The careful student of particular registers soon learns where they are deficient and works accordingly.

In Devon about thirty registers seem to be complete from 1538 onwards, several more begin in the 1540s, many more in the 1550s, so that one could write a history of public health over a good deal of Devon during a period of more than 400 years. Only in exceptional cases, such as St Leonard's (Exeter), where the surviving register begins only in 1704, or Nymet Rowland, beginning in 1719, are we seriously frustrated by the loss of several generations of these records.*

Epidemics before 1546

According to Creighton, the summer of 1540 'was a sickly one throughout England'. This was not bubonic plague, which was endemic in this country for more than 300 years after the first outbreak in 1348 – usually known as the Black Death – but was described as 'hot agues' or 'laskes' or dysentery. Stow called it 'the bloody flux', which makes its nature even clearer. The summer of 1540 was one of great drought. Wells and brooks dried up, and produced ideal conditions for conveying infection by contaminated food and garbage.

It remains to be seen how many of the early Devon registers reflect this particular outbreak. There is no trace of any excessive mortality in the Colyton parish register, which purports to be complete from 1538; but one cannot help noticing that the number of burials recorded in three years – 1540, 1541, and 1542 – is suspiciously low. Thus in 1539 (actually from March 25th, 1539, to March 24th, 1540) twelve burials were recorded. In 1541 there were only four (from August 9th to October 9th), and in 1542 only five. In 1543 twenty burials are recorded. It is clear, therefore, that though the Colyton register appears on the face of it to be a perfect record, it is not so. For some reason the register was badly kept during these years, and the baptismal registers show the same laxity, certainly in 1540 and 1542. Thus in looking for evidence of known outbreaks of illness in local registers one must be continually on the watch for faulty

---

* The Devon & Cornwall Record Society has a collection of transcripts of several hundred parish registers for these two counties, available to members, which make this kind of historical search easy. But students working on one parish should always check the transcript against the original register wherever possible.

keeping of the record by the parson. Not a single burial is recorded at Colyton between April 8th, 1540, and August 9th, 1541. Did the parson or curate himself die of dysentery in the summer of 1540, or what happened?

The registers of Bovey Tracey show an outbreak of some sort in 1541. For the years 1539–45 (but excluding 1541) the average number of burials was just about thirteen per annum. In 1541 there were twenty-one burials, rather more than 50 per cent above the average. Bridford, on the other hand, shows no increase in this year; nor does the equally isolated parish of Clayhanger near the Blackdown Hills. A number of other parishes, well scattered throughout the county, similarly show no perceptible increase. We may conclude that the epidemic of dysentery did not hit Devon, with its generally higher rainfall and multitude of copious streams.

Some parishes showed a marked increase in the year 1542. At Shobrooke the burials shot up to eleven, just about twice the annual average for the decade of the 1540s. Indeed, if we exclude the bad years of 1542 and 1545 the average number of burials at Shobrooke was 4.4 a year. So the bad years showed nearly treble the ordinary number of burials (eleven in each year). At Georgeham, similarly, there were fifteen burials in 1542, well over two and a half times the average for normal years. And of these fifteen deaths, seven took place in the summer, between May and July. At Kenn also there was a mild epidemic in 1542, as in 1545, with deaths rising to about twice the average level. Perhaps these small, scattered outbreaks were dysentery rather than plague, due to local infections. One might have expected plague to be more general, though not necessarily to hit every parish, as we shall see shortly.

The plague of 1546–7

The first large-scale epidemic we can study in the Devon registers is the plague of 1546–7. London, being better documented and reported on by visitors and others, provides a good source for identifying the nature of epidemics that are un-named in the burial registers of provincial parishes. According to

Creighton, there was plague in London in the late autumn of
1547, and in 1548 a 'great pestilence'. That there was plague in
Devon by the autumn of 1546 is made clear in a letter from
certain commissioners of musters to the Privy Council in
London. They report about the danger of mustering a large
number of men 'while plague reigned so fervently' in the county,
and receive permission from the Council to delay matters until
the epidemic had ceased.

In Devon we have sufficient information at this period from
some twenty-five towns and villages all over the county. In
some places the visitation was very severe, in others there is no
observable trace in the registers in these years.

Perhaps the most striking evidence comes from Barnstaple,
in North Devon. Here the average number of burials per
annum in the seven years 1539–45 inclusive was exactly forty.
During the first few months of 1546 there was no marked increase, with thirty-seven burials recorded down to the end of
August. The plague claimed its first victim on September 6th,
so the parson records, but earlier cases may have escaped his
notice. Indeed, there had been thirteen burials in the preceding
three months, an abnormal number which may indicate the
slow beginnings of the epidemic.

From September 6th until October 18th, no fewer than
seventy-four people were buried; about two years' deaths in the
space of six weeks. There were several days in October when
four or five people were buried. For a week there is a gap in the
register (no wonder the parson could not keep up with it) and
then four days in which another ten people were buried.
Another gap of thirteen days, and then a sequence of forty-five
burials between November 10th and 30th: over a year's deaths
within three weeks. In December there were eleven burials in
the first nine days, and then follows a gap of eleven weeks in the
register (until February 25th, 1547). Altogether, 176 burials
are actually recorded. The gaps in October and November can
easily be allowed for as burials were averaging 2.5 a day from
October 1st to November 30th. On the eighteen missing days
we can assume a minimum of forty-five burials. By December

the burial-rate was moderating, but we can assume at least one per day for the missing twenty-two days of the month. The total number of burials for the calendar year 1546 was therefore 244, possibly slightly higher if the breakdown of the entries in October and November reflects a particularly critical spell when the harassed parson could not keep pace with his records. At any rate, the number of deaths at Barnstaple in that year was more than six times the average of the normal years that had preceded it.

Mortality was still high in 1547. How high we cannot be sure for the burials register remained unwritten until near the end of February; but in the next ten months sixty-nine people were buried. There are strong indications that plague flared up again that spring, for there were no fewer than forty burials in March, April and May. There were probably well over 100 deaths in the complete year. Over the eight years 1548–55 the burial-rate returned to its pre-plague average of forty per annum.

The visitation of plague at Barnstaple was a major one. More than 200 people died from it – rather more than a tenth of the entire population of the town – assuming that forty people would have died in the normal course of events. Yet in the large village of Braunton, five miles to the west, there was only a slight trace (if any) of plague during 1546. Here the average number of deaths per annum in 1539–45 was 14½. In the course of 1546, twenty-three people died – about eight more than the average. But the plague, which had flared up again at Barnstaple, suddenly spread to Braunton in the early spring of 1547. There were seventeen burials during April, sometimes three in one day: a year's deaths in four weeks. It was a short attack, dying away by the end of June, but it may have flared up again a year or so later. For while the number of deaths during 1548 returned to normal, the figure for 1549 jumped to thirty-three. Thereafter it fell to near the pre-plague level again.

What happened in the remoter North Devon villages? North Molton, a large village on the southern foothills of Exmoor, was hardly touched in 1546–7. The parish of East Down, at the western end of Exmoor, escaped in 1546–7 but was badly hit

by the Great Sweat four years later (in 1551). This will be
referred to more fully a little later. Parkham, well to the west of
Bideford, was only lightly touched in 1546 and not at all in
1551.

There are two other villages in these parts – Georgeham and
Northam – for which information is forthcoming. Here the picture is confused and complicated. At Georgeham in a 'normal'
year between 1540 and 1550 there were five or six burials (5.7),
but in 1542 this rate trebled (to fifteen). There were seven
deaths between May and July: probably a quite local outburst
of plague. Here, too, the late spring of 1547 produced another
outbreak; six deaths in May, and sixteen altogether during the
year. Georgeham therefore suffered two minor outbreaks of
plague in the 1540s. In these two years thirty-one people died,
as against the eleven who would have died normally: an additional loss of twenty people due to plague. The village also
had a touch of the sweating sickness in 1551, with several additional deaths in the summer months.

The populous village of Northam, on its hill just north of
Bideford, usually had ten burials a year in the 1540s; 1546–7
passed off quite normally here, but in 1549 the burials multiplied by nearly four (thirty-six during the year). This, too, must
have been a purely local epidemic of some sort, for one does not
find it repeated elsewhere in the parishes for which we have the
necessary records, and two-thirds of the thirty-six deaths took
place in the three winter months from November 1549 to January 1550. What this infection was we cannot even guess.

The health picture in North Devon during the 1540s, the
first complete decade for which we have the records, is therefore a complex one. Plague was, more often than not, a highly
local thing: one village could be suffering sharply from it,
whilst its neighbours were free. Their turn usually came later,
but after a long interval which suggests that the outbreak was
spontaneous and not carried from somewhere else.

How does this pattern compare with what we find in South
Devon? We may begin with the city of Exeter, by far the
largest town in the West of England. Unfortunately only two of

the city's twenty or so parishes (including the suburban parishes of St Thomas and St Leonard) can produce registers
going back to 1538. These are St Petrock and St Mary Arches,
both crowded central parishes. In St Petrock there were twenty
burials during 1546 as compared with the normal three or four.
Ten of these fell between June 8th and July 17th. Yet in St
Mary Arches, only 200 or 300 yards away, there is no sign at all
of plague at this time. Normally there were three burials a year
in this parish: in 1547 there were nineteen, but with a curious
incidence that makes it difficult to be certain of plague. It has
been suggested by a medical authority that it may have been
typhus or sweating-sickness.* It is a matter for regret that we
have no other Exeter parish registers to throw more light on
this confusing picture of public health in 1546–7: but what is
clear is the surprising fact that even in a crowded city one
parish could be afflicted while another only two or three
minutes' walk away could escape. Did townspeople, as well as
perhaps country-people, instinctively take sensible precautions
when plague was known to be about, even before the authorities
had advanced to the point of quarantine regulations?

The Dyetary of Helth, published by Andrew Boorde in the
1540s (most probably in 1542), gives advice on this subject:

A man cannot be too ware, nor can not keep himself too
well from this sickness, for it is so vehement and so parlous,
that the sickness is taken with the savour of a man's clothes
the which hath visited the infectious house, for the infection
will lie and hang long in clothes. And I have known that
when the straw and rushes hath been cast out of a house
infected, the hogs the which did lie in it, died of the pestilence; wherefore in such infectious time it is good for every
man that will not flee from the contagious air, to use daily,
specially in the morning and evening – to burn juniper, or
rosemary, or rushes or bay leaves, or marjoram or frank-
incense or bengauyn. But let him use this diet: let the

* Ransom Pickard, *Population and Epidemics of Exeter* (1947),
p 30.

chamber be kept close, and keep a continual fire in the chamber of clear burning wood or charcoal without smoke; beware of taking any cold, use temperate meats and drink, and beware of wine, beer, and cider; use to eat stewed or baked wardens, if they can be got; if not, eat stewed or baked pears, with comfits; use no gross meats, but those the which be light of digestion.

East Devon escaped either lightly or completely the plague of 1546–7; but parishes to the south and south-west of Exeter generally suffered severely. Remoteness had little or nothing to do with the incidence of the outbreak.

Four early burial registers (from 1538) survive in East Devon: Clayhanger, Uffculme, Plymtree, and Colyton. Clayhanger, a parish of scattered farms to the east of Bampton, had a remarkable record of freedom from epidemics. The registers, which were well kept and are complete from the autumn of 1538, do not show a single year down to 1600 in which burials were abnormal, with the slight exception perhaps of 1592 and 1597. In each of these years eight people died – four or five more than the average – but the total number of burials for the decade was no greater than it had been for twenty or thirty years.

Clayhanger, 1540–99

Decade	Average burials per annum	Exceptional years (twice the average rate or over)
1540–49	2·3	1543 (5 burials)
1550–59	3·1	—
1560–69	2·6	—
1570–79	3·3	—
1580–89	3·4	—
1590–99	3·3	1592(8), 1597(8)

Uffculme, a large village at the western end of the Blackdown Hills, escaped any epidemic throughout the 1540s, but had a very sharp visitation from the sweating-sickness in 1551, as we shall see, and a very chequered medical history thereafter until the end of the century. Plymtree, also in East Devon, had a touch of the plague in 1546 but escaped entirely the sweat of 1551. In the seven years preceding 1546 the average number of burials in the parish was 4.1. This figure trebled in 1546–7 (thirteen), half the burials taking place in the first four days of January 1547. Colyton, near the East Devon coast, was a mixed parish: a compact village in the middle of a large fertile area with perhaps eighty or ninety scattered farms. The mortality-pattern is much more complex than that of most parishes, with far more abnormal years which almost make nonsense of any average burial-rate per annum, but even so some kind of pattern emerges in the second half of the century at least.

Decade	Colyton, 1540–99 Average burials per annum	Exceptional years
1538–49*	21·0	1546(36)
1550–59	33·3	1552(50), 1557(61), 1558(79)
1560–69	13·7	1566(25)
1570–79	21·1	—
1580–89	31·8	1587(44), 1588(44)
1590–99	42·1	1592(62), 1596(64)

Nine years only. The years 1540, 1541, 1542, are incomplete.

Colyton suffered noticeably but not severely in the epidemic of 1546–7. The number of burials was nearly twice the average for the whole decade. But there was no spectacular mortality in any one short spell, the peak months being May (six) and September (six), and five in June 1547: much the same picture as at Exeter (St Mary Arches). Nor was the visitation of the sweat in 1551 particularly severe. The real blow fell on Colyton in 1557–8, an epidemic (influenza?) which most places in Devon never noticed but which at Colyton carried off probably about 100 people. This is discussed below.

Judged by these four parishes, and to some extent by Exeter, East Devon escaped very lightly in the plague epidemic of 1546–7. Beyond Exeter, to the west and south, the visitation

was severe. At Kenn, no fewer than sixty people died in
1546–7 (March 25th–March 24th) as against an average for the
preceding six years of about seven burials per annum. Here the
death-rate multiplied by over eight, and some fifty-three
people died prematurely. The epidemic began at the end of
July 1546 and burials mounted rapidly: August (eight), September (seven), October (five), November (fifteen), and December (eleven). By January 1547 it seems to have been over,
perhaps killed by the onset of winter. Novembers and De-
cembers in Devon are usually very mild and very wet, a muggy
combination which probably kept the plague nicely incubated
until the first real frosts set in.

Bridford and Hennock are two hill-parishes to the south-
west of Exeter, consisting mostly of scattered and remote
farms. Yet they both suffered cruelly. At Bridford the average
number of burials from 1539 to 1545 was 2.3 a year. Then, in
one year between October 1546 and October 1547 no fewer
than thirty-one people died, the peak months being October
1546 (nine) and August–September 1547 (eleven). The epidemic died away in December 1546 but slowly reappeared in
the summer of 1547, dying away again by the following December. Altogether forty-three people died in the two years
1546–7 as against the four or five who would normally have
died. In a thinly populated hill-parish the premature loss of
nearly forty people must have been an economic disaster as well
as a personal grief. At Hennock, a similar sort of parish four
miles to the south of Bridford, the parson records that 'a pestilence' began at Huish, a hamlet on the edge of the parish, in
September 1546. Here, too, it died away in the winter and
burst forth again in the following summer when twenty-three
people were buried between July and early September
(1547).

Adjoining Hennock on the west was Bovey Tracey, a large,
closely knit village in a parish of many scattered farms. Again,
the early registers survive, and show a massive outbreak of
plague in 1546–7. From 1539 to 1545 there were fourteen
burials a year. In the two years 1546 and 1547 there were 118

burials, some ninety more than normal. It looks as though plague began at Bovey and spread over the hills to Hennock, for July and August of 1546 saw eleven burials. By early September Hennock was infected, as we have seen. Bovey Tracey was a local market and probably served to spread plague all over the adjacent hill-parishes. The incidence of plague at Bovey is different again, the peak months for burials being November 1546 (twelve), January 1547 (twelve), and then a dying-away of infection until the following May (five), June (ten), July (ten), August (thirteen), and September (eight). But the main point is that Bovey lost some ninety men, women, and children prematurely in little over twelve months between the summer of 1546 and the autumn of 1547.

At Stoke-in-Teignhead, eight miles south-east of Bovey Tracey, the plague appeared in mid-May (1546). Four of the Martin family were buried in a week (May 19th–26th). In June and July no fewer than forty-nine people died. Altogether 101 people died in this parish in the year 1546–7 (March 25th–March 24th), as against a normal rate of sixteen or seventeen, a net loss of some eighty-five people out of a total population of about 500–525. What is very noticeable also is the heavy incidence of plague in relatively few families. Altogether, eight Martins died, nine Simons, six Taskers, five Yenlings: well over a quarter of the deaths occurred in only four families. Nearly half the deaths (forty-seven) occurred in eight families. Plague was not only haphazard in its incidence from parish to parish, but it struck very unequally within any given village or town. What proportion of families contracted the plague we can never know, but it would be a profitable line of inquiry for social history to discover to what degree deaths from epidemic diseases were concentrated on a minority of the local population and whether this minority comprised an undue proportion of the poor, even by the mid-sixteenth century. If so, the economic significance of plague and other large-scale killer-diseases would be greatest in the sector of labour-supply.

Other South Devon parishes affected by the 1546–7 epidemic can be dismissed briefly since they reveal no facts not

already discussed. At Stoke Fleming, near Dartmouth, normal
burials were eight or nine a year. The plague killed an additional twenty people. At Ugborough, a large village in the
South Hams, there were 106 burials in the year 1546–7 as
compared with an average of sixteen to seventeen in ordinary
years – a sixfold increase and an additional loss of some ninety
people beyond those who would normally have died. Occasionally the devastating plague-year was followed by a year or two
of low death-rate, as though nature might be seeking to restore
the balance, but generally there was no such bounty. The post-
plague years in most parishes merely revert to the pre-plague
norm. At Ugborough the epidemic lasted from May 1546 to the
end of January 1547. In the six months from July to December
1546 the parish lost as many people as would normally have
died in five years.

The Great Sweat of 1551

The sweating-sickness was a new type of infection which first
reached England in the autumn of 1485. It has been suggested that it was probably a new and virulent form of
influenza. Further outbreaks occurred in 1508, 1517, and 1528.
The fifth and final outbreak came in 1551. Death was swift, and
mortality was high.

The epidemic of 1551 began at Shrewsbury in the spring. By
June it had reached Loughborough in Leicestershire, where the
parish register records that 'the swat, called New Acquaintance, alias Stoupe Knave and know thy Master' began on the
24th of the month. It was sometimes called Stop-Gallant because it was supposed to attack the rich and young, and to kill
them within a few hours.

In Devon the parish of Uffculme suffered severely, though it
had escaped all the epidemics of the 1540s – perhaps because of
that. Usually there were about ten burials a year, but in 1551
there were no fewer than thirty-eight and it is possible that this
is not the complete story as there are no burial entries until
June 25th. The Sweat seems to have reached Uffculme at the
very end of July. Between August 2nd and August 11th there

were twenty-seven burials, sixteen of them in three days.

What happened in other Devonshire parishes? At Bovey Tracey, which had been severely hit in the plague of 1546-7, there was a noticeable increase in burials but nothing spectacular. At Bridford, too, there had been great mortality in 1546-7 and nothing abnormal in 1551. Clayhanger also escaped the Sweat entirely. Its incidence is inexplicable, except that often a place that had escaped in 1546-7 suffered acutely in 1551, and vice versa. In the lonely parish of Shirwell, on the edge of Exmoor, there had been six burials during 1550 but sixteen in the following year, of which eight took place within seven days in August. North Molton escaped both epidemics; but East Down, remote enough one would have thought, escaped in 1546 and was badly hit in 1551. Usually there were four or five deaths a year here; but in August 1551 there were no fewer than fourteen deaths in fourteen days.

Both Kenn and Hennock suffered in 1546 and escaped in 1551. So also at Barnstaple. Colyton suffered noticeably in 1546-7, and again noticeably but not severely in 1551. But Colyton's turn came in the great influenza epidemic of 1557-8. It certainly looks as though there is a connexion of some kind between various epidemics. A heavy mortality in one epidemic usually meant an escape from a later epidemic (even of a different disease) as though nature had culled the flock once and would not do it again immediately. But what was the precise mechanism of this connexion? This remains to be discovered.

The Influenza Epidemic of 1557-8

The 1550s were an unhealthy decade all over the country. They also saw a sequence of harvest failures in the same years which must have left a considerable part of the population undernourished, even if not actually starving at times, and ready victims to any infection. The harvest of 1549 was deficient. Those of 1550 and 1551 were both bad. Those of 1552 and 1553 were good; 1554 average. Then came the famine years of 1555 and 1556. Though 1557 was good, and the following year abundant, the physical damage had already been done when the influenza epidemic struck.

At Colyton there were 140 deaths in the years 1557 and 1558, of which forty or so would have occurred anyway. So about 100 people died in this epidemic, which seems to have struck in August 1557 when thirteen victims were buried. With slight intermissions this epidemic lasted until the spring of 1559, finally dying out at the end of March after some twenty months.

At Bovey Tracey the pattern of deaths is different. Here, after the heavy mortality of 1546–7, the burial-rate settled down to an average of twenty-six or twenty-seven a year between 1548 and 1554. But in the bad harvest year of 1555 it jumped to thirty-seven, and in the famine year of 1556 to no fewer than fifty-eight.* In the two years together some forty or so additional people died beyond the normal number. Did they really die of starvation because of the two dreadful harvests, one after the other? The influenza years of 1557 and 1558 passed by almost unnoticed here, for death had already perhaps carried away the weaklings. But it would be interesting to discover the age and sex of those who died in 1555–6 (actually the high death-rate persisted into April 1557 and then dwindled sharply), and how they differed, if at all, from those who would normally have died. It is in detailed analyses like these that the local historian can use his microscope most fruitfully.

At Bridford, again, the great epidemic of 1557–8 passed unnoticed. After the mortality of 1546–7, Bridford experienced no further killing epidemic until 1570–1 – an interval of nearly a quarter of a century; and then again in 1591–2, after another twenty-one years of comparative normality. The epidemic of 1570–1 lasted from October until the following January, a winter illness of some kind. On the other hand, the Uffculme registers show the 1570 epidemic at its worst from April to September, with a doubled mortality-rate for the year.

Georgeham registers show an odd picture. The epidemic of

* The years all run from March 25th to the following March 24th.

1557–8 seems to have passed over it (though the record for 1558 is missing); but 1551, 1554, and 1555 were all bad years in the burial register. At Northam, also in North Devon, there was nothing very striking in 1557–8; but Shobrooke, not far from Exeter, saw a major epidemic in 1557–8 with nineteen deaths as against the normal four or five.

The influenza epidemic of 1557 was European in scale. Generally speaking the death-rate throughout England in these two years was at least four times the normal; but once again the impact varied from parish to parish. Isolated parishes often escaped, but if so their turn usually came later. One continually sees in the registers how years of low mortality are followed by a sudden leap in burials.

Epidemics after 1560

After the bad years of famine and the massive epidemics in the 1550s, there was no epidemic on a considerable scale until 1570. Ransom Pickard, in *The Population and Epidemics of Exeter* (privately printed in 1947) calculated that the plague outbreak in that year killed about 600 people in nine Exeter parishes alone. These are the parishes for which the necessary registers survive. On an average 118 people should have died in these parishes; but in fact deaths totalled 729. So we may assume that some 600 people died of plague in less than half the city for which we have the necessary records.

However, it would not be accurate to double this figure to arrive at the true total. Ransom Pickard shows clearly that deaths from plague were heavily concentrated in the large, poor, and overcrowded parishes of St Sidwell, St Mary Major, and Holy Trinity. In these three parishes alone there would have been about seventy-seven 'normal' burials; whereas in 1570 there were no fewer than 521, an excess of 444. In the wealthy parish of St Petrock, on the other hand, there were only eight burials as against a normal four or five.

Plague and other killer-diseases were very much concomitants of poverty. One can trace this pattern right through

from the sixteenth century to the cholera epidemics of the nineteenth century, and no doubt it has always been true.

The same pattern is observable in the next serious outbreak
of plague at Exeter in 1590. By this date we have eleven parish
registers, which show a total number of burials amounting to
735, as against a normal expectation of 144. Ransom Pickard
estimates the total deaths for the whole city at 1,030, and in
1591 – when plague recurred – at 418. Altogether nearly 1,450
people died in these two years out of a total population of
perhaps 9,000 to 10,000 at most: one in every six or seven. And
once again the plague deaths were heavily concentrated in the
poorest parishes, whereas the wealthy got off lightly. Thus the
three rich central parishes of St Petrock, St Mary Arches, and
St Martin would normally have had fifteen deaths per annum
at this date. In 1590 they totalled only nineteen, and in 1591 –
plague came again the following year, a familiar pattern – there
were twenty-two burials. Roughly speaking, burials only rose
by one-third in the richer parishes even in a bad plague-year;
whereas in the three poorest parishes they rose from a 'normal'
ninety-six to 559 in 1590. Here the death-rate multiplied by
between five and six. In the second year, the total in these parishes fell to 168. Clearly, the first wave of plague had been
devastating in the stinking crowded streets of the poorer areas,
but thereafter the survivors acquired some degree of immunity.
Even so, whereas about 200 people would have died in these
two years in any event, the actual number of deaths was 727. So
well over 500 people died of plague in these three parishes
alone. In 1570–71, a similar calculation suggests that some 380
had died of plague.

What happened in the country parishes? At Colyton which
had suffered severely in the great influenza epidemic of
1557–8, there was no noticeable plague in 1570–71. The rising
number of burials in the late 1570s and early 80s may merely
reflect a growing population; but the late 80s and early 90s
show a sharp rise in burials as though there were pandemic
diseases at work. The two years 1592–3 were certainly plague
years, with total deaths at 113. It is hard to estimate what

'normal' deaths might have been as the Colyton figures really call for a more detailed analysis than one can give them here.

Two other bad years at Colyton call for a comment. These were 1596–7, when no fewer than 115 people died as compared with only sixty in the two years 1594–5. Here the death-rate roughly doubled. Why? The answer may be: simple starvation. The harvests of 1594 and 1595 were both very bad; but worse was to come. The harvest of 1596 was disastrous, even worse in the West of England than elsewhere. At Exeter the average price for wheat reached the highest level ever recorded (nearly 63s a quarter). The year 1597 saw the fourth harvest failure in succession, though in the West it was not quite so disastrous as in the rest of the country. It is a moot point among historians whether people actually starved to death in Tudor England (they had certainly done so in medieval times), but the mortality at Colyton in 1596–7 suggests that it was still possible. One cannot be sure that plague or some other killer-disease was not present also, and it is a nice point where malnutrition ends and starvation begins.

At Bovey Tracey the plague years of 1592 and 1593 were very marked in the burial register. Once again we have the familiar sequence of two successive bad years, but in the second year not nearly as bad as the first. In the preceding five years, deaths had totalled 152, an annual average of just about thirty. But in 1592–3 (March 25th–March 24th) there were no fewer than eighty-seven burials, roughly three times the normal. The epidemic clearly began in early April: one can pin it down to the very house. In February and March there had been three deaths in each month, about the normal. In April there were eleven, of whom six were in the Voysey family. The Voyseys lost four of their number in two days. In the early weeks of 1593, similarly, there were five deaths in the Wetherdon family. Richard Wetherdon lost his wife, two sons, and a daughter in a little over a fortnight; and possibly John Wetherdon who died on the same day as Richard's wife was a close relation also. A microscopic analysis of the parish register resurrects these terrible family tragedies after nearly 400 years.

One tends to grow hardened to the word 'plague', to use it over and over again, forgetting what it really meant in terms of human suffering. At Bovey Tracey, forty-nine people were buried in the first three months of the year 1593. On the other hand, the famine years of 1596 and 1597 passed without any reflection in the burial register.

At Bridford, 1591–2 was the bad year, the plague beginning here in September 1591. At Uffculme the epidemic history is different again. Here there was an outbreak of some sort in January-February 1588, with twenty-two people buried in the two months; and 1597 showed a big jump in deaths also, the sequence being as follows:

1596	11 deaths
1597	30 deaths
1598	11 deaths

In my book *Devon*, I analysed some of the burial figures for the crowded little cloth town of Crediton. Here the plague of 1571 began in early April and by the end of July had killed 400 people. Altogether the enormous total of 535 people died during the year, of whom some 500 died of plague. This was perhaps one-third of the total population of the town. The plague of 1590–91 was equally devastating. It lasted for two years all but a month, and killed 535 people. Altogether Crediton lost well over 1,000 people in two major visitations of bubonic plague. In the neighbouring country parish of Newton St Cyres more people died in three months in 1571 than normally died in four years; and in the winter of 1604–5 there were thirty-five plague deaths and only one 'normal'. Newton St Cyres was on the busy main road between Crediton and Exeter and must have been exceedingly vulnerable to infection from travellers in either direction.

Isolation from traffic routes certainly helped to keep down the worst infections. At Hartland, a very remote parish in North-West Devon, the registers are complete from 1558 onwards. They show no great extremes. It was a large area with widely scattered farms, an environment that helped, unlike that of crowded villages such as Colyton and Uffculme, or congested towns like Crediton. From 1558 to 1600 the average number of burials was twenty-three a year. In all this long period there were only three outstanding years – 1569 and 1591 with forty burials each, and 1597 with thirty-six.

The epidemic picture of Devon parishes in the sixteenth century is not always a clear one. Certain major epidemics were fairly general, but even these missed some parishes completely. The picture for the seventeenth, eighteenth, and nineteenth centuries has never been drawn. Even here I have not exhausted the evidence for the Tudor period. A comprehensive study of one large parish, or better still a group of contiguous parishes, over the whole period of 400 years would be a valuable pioneer work, and a contribution to medical history in general.

CHAPTER EIGHT

The Winter of 1963

THE WINTER of 1963 was one of the historic winters of the past 200 years. In years to come we shall bore our grandchildren with tales of what we endured, despising their winters as nothing to be compared. James Cossins, writing his delightful *Reminiscences of Exeter* in 1877, says (true to form of all old people):

> The young reader must understand, in those days, the winters were much more severe than now; skating almost a certainty, and snow falling at various times for two or three days, and remaining on the ground for several weeks. I have seen birds lying dead on the ground for want of food. My father informed me that the snow had been so high on Haldon that men were sent from Exeter to cut a passage through it, to allow the mails to pass.

He spoke too soon, for the winter of 1881 was as fierce as anything he could have remembered. And then came the great snows of 1891, and the intense cold of 1895. Already, old men still alive are telling us that the winter of 1891 surpassed that of 1963 in ferocity; but their subjective recollections, like those of James Cossins, will not bear a close scrutiny.

The Meteorological Office announced that January 1963 was the coldest January in London since 1838. But in the South West it was the coldest January since 1814. The records kept at the Devon & Exeter Institution, continuously since January 1817, reveal that at Exeter the average temperature for January 1963 was 28·9 degrees F, more than three degrees colder than the average for January 1838.

The coldest months at Exeter have been (average for month):

February	1947	31·5°F	January	1880	35·2°F
January	1945	35·2°F	January	1879	34·5°F
January	1940	35·5°F	February	1855	31·3°F
January	1917	35·9°F	January	1853	34·2°F
January	1895	35·1°F	January	1838	32·2°F
January	1881	32·1°F	January	1830	32·7°F

It will be noticed that the coldest month until January 1963 was not in 1838 at all, but February 1855, with February 1947 a close second. The 1830s produced two memorable winters, and so did the early 1850s. It is probably of these that James Cossins was thinking when he wrote in the 70s, and to this extent his memories were well founded.

But January 1963 beat all previous records by a substantial margin. It is worth noting, too, that the average January temperature at Exeter Airport, normally several degrees colder than central Exeter, was 27·6 degrees F. Thus the cold was so intense and all-pervading that the centre of the city was not noticeably warmer than the exposed airfield.

Unfortunately, the records of the Devon & Exeter Institution do not reach back to the great winter of 1814. But before considering the claims of that winter, we must dismiss those of 1891, whatever its survivors may say. It was certainly very cold. By early January the Exe was frozen at Exeter and Topsham, and the Teign from Shaldon Bridge up to Newton Abbot. Several ships were frozen at the entrance to the Exeter canal. But the average temperature for the whole month did not fall as low as that of several other Januarys. Then came the great snows of March 9th–10th, and the blocked railways and roads and fallen telegraph lines; but the winter of 1963 repeated that story over and over again.

The winter of 1895 was more severe than that of 1891: not so much snow, but, according to the Devon & Exeter Institution records, a 'great frost practically unbroken for 26 days' in January and February.

January 1881 produced the coldest night ever recorded in Exeter since records began. On the 21st, the minimum exposed temperature fell to 2 degrees F, (thirty degrees of frost). In

January 1963 the corresponding lowest temperature was 12 degrees F on the night of the 14th – twenty degrees of frost.

Looking backward yet further, the winters of 1879 and 1880 were very cold, and so were those of 1853, 1854 and 1855. It was the February of 1855 that produced the lowest average temperature for any month until January of 1963. There were two severe frosts, one of eighteen days' duration and one of fifteen days. But the thermometer never fell below 20 degrees F (twelve degrees of frost) even so.

Prior to 1817, when the Exeter records begin, we have to rely on records from other parts of England and it does not follow that the South West experienced the same weather as the rest of the country. As said above, the London figure for January 1963 was not quite as bad as that for 1838; but at Exeter it was worse.

It seems certain that the winter of 1814 was very fierce in the South West also, for the national records speak of a severe frost lasting from January 8th, with little intermission, until March 20th. This intense cold prevailed in every part of England. An exposed thermometer in one place recorded fifty-one degrees of frost. But in the absence of local meteorological records we have no accurate means of comparing the winter of 1814 with that of 1963 in the South West. The local newspapers do not help greatly, beyond saying that the snowfall of early January was greater than anything within living memory, that all travelling ceased, and the shops of Exeter nearly all remained shut and the streets empty. In many streets the snow was said to be 3–4 ft deep. But the real test of severity is the average temperature over a whole month, and this we do not know for 1814.

It is probable that the closest parallel to the winter of 1963 in the South West was the hellish winter of 1740. An intense frost lasted for eight weeks, beginning on December 24th, 1739. From January 1st to February 5th the temperature rarely rose as high as freezing-point. This reminds us of our own January and early February exactly. A contemporary account of this winter of 1740 brings it home to us vividly:

An unheard of frost seized with extraordinary severity on the world ... Men felt so oppressed that days passed by unheeded. One would and could hardly speak. One sat and thought, yet could not think. If anyone spoke a word, it was with a hard, set face ... Even the cattle in their stalls died of cold. The trees split asunder. Not only beer, but wine in cellars froze ... Crows and other birds fell to the ground frozen in their flight. No bread was eatable, for it was as cold and hard as stone.

Dr John Huxham, a Plymouth doctor, kept a weather record for the years between 1727 and 1748, published in his book *Observations on the Air and Epidemic Diseases*. He details the Great Cold of 1739–40. The wind began to blow from the east and north-east on December 22nd. There followed

a most severe Storm from the East, with an exceeding severe Frost, and a constant exceeding small Snow to the very End [of the year]. In an Instant a most piercing Cold froze up every Thing, both within Doors and without ... whatever was exposed to the Air instantly turned into Ice. People even shivered by the largest Fire's Side, nor could they keep themselves warm in their very Beds; indeed so very greatly were we benumbed by the Excessive Cold that we scarcely seemed alive.

A great thaw, with rain, on January 1st, 1740, was followed by the immediate return of the frost to the end of the month. The severity of the cold had never been known before in this country, so they said. The sea froze on the shore. Trees and shrubs were killed, even 'the very hardy Furzes themselves'. Dr Huxham's account is full of the medical consequences of this awful cold, including the information that 'a nasty Itch was now universal amongst the lower kind of People', clearly due to the prolonged absence of washing.

Reading these accounts of the winter of 1740, even in the absence of accurate thermometer readings, we may safely say that that winter was even more piercing than our own of 1963, though there may not have been much to choose between them. When we read the circumstantial details – unable to think, difficulty in uttering a word, the days going by unheeded – we know exactly how our ancestors felt. It seems probable that we in the South West passed through the hardest winter since 1740, certainly since 1814; and we are entitled to feel a melancholy satisfaction at the thought.

The winter of 1963 actually began to develop in the last week of December 1962. On December 23rd and 24th the night temperature at Exeter fell on both nights to 21 degrees F, and on Christmas night to 20 degrees F. On the 26th there were snow showers, and then sleet at night with a minimum temperature of 22 degrees F. On the 27th there was a heavy snowfall at night, and a minimum temperature of 21 degrees F. Snow also fell on the 28th, and on the 29th there came, to quote the Devon & Exeter Institution meteorological records, a 'blizzard at night'. The last two days of the Old Year saw more snow fall, and from then on the winter slowly increased its grip until we thought the world would never again look any different. The sky remained leaden for week after week, and an icy wind blew continually from the east.

Towards the end of January a slight thaw arrived, but by the first days of February the intense cold returned. Nobody moved outdoors after dark; everywhere it was silent. Again there was a slight letting-up in mid-February. The snow disappeared after lying for seven weeks without a break. Later in February it became cold again, with the easterly winds creeping in everywhere; but the winter was really over and on March 2nd the maximum shade temperature reached 53 degrees F. On Sunday, March 3rd, the sun shone all day, and the thermometer touched 62 degrees F in the sun. The worst winter for more than 200 years was finally over.

CHAPTER NINE

The Wealth of Medieval Devon

TAX ASSESSMENTS usually make melancholy reading. But the great assessment of personal property made in 1334, searching out every corner of England except Cheshire and Durham (which were separately pursued), is of unusual interest to economic and local historians. From it they can reconstruct a picture of the economy of England, or of one particular part of it if they are so minded, as it was just before the Black Death. It is true that many important things are missing from this picture and that it portrays only one kind of economic information – the distribution of taxable wealth between one region and another, between town and town, and from parish to parish. But it gives us, for all its deficiencies, a picture which we could not derive from any other source. Or perhaps it is better to look upon it simply as a valuable frame, into which we can afterwards fit a whole multitude of economic, social, and political facts that would otherwise lack coherence and perspective.

During the thirteenth century a new kind of taxation, the taxation of personal property, appeared as an extraordinary levy. This tax was levied upon every individual in the country with movable goods or personal property, unless he was specifically exempt, at the rate of a tenth or a twentieth, sometimes a sixth, of the assessed value of his goods. Houses and lands were not assessed under this tax. In 1334, however, a new plan of assessment was adopted.

It was obviously meant to be temporary, and was used to avoid the corrupt practices that were said to have prevailed when the tax of 1332 was assessed and collected. Exchequer and other government officers were sent into the counties to serve with resident heads of religious houses as assessors of the fifteenth and tenth. They were to proceed by the method of collective agreement with the people of the townships and boroughs. The result of this collective bargaining plan was that each administrative unit of taxation agreed, or was forced to agree, to pay a definite sum of money. The government officers did not go behind this agreement, but left the people of the district to apportion the sum in a manner satisfactory to themselves. Whereas the rolls of the tax of 1332 contain the names of the property holders of the townships and boroughs and a statement of the sum each man was to pay, the rolls of the tax of 1334 contain simply the names of the townships and boroughs and the sums for which those units were responsible.

There was nothing inherently inelastic in the new plan of assessment, since succeeding years might have seen other negotiations and other agreements, with a resulting rise or fall in the amount due from townships and boroughs. It was not tried again; the sums agreed upon in 1334 became the basis of a standardized fifteenth and tenth that lived until 1623. The amount that each community had to pay in 1334 had been reached by what was, in theory at least, a mutual understanding between men whose probity could hardly be questioned and the property owners of each district. The result was a schedule of taxes that might be regarded as an approximation to justice.*

The assessment of 1334 became standardized for nearly 300 years. Boroughs and ancient demesnes were assessed at the rate of one-tenth, and townships and tithings at a fifteenth. These assessments could be reduced, and were indeed reduced from time to time, in cases of exceptional hardship or impoverishment. We shall examine in due course the widespread reductions allowed in 1445; but no assessment was increased after 1334. The utmost the Exchequer could do was to try

* Willard, *Parliamentary Taxes on Personal Property*, 1290–1334, p 5.

to restore the assessment of 1334 wherever reductions had been allowed at some time.

The assessment of 1334, county by county – with an occasional large town listed separately – is therefore a most valuable record of the relative taxable capacity of the English counties before the economic dislocation and changes brought about by the Black Death; and within each county the varying assessments on each town, village, and tithing enable us to draw a fairly detailed picture of the distribution of taxable wealth as it was in that year: to see which towns were important and which were already stagnant or decaying, and to discover which of the rural districts were fertile or at least being fully exploited, and which were not. Coming as it does at the end of the great agricultural boom of the thirteenth century and just before the Black Death, the assessment is a useful landmark both for the student of English local history and for the general economic historian.

This record has occasionally been used by historians and others. Topham printed an inaccurate transcript of the county totals in *Archaeologia* in 1785, and Thorold Rogers used a later version, made in 1341, as the basis for some general comments on the distribution of wealth in England in the early fourteenth century. The detailed Norfolk assessment was separately printed, with a short introduction, by the Rev W. Hudson more than fifty years ago; and the details of the Devon assessment were privately printed by C. L'Estrange Ewen in 1939. Since Norfolk was by far the richest county in the 1334 assessment, we shall be able to make some instructive comparisons between it and the county of Devon from these two detailed lists; but it is necessary first to say something of the relative position of Devon in the national list.

The chief taxers for Devon in 1334 were the abbot of Torre and Geoffrey Gilbert, and their assessment was arranged by hundreds under 682 heads. Besides the city of Exeter, there were 19 boroughs, 11 ancient demesnes, 582 tithings, 49 hamlets, 10 manors, 1 parish, 4 vills, and 5 groups of tenants. The city, boroughs, and ancient demesnes (all paying a tenth)

yielded £241 2s 4d, and the rest, paying a fifteenth, yielded
£712 12s 8d. The total yield from Devon was therefore
£53 15s 0d.

Since Topham's list is inaccurate, and appears to be the only
one in print, it will be useful to set out here a transcript of the
county totals as given in an Enrolled Account at the Public
Record Office. The counties are rearranged in the following list
in order of magnitude, with the few towns which are separately
distinguished in the record placed together at the end.

Gross Yield of Fifteenths and Tenths in 1334

		£		
1.	Norfolk	3,485	16	7
2.	Kent	1,927	6	11½
3.	Gloucestershire	1,642	0	7
4.	Wiltshire	1,595	13	7¾
5.	Lindsey	1,526	2	11½
6.	Suffolk	1,439	5	0¾
7.	Oxfordshire	1,403	8	6
8.	Somerset	1,357	19	2½
9.	Essex	1,234	14	7¾
10.	Hampshire	1,187	16	2¾
11.	Northants	1,161	0	6¼
12.	Sussex	1,104	7	8½
13.	East Riding	1,053	13	0
14.	Berkshire	1,036	3	9
15.	Cambridgeshire	1,011	10	6½
16.	Devon	953	15	0
17.	Kesteven	953	9	4
18.	Dorset	851	9	0½
19.	Warwickshire	841	18	3¾
20.	Leicestershire	757	12	10½
21.	West Riding	738	10	8½
22.	Nottinghamshire	706	2	3¼
23.	Buckinghamshire	688	5	4
24.	Bedfordshire	674	7	7¾
25.	Holland	665	11	8
26.	Shropshire	644	12	0¼
27.	North Riding	617	4	1
28.	Hertfordshire	610	3	6¾

29.	Surrey	584	5	9¾
30.	Staffordshire	575	18	3¾
31.	Worcestershire	502	17	10½
32.	Cornwall	478	17	9
33.	Derbyshire	471	3	4¼
34.	Huntingdonshire	444	7	10¾
35.	Herefordshire	437	5	11
36.	Lancashire	377	9	5½
37.	Middlesex	341	19	7¼
38.	Northumberland	333	10	7½
39.	Cumberland	249	4	5¼
40.	Rutland	215	18	6½
41.	Westmorland	190	15	7¼
42.	Isle of Wight	153	2	3
	London	733	6	8
	Bristol	220	0	0
	York	162	0	0
	Newcastle	133	6	8
	Hull	33	6	8
	Bath	13	6	8
	Sum Total	**38,170**	**9**	**2½***

* The Palatinates of Chester and Durham are the only counties missing from the above list. All towns not seperately listed are included in the totals of their respective counties.

Within each county, if we examined the detailed assessments, we should find districts of even higher taxable value, as for example, in the marshland of western Norfolk, where all those splendid medieval churches stand and where the assessments for the purely agricultural townships of Terrington, Wiggenhall, Walpole, Tilney, Walsoken, and West Walton are all higher than those of the great majority of English towns at this period. Terrington, assessed at £40 9s 0d, paid more than the ancient trading city of Exeter, which was assessed at £36 12s 4d. All these townships, except West Walton, paid more than the second town of Devon, the port of Plymouth, which had an assessment of £24. This marshland district, comprising seven townships divided into fourteen parishes, covered some 51,235 acres in all and was assessed at £205 7s 0d – an average of almost exactly 80s a thousand acres.

The counties with the greatest agricultural wealth (for urban wealth plays only a small part even in Norfolk) correspond roughly with those having the greatest density of population in 1377, as we might expect, though there are some interesting differences that would be worth further exploration. In general, the assessment of 1334 reflected with a considerable degree of accuracy the relative wealth of the different regions of England, the varying degrees of fertility of the soil or the varying extent of its exploitation at that date, and the relative fortunes of the trading centres, large and small. And within each county, the assessment reflected the local variations from borough to borough and from township to township.

Rural Devon in 1334

If we now turn to Devon in particular, the most striking fact is that while it is the largest county in area (Yorkshire and Lincolnshire each being divided into their constituent parts in the assessment), its taxable capacity is very low: it is sixteenth in its gross yield, and even lower in its rating per thousand acres. It paid almost exactly the same amount of tax as Kesteven, though it was rather more than three and a half times as large in area. The rich county of Norfolk paid nearly five times as much as Devon, acre for acre. Even if we take the richest agricultural district in Devon, that of the fertile sandstone and limestone country of the South Hams, stretching westwards from the Dart to the Plym, it makes a poor showing beside the richer regions in the Midlands, the Fens, and East Anglia: it is assessed at only 15s a thousand acres. This is less than one-fifth of the assessment of the marshland of western Norfolk.

The next wealthiest agricultural district in Devon was that centred upon Barnstaple in the north: the lower Taw and Torridge valleys, stretching as far as the north coast and eastwards to the foothills of Exmoor, a district composed mostly of a dark red loam derived from the Devonian sandstones. Here the assessment averaged about 13s a thousand acres. Third in value came the famous deep red lands of the Exeter region, comprising the lower Exe and Culm valleys, with a long tongue running westwards as far as Hatherleigh: but even this land was assessed at only 12s a thousand acres. The country behind Torbay, some of it very fertile today, produced about 11s a thousand acres, and the East Devon region – an infertile and cold greensand plateau scored by deep valleys in the red marls – about the same. We should expect the exposed foothills of the Dartmoor and Exmoor borders to be poor and indeed they are, producing less than 5s a thousand acres for the national exchequer; but large tracts of central and western Devon were little better, yielding only 6s to 9s on an average. The average yield for the county as a whole – including the towns, which do not affect the figures much – was as low as 11s 6d a thousand acres.

To some extent this low figure, like that of the Northern counties or of Cornwall, can be explained by the exceptional amount of irreclaimable waste, defying all colonization but the sparsest and most primitive. But the fact that even the South Hams and the Vale of Exeter, blessed as they are with rich deep soils and a more genial climate than almost any other region in England, stood no higher than this in taxable value, cannot be explained except by the assumption that Devon as a whole was agriculturally one of the most backward counties of England. Here and there the picture is better, as in the large parish of Kenton to the west of the Exe estuary, where the average assessment is about 27s, or at Ottery St Mary, in the warm Otter valley, with an assessment of about 40s a thousand acres; but taken as a whole the county presents a picture of a rather poor peasantry, without much in the way of movable goods (grain, livestock, or household equipment) as compared with the Midlands or East Anglia. Devon was a county that was colonized late, beginning some two to three centuries after the East Midlands and East Anglia, and it is evident that even in 1334 there was still a vast amount to be done before its agricultural resources could be said to be fully exploited. A late start and a more difficult terrain, for the greater part of its surface, must explain the lowly position of Devon in the tax assessment.

Before we adopt this explanation without further thought – for if true it affects our whole idea of Devonshire farming in the thirteenth and fourteenth centuries – there is one other possibility that calls for consideration. This is that the county as a whole (with an exception here and there) was under-assessed to a truly remarkable degree.

This appears to me to be unlikely for a number of reasons. The chief taxers were, as elsewhere, a government official and the head of a religious house. It is difficult to conceive in the first place that these connived at deception on such a scale as to produce under-assessments over thousands of square miles, or that they were systematically deceived on a grand scale all over the county. More to the point, perhaps, is the fact that the Devon assessment of 1334, when it is mapped parish by parish according to its yield per thousand acres, reflects pretty faithfully the variations in the fertility of the soil and the exposure of various districts; in other words, the agricultural possibilities of the different regions of the county. Not only that, but such a map also follows very closely the Domesday maps of the county – the density of population, the value of the land, the number of plough-teams per thousand acres, and all the other indices of comparative wealth. This being so, we must also believe, if we assume a widespread under-assessment by the local assessors in all the villages and tithings in 1334, that it was so systematic over nearly 700 assessments that in the end it still reflected with substantial accuracy the variations of agricultural wealth that the geographers and the Domesday historians would lead us to expect.

We must accept the 1334 assessment at its face value, surprising as it may be in its low estimate of the agricultural wealth of Devon. It puts the richest agricultural lands of the county, those in the South Hams and the Vale of Exeter, on a level with some of the poorest in western Leicestershire at that date. Many Devonshire farmers were still in the early stages of their farming; they were at the most only three or four generations removed from the first colonists of their farms. The high reputation which the county enjoyed for the standard of its farming in the late sixteenth century and the seventeenth, was far from being true of the early fourteenth. At that date few counties were lower than Devon: there were Cornwall (slightly poorer as a whole), and the counties of Northumberland and Cumberland, Westmorland, and Lancashire, and the North and West Ridings of Yorkshire, the assessments of which ranged from 5s to 9s a thousand acres.

The poor position of Devon has already been accounted for by its late start in the work of colonization and by the large amount of land still uncolonized in the first half of the four-teenth century. Similarly, we can account for the very high position of such counties as Oxfordshire and Rutland by the fact that they had colonized almost every acre of their land by the end of the thirteenth century. Rutland, at least, had begun the work of clearing the virgin land before the end of the fifth century, fully 200 years before the Saxons entered East Devon. Moreover, much even of the colonized land in Devon was not capable of high productivity in the thirteenth and fourteenth centuries: a valuation made in 1343 showed that the poorest wool in England was that of Cornwall and Devon, and the contemptuous remarks of William of Malmesbury in the early twelfth century about the barrenness of the soil around Exeter, which hardly produced a poor quality of oats, are echoed later by Richard of Devizes, who alleged that at Exeter men and beasts were fed on the same grain.

The boroughs in 1334

Let us now turn to the Devonshire boroughs – that is, the places that ranked as boroughs for taxation purposes, though they were not necessarily parliamentary boroughs.

The city of Exeter was assessed at £36 12s 4d and was by far the most important town in South-Western England. To this figure we may add the assessment of Exe Island (£4) between the city walls and the river, and already a built-up suburb of the city. Exeter was the ecclesiastical, political, and economic capi-tal of the South West, and its great importance as the seat of a rich and extensive bishopric, and as the centre of political government for a wide province, is not entirely measured by its tax assessment, however accurate this may be. Its prominence was not just a matter of its merchants' wealth.

Yet, even when we make due allowance for this, it is still small when compared with the other provincial capitals. London already overshadowed all other towns. It stood higher than twenty-one English counties in taxable wealth, assessed at very nearly as much as the whole of the West Riding of Yorkshire. Bristol, York, and Newcastle were the three largest and wealthiest towns in the provinces. Bristol's assessment was five times that of Exeter (including Exe Island), York's was four times as high; and Newcastle's three times. Few towns are separately distinguished in the 1334 roll, but from the detailed Norfolk assessment we learn that Yarmouth was assessed as highly as £100, and Norwich at £94 12s 0d. Lynn was put at £50, but there was South Lynn also (£18), contiguous to it, so that the whole town was assessed at £68.

Though we cannot say, without an examination of all the separate county assessments, where Exeter stood in the list of English towns in 1334, it is clear that she was surpassed by many, and did not compare in wealth with the other great provincial capitals, Bristol, York, Newcastle, and Norwich, despite William of Malmesbury's encomium on her riches as a trading city 200 years earlier. The historian of the reign of Stephen had also reckoned Exeter to be the fourth city of the kingdom, after London, York, and Winchester. It looks as though the city had fallen behind several others during the course of the thirteenth century; but this is a piece of history which still requires exploration.

The taxation boroughs of Devon were nineteen in number, and they range downwards from the growing port of Plymouth, assessed at £34 12s 8d, to the miserable, decaying town of Lydford, on the western edge of Dartmoor, which had been going downhill ever since Domesday or at least since the twelfth century, and was now assessed at only £1 3s 4d – lower than a great number of villages. The list of the Devonshire towns (other than Exeter) in order of their economic importance, is as follows:*

	£	s	d
Plymouth	34	12	8
Barnstaple	18	14	0
Dartmouth	16	0	0
Tavistock	9	0	0
Totnes	8	7	8
Torrington	7	17	2
South Molton	6	5	5
Bideford	6	0	0
Plympton	4	6	8
Crediton	4	1	1
Kingsbridge	3	10	0
Modbury	3	10	0
Ashburton	3	6	11
Bradninch	2	16	8
Honiton	2	16	8
Dodbrooke	2	3	4
Tiverton	2	0	0
Okehampton	1	12	8
Lydford	1	3	4

The rapid rise of Plymouth during the thirteenth century is worthy of a separate study. In 1086 the manor of Sutton had been a small, poor place populated only by four villeins, two bordars, and a slave (*servus*), worth only 20s a year to the king, who held it in demesne. On the shores of Sutton Pool in the twelfth century a few fishermen dried their nets and sails and sold their fish, paying £4 yearly to the king for these privileges. Leland's description of Plymouth in those days is true

* The Plymouth figure includes that for the borough of Sutton Prior (£24) and that for the tithing of Sutton Vautort (£10 12s 8d). It is not certain that the two townships had coalesced by this date, but they were not far from doing so and since later assessments treat them as one I have done so here. The Dartmouth figure includes that for Southtown (£5), which adjoined the borough of Clifton-Dartmouth on the south and was physically a part of the town.

enough: 'This Town about King Henry the 2 tyme was a mene thing as an Inhabitation for Fischars, and after encreasid by a little and a little'. The port of Plymouth, which grew up around Sutton Pool, at the mouth of the river Plym and on the lands of the prior of Plympton, is first mentioned by name in the year 1205. By the fourteenth century it was being used as a rendezvous for naval and military operations against France, and its commerce also had greatly extended. By 1334 the borough of Sutton Prior *alias* Plymouth had far surpassed the Domesday borough of Barnstaple and was second in importance only to the city of Exeter. All this growth had taken place in the past 150 years or less.

Barnstaple, Totnes, and Lydford had been Domesday boroughs. Of these Barnstaple still maintained a leading position among Devonshire towns: it was the only port of any consequence in North Devon, it had the largest annual fair, and it was the weekly market-centre for a large part of one of the most fertile and populous parts of the county. Its economic life was unshakably rooted in the soil.

Totnes was a walled town and an ancient market and fair-town for another of the richest parts of Devon; but as a port it was already losing trade to Dartmouth which had come up rapidly, like Plymouth, since the early years of the thirteenth century. The mouth of the Dart had been an important gathering-place for naval and military operations since the twelfth century. In 1147 a great European fleet had set out from here on the Second Crusade, and in 1190 more than 100 ships were assembled here for the start of the Third Crusade. The Dartmouth records make it clear that by 1200–10 a borough had been created here to cope with, and take advantage of, the growing military and commercial traffic of this magnificent harbour; and by 1334 Dartmouth stood fourth among the Devonshire towns, with the same assessment, for example, as the ancient capital town of Thetford in Norfolk.

The four leading towns of Devon in 1334 were all sea-ports. Next in order of importance came a scattered group of inland towns whose growth and position in the early fourteenth century depended very largely on their functions as market-centres for the purely agricultural districts around them. Of these, Tavistock, whose rise during the twelfth century had brought about the decay of both Lydford and Okehampton, was the largest urban centre on the westen side of Devon. Totnes was the most important market-town between Exeter and Plympton; and Torrington, South Molton, and Bideford served smaller agricultural districts in their own parts of North Devon. The remainder of the towns in this list had mainly come into existence as boroughs in the later years of the twelfth century and the very first years of the thirteenth, and were all little market-towns.

As to the population of the Devonshire boroughs in the early fourteenth century, we can form only an approximate idea about some of them; but, such as it is, it will serve to show on how small a scale they were constituted. We know, for example, that the walled area of the city of Exeter was only ninety-one acres, and that of Totnes as little as ten acres, though by the early fourteenth century both possessed considerable suburbs outside their walls. We also know that in 1300 the decayed borough of Lydford had forty-eight burgesses and Bradninch 120.

It will be noticed that the 1334 assessments for Lydford and Bradninch bear a fairly close relationship to their respective burgess populations (Lydford 23s 4d, Bradninch 56s 8d). On this basis Totnes, whose assessment was almost exactly three times that of Bradninch, would have had about 360 burgesses in the early fourteenth century, possibly somewhat fewer as the town had a number of considerable merchants whose individual assessments would have swollen the total tax more than proportionately. But we shall probably not be far wrong if we put the burgess population of Totnes at about 350 in the year 1334,* and we must envisage Barnstaple at the same date with

---

* In the year 1255 there seem to have been 277 burgages in Totnes. We are told that each burgage paid 2d yearly at Easter as 'Ester-gavell' and the total is set down as 46s 2d in that year (Watkin, *Totnes Priory and Medieval Town*, 1, pp 152–3).

about 700–750 burgesses, Plymouth (the borough of Sutton Prior only) with about 900–950, and Exeter about half as big again with about 1,300–1,400 burgesses. (The figure of 4,837 taxed persons at Plymouth in 1377, which has been repeated in all the histories of Plymouth and in countless other books, including a recent work on *British Medieval Population*, since Topham printed it in *Archaeologia* for 1785, is a pure invention by Topham. It appears nowhere on the roll he purports to transcribe. It has bedevilled all accounts of the early history of Plymouth.) It is also safe to say that some eleven of the twenty Devon boroughs in the 1334 list probably had fewer than 200 burgesses. These figures are at the best only an approximate guide, but they are useful as throwing a feeble light into a subject otherwise wholly obscure.

The Ancient Demesnes and the Tithings

Of the eleven estates in ancient demesne, there is little that can be said beyond what has already been said of the rural areas in general. They tend to be more highly assessed than the other rural estates, even allowing for the fact that they were rated at a tenth, like the boroughs. Thus Kenton was assessed at something like 27s a thousand acres, Ottery St Mary at 40s, Budleigh at over 50s (the highest in Devon), Northam at 24s, and Braunton and Shebbear at 20s. But such higher values can be explained simply by the fact that these are all old estates, most of them in fertile and sheltered valleys, such as Budleigh and Ottery, Kenton and Axminster. They have been longer under cultivation than the great majority of townships in Devon and, being among the original settlements of the Saxon Conquest, they generally occupy the most fertile and rewarding lands. As soon as we leave these warm lands of East Devon and go to the western side, we find that the ancient demesne is as poor as anything around it. Lifton's 5,982 acres produced only 40s — only 6s 8d a thousand acres even at a tenth. At a fifteenth, Lifton would have yielded only about 4s 6d a thousand acres. Ancient though Lifton was as a settlement, it was younger than the large villages of East Devon, and it was in the midst of a cold, exposed, and unrewarding countryside.

Outside the boroughs and the ancient demesne lay the 651 tithings, hamlets, and vills. The general picture presented by their assessments has already been examined, and the impression we get is one of a low standard of agricultural wealth as compared with all the rest of England except the North. Within the county the highest values are in general found where we should expect to find them, on the low-lying and well-drained soils, in the sheltered valleys. But we also come across frequent and interesting contrasts between parishes that adjoin one another. Kenton and Kenn present such a contrast; and elsewhere we find equally striking contrasts even where the soils appear from the geological map to be much the same. In a small group of adjoining parishes on the Culm Measures of North West Devon, we find the parish of Langtree assessed as high as 19s 6d a thousand acres, Buckland Brewer at 12s 6d, Peters Marland at 8s 2d, and Petrockstow at only 5s. Some of these differences we can readily explain from the details of the geological map and others from the contour map of the district; but there remains a residue which calls for further explanation, for a minute examination of the process of colonization in each parish. In such an examination the assessment of 1334 is the most useful starting-point, and a great deal of exploration remains to be done by the devoted band of local historians and topographers, whose work, though it may be bounded by their own parishes, is nevertheless of great potential value. The history of each parish, viewed in this way, is a contribution to the history of England: it no longer remains a collection of unassimilated facts but has its own peculiar theme and continuity. From the histories of such remote and unknown parishes, wherever they may lie, the economic and social history of the county will one day be written with a full mastery of the facts; and from these histories of the counties and provinces we shall then be able to write the general history of England that calls to be written.

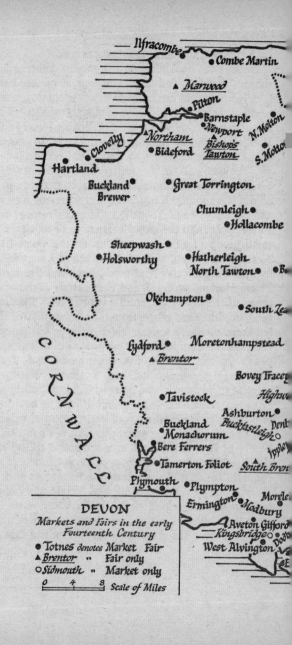

DEVON
Markets and Fairs in the early
Fourteenth Century

● Totnes denotes Market Fair
▲ Brentor " Fair only
○ Sidmouth " Market only

0   4   8 Scale of Miles

The Reassessment of 1445

The assessments fixed in 1334 were not touched for nearly a
century, though they became increasingly unreal with the economic changes brought about by the Black Death and the
deepening depression of the later years of the fourteenth century. By 1433 the continuance of this depression made it evident that a complete reassessment was necessary to take
account of the changed conditions. The total yield of fifteenths
and tenths had been fixed at £38,170 9s 2½d. In 1433 this was
cut by £4,000, and the reduction was distributed proportionately among the county totals. This proved inadequate
to meet the circumstances of the more impoverished towns and
districts, and in 1445 the total was cut by £6,000 (15.7 per
cent), a reduction which thereafter held good until the
seventeenth century. This reduction, too, was distributed
proportionately among the counties. Each was allowed a cut of
15.7 per cent on its former assessment, but within each county
the reduction was carefully apportioned according to the special
circumstances of each place. A number of places got no reduction at all; others received a reduction two or three times the
average for the county as a whole. This involved a minute
reassessment of every town and township, hamlet and tithing,
and the result is a revised list which reflects very closely the
changed circumstances of economic life within each county in
the middle years of the fifteenth century.

The Devon assessment for 24 Henry VI is to be found
among the lay subsidy records at the Public Record Office. It is
in the form of a schedule of deductions from the assessment
fixed in 1334, containing the names of the 227 boroughs, ancient
demesnes, hamlets, and tithings which received some reduction
in their assessments, however small. The remaining 455 places
were allowed no reduction, a point to which we shall return
shortly.

The total reduction of the Devon assessment amounted to
£149 19s 2d – ie, 15.7 per cent of the total of £953 15s 0d fixed
in 1334 – but inside the county the reductions from place to

place ranged from nil to as high as 74 per cent.

The towns of Devon, sea-ports and inland market-towns alike, were most of them in a bad way by the middle of the fifteenth century. All but one – Lydford – were allowed a reduction of assessment, and Lydford had been so poor and decayed in the fourteenth century that it could hardly be worse 100 years later. There were, however, four towns that were relatively prosperous by comparison with the others, towns whose assessments were reduced by less than the county average. These were Torrington, Ashburton, Tavistock, and Plympton, where the reductions were 4, 10, 13.3, and 15 per cent respectively. The comparative prosperity of Torrington must reflect its continued growth as a market-centre for that part of North Devon: it was indeed to become the largest market (except Exeter) in all Devon before the end of the sixteenth century, especially notable for its cattle market. The other three towns are stannary towns and it seems likely that, even if the tin trade was depressed also, it still helped to add to the taxable wealth of what would otherwise have been purely agricultural centres.

Towns like Crediton, Okehampton, and Tiverton, which were nothing but markets for the surrounding countryside, were severely depressed: their assessments were cut by 74, 61, and 50 per cent respectively, the highest cuts in the whole county. The south-coast ports were suffering also, partly from the interruption of their overseas trade by the war with France, and partly because of their physical destruction in some cases by the enemy. In 1403, for example, a Breton force had landed at Plymouth one August afternoon and burnt a considerable part of the town before re-embarking the next morning. The attack on Dartmouth in the following year was, however, repulsed and the town escaped the burning which had been planned for it. Even so, Dartmouth was hard hit by the decay of its trade: its assessment was reduced by almost 40 per cent, and that of Southtown by fully one half. The boroughs of Kingsbridge and Dodbrooke, which adjoined each other, were also much impoverished, and the inland market-town of Modbury equally so.

The city of Exeter and the borough of Plymouth were about equally reduced (27 to 28 per cent). The full list of reductions in the boroughs is as follows:

Crediton	74 per cent
Okehampton	61
Tiverton	50
Kingsbridge	43
Dartmouth	$39\frac{1}{2}$
Modbury	38
Dodbrooke	37
Bradninch	28
Plymouth	28
Exeter	$27\frac{1}{2}$
South Molton	$26\frac{1}{2}$
Totnes	24
Honiton	23
Bideford	22
Barnstaple	18
Plympton	15
Tavistock	13
Ashburton	10
Torrington	4
Lydford	nil

Altogether, about 28 per cent of the total tax reduction for Devon was applied to the city of Exeter and the boroughs. It is evident that the towns were the greatest sufferers in the *malaise* of the fifteenth century. The eleven estates of ancient demesne also received a liberal reduction: the assessments of all of them were reduced by amounts varying from 15 per cent in South Tawton to 44 per cent in Budleigh. Substantial reductions were made in Northam (40 per cent), Ottery St Mary and Exe Island (33 per cent each), Kenton and Shebbear (29 per cent), and Lifton (25 per cent). In all, 16 per cent of the Devon reduction was applied to the ancient demesne. Thus fully 44 per cent of the whole reduction for Devon was allotted to the boroughs and the ancient demesne.

The remainder of the cut was distributed among 197 rural vills. The most considerable reductions are found in the three south-western hundreds of Ermington, Plympton, and Roborough, and in the fertile country to the south and east of Exeter (the hundreds of Exminster, East Budleigh, Clyston, Ottery, and Colyton), and in a small inland block comprising the hundreds of Crediton, West Budleigh, and North Tawton. These reductions are nowhere very striking, and do not compare in magnitude with some of the heavy cuts in the Leicestershire villages, for example, where nearly thirty places had reductions of between 30 and 60 per cent.

More remarkable still, fully 70 per cent of the rural townships and tithings in Devon were allowed no reduction at all. Again this is in striking contrast to Leicestershire where, out of a total of 328 assessments, only twenty-six fail to show some reduction – less than 8 per cent. In Norfolk nearly five-sixths of the 658 assessments show some reduction; about one in six do not.

Before we leave the subject of the reassessment of 1445 there is one curious fact to which attention must be drawn, and for which no explanation can be given. The borough of Totnes had been allowed a reduction equivalent to 40s on a full tenth. Theoretically, it should have paid only £6 7s 8d thereafter, when a full tenth was demanded. But the surviving assessments among the Totnes records for 1448 and 1449 show that the full amount was collected and paid over to the tax-collector. Thus in November 1449 a levy was made for half a tenth in the town. Altogether 255 assessments were made, and the sum of £4 10s 3d raised. We are then told that the mayor and receiver paid over to the king's tax-collector £4 3s 10d, which is exactly one half the full assessment of £8 7s 8d, with no deduction. Similarly, the levy of September 1448 raised £4 8s 3½d. Though we are not told what was handed over to the collector on this occasion, the total sum raised in the town suggests that again no account was taken of the reduction allowed in the reassessment. We must leave this mystery unsolved for the time being.

These detailed assessments of 1448–9 are interesting also as showing how much the town had outgrown its thirteenth-century walls. There were only eighty-two assessments within the gates in 1449, eighty-six outside the east gate (on the river side of the town), forty-one outside the west gate, and sixteen in 'Little Totnes'. Nearly two-thirds of the town was outside the walled area by the middle of the fifteenth century. A levy for a tenth in 1416 gives 209 assessments, of which seventy-five were 'within the gates' – about the same proportion as a generation later. There is, however, one marked difference between the two assessments: in 1416 the people outside the walls contributed 57 per cent of the total tax, in 1449 only 47 per cent. Whether this is due to a greater decay of wealth outside the walled area in these thirty years or so, or whether it merely reflects the vagaries of the local assessors, we cannot say.

The Prosperity of Devon in the Fifteenth Century

Devon appears to be a comparatively prosperous region in the earlier half of the fifteenth century, quite unlike the Midlands, where the evidences of depression both in town and country are abundant. A good deal of the explanation for this apparent prosperity lies no doubt in the fact that large areas of rural Devon which were not being fully, or indeed at all, exploited agriculturally in the early fourteenth century, had now been developed. The taxable capacity of these districts had increased in the three generations between the 1330s and the 1440s, and they were now relatively under-assessed. Even if there were signs of economic depression in these parishes, therefore, their assessments called for no reduction. It is significant that the districts where reductions were allowed on any scale in 1445 (outside the boroughs) were, by and large, those parts of the county which had been most highly assessed 100 years earlier. The failure of 70 per cent of the Devonshire townships and tithings to secure any reduction at all in the second quarter of the fifteenth century must be attributed, in part at least, to their comparative under-assessment at that date, and is not in itself sufficient evidence of 'prosperity'.

But this is not the whole story. There is more positive evidence in Devon, if not of prosperity, at least of the absence of any depression such as afflicted most of England during the greater part of the fifteenth century, and that is the evidence of widespread building activity.

Although most of the finest church-building in Devon, as elsewhere, was done in the last and greatest phase of the Perpendicular style – from about 1480 to 1540 – and most of the rich Devonshire screens belong to this period also, there is, nevertheless, abundant evidence of the rebuilding of many churches, and of substantial additions to many others, during the first half of the fifteenth century. The episcopal registers of Bishop Stafford (1395–1419) and of Bishop Lacy (1420–55) contain a great number of indulgences granted to those who would contribute to the rebuilding of churches all over the diocese, and not only parish churches but chapels, bridges, roads, and leper hospitals also, in considerable numbers.

It is true that indulgences are primarily appeals for funds on behalf of parishes which cannot afford to complete their pious works single-handed, and they might on that ground be construed as evidence of poverty. Sometimes, indeed, this is so. When Bishop Lacy granted forty days' indulgence to all contributors to the repair or rebuilding of the sequestered church of Satterleigh, a parish of barely 500 acres up in the hills between the Taw and the Bray, and populated only by half a dozen farmers and a few labourers, we may be sure that the parish was too poor to erect single-handed even the simple little structure we see today. It is also true of Down St Mary, farther up the valley, for the rebuilding of whose tower and nave, destroyed by a high wind, Bishop Stafford granted an indulgence in 1413. So, too, in the tiny parish of Landcross – a little over 300 acres in the Torridge valley above Bideford – where the church was being rebuilt in 1435. All these buildings are small and plain today.

But there are also several parishes where the motive for granting the indulgence is quite different: it is to ensure that the new building shall be even more splendid than the par-

ishioners alone could make it, a monument worthy of the whole
diocese. Such, above all others, was Totnes church (Illus. 9),
for the complete rebuilding of which Bishop Lacy granted an
indulgence in 1432. Here the nave was rebuilt between 1432
and 1444, the chancel between 1445 and 1448, and the beautiful blood-red tower of sandstone from Stoke Gabriel between
about 1449 and 1459. We may assume that the magnificent
stone screen, which was erected in 1459–60, was the climax of
the building of this noble church.

The amount of church-building that was going on simul-
taneously in Devon, as revealed by the indulgences and other
evidence, is most striking. Apart from a noticeable gap in the
1420s when no indulgences were granted (or none have survived) except for the repair of one or two bridges, the work of
reconstruction was going on in all parts of the county. In the
last decade of the fourteenth century we have evidence of it at
Poltimore (1390), Bradworthy (1395), and Buckland Brewer
(1399), and the chapel of St Mary at Dartmouth, 'newly built'
in 1400. In the following decade we hear of work going on or
completed at Broadhempston (rebuilt 1400–01), Buckerell
(completed in 1403), Woodbury and Lympstone (both completed and rededicated in 1409), and possibly at Upton Hell-
ions, where the high altar was consecrated in 1409 and where
examination today shows a twelfth-century church recon-
structed to some extent in the fifteenth century.

In the decade 1410–20 we hear of work going on at Down St
Mary (from 1413), at Honiton (St Michael's, from 1418), and
at Moreton Hampstead, where a new tower was under construction in 1418. A good deal of the stately church of Broad
Clyst, near Exeter (Illus. 11), was also rebuilt during the episcopate of Bishop Stafford, but we cannot give it a more precise
date than that. The superb Norman church of Crediton, almost
cathedral-like in its proportions and beauty, was also being rebuilt in these years. We know that the great nave was building
between 1413 and 1418, following the completion of the choir
in the early 1400s.

During the same decade there was a notable amount of

bridge-building: some of the best medieval bridges surviving in Devon date from these years. Indulgences were granted for the rebuilding of the bridges over the Dart at Staverton and Holne, both in 1413, and for Lee Bridge over the Yealm in 1414; and in 1415 Thomas Barton, a canon of Exeter, left £10 in his will 'towards rebuilding the bridge at Thorverton with arches of stone, if the inhabitants set about the work in earnest within a year and persevere with it'. He also left 100s for the construction of a stone bridge over the Creedy at New Mill, near Crediton, 'if the inhabitants are willing to contribute and complete the work within a year'.

The falling-off of building activity in the 1420s is very noticeable: the only indulgence of any importance was that granted in 1425 towards the repair of the bridge at Bideford. It is true that a great deal of building of churches, bridges, and poor-houses or leper hospitals went on without the aid of indulgences (as we shall shortly see) and that this silence in the episcopal records is not therefore conclusive. Nevertheless, it is striking when compared with the records for the decades on either side; nor is there any other documentary evidence of building on any noticeable scale in this decade. With the 1430s it is quite different. Much new building was undertaken, and the pace does not seem to have slackened throughout the 1440s – precisely when the country as a whole was so impoverished as to call for a complete reassessment of its taxable capacity.

The work at Totnes, begun in 1432 and probably completed by 1460, has already been referred to. A number of other town churches were going up in the 1430s: at South Molton the fine Perpendicular tower was in course of construction in 1435, that at Bradninch was rebuilt in 1437–9; and it seems very likely that the towers of Ashburton and Tavistock were built in the 1430s as they appear to be by the same master mason as that of Totnes. Moreover, when the building of Totnes tower was under way in 1450, the towers of Ashburton, Tavistock, and Buckland Brewer (together with Callington, just over the Cornish border) were viewed as possible models for Totnes, sug-

gesting that they had just been completed in the latest style.
During the 1430s indulgences were also granted for the complete rebuilding or substantial alteration of the churches at Satterleigh and Landcross (both in 1435); Harberton (Illus. 10)
and Ilfracombe (both in 1436); Paignton, St Petrock's at Dartmouth, and Teigngrace (all in 1438); and Little Torrington
and Huntshaw (both in 1439).

Much of this work naturally continued through the 1440s: at
Totnes, Ashburton, and Tavistock the complete reconstruction
of these large town churches went on unabated. In the last of
these, a second south aisle – known as the Clothworkers' Aisle –
had been completed by 1450. A second aisle like this was a pure
luxury: there is no evidence of depression here. In the great
town church of St Andrew, the only church that Plymouth yet
possessed, a new north aisle was dedicated in 1441, and by
1460 the splendid Perpendicular tower had gone up, the materials provided by the townspeople and the cost of building by
the merchant Thomas Yogge. The receivers' accounts, however, show work still going on in the 1480s.

Then there is the architectural evidence of the towers of such
country churches as Molland, Lapford, and Stoke Rivers, all
built by the same master mason in the second quarter of the
fifteenth century. We cannot date the work more precisely than
this, beyond observing that at Lapford the manor came to the
St John family about 1430 and that we may attribute the substantial rebuilding of the fabric to the new lords. Again, we
know that the Perpendicular work at Sidbury, which involved a
large-scale reconstruction, was going on in the 1440s. In the
accounts of the Dean and Chapter manor of Salcombe Regis
for the year ending Michaelmas 1445, there are no returns from
the quarry at Dunscombe in that year because the Chapter had
handed over the quarry to the parishioners of Sidbury for the
purpose of getting out the stone they needed.

There is not much doubt that other rebuilding was going on
during Bishop Lacy's episcopate (1420–55) of which we have
no documentary evidence. The appearance of his arms in the
glass or on the fabric of other churches in Devon implies that

some of the Perpendicular refashioning or complete rebuilding was done during his reign at Exeter. His arms appear in the glass at Ashton, in the Teign valley, one of the most attractive village churches in all Devon, where the fabric was completely rebuilt in the fifteenth century; and they appear also on the font at Ipplepen, where he is said to have provided the chancel screen about 1430. The fine medieval oak pulpit is of the same date, and so, too, is the chancel screen in the neighbouring church of Torbryan, where it probably marks the completion of an early fifteenth-century rebuilding.

Although most of the beautiful rood-screens of Devon date from the closing years of the fifteenth century and the first half of the sixteenth, a number of fine examples belong to the earlier period we have been discussing. Besides the screens at Ipplepen and Torbryan, there are those of Halberton, Uffculme, Pilton, Exbourne, Trusham (dated 1431), Bishop's Tawton, Nymet Tracy, Burlescombe, Calverleigh, Willand, and Atherington (the nave screen only). Probably all these screens, which may be assigned to the period 1400–50, are to be associated with the completion of some reconstruction of the fabric, such as the enlargement of the nave or the chancel (or both) which made the provision of a screen necessary or desirable.

At Swimbridge, near Barnstaple, the north aisle of the nave was newly completed in 1443. Oliver says that the church of Little Hempston near Totnes was completely rebuilt in 1439, and that the tower of Bradford, near Holsworthy, was rebuilt in 1438.* Other churches which are said to have been wholly rebuilt during Lacy's episcopate are Plympton St Maurice, Morchard Bishop, and Okehampton, besides the two small city churches of St George and St Edmund in Exeter. The nave and tower of Stockleigh Pomeroy, in the beautiful remote country beyond the Raddon Hills, belong to this period also. So, too,

* Oliver, *Monasticon,* pp 445, 449. I can find no mention in the printed portion of Lacy's register (to 1441) of the rebuilding of Little Hempston, however, and Oliver's reference to Bradford is probably a slip for Bradninch, for which we know an indulgence was granted at the end of 1437. There was no indulgence for Bradford.

does the main portion of Hartland, a cathedral-like parish church in the far west, overlooking the Atlantic; and the work on the great church at Crediton also continued well into Lacy's time.

The number of bridges built or rebuilt, or substantially repaired in the 1430s and 1440s is too great to catalogue: most of the important bridges, used by travellers over a wide area and therefore considered to be a wider responsibility, are the subject of indulgences in these decades, such as Barnstaple, Bideford, Tawstock, Teignbridge, Totnes, Greyston (over the Tamar, near Tavistock), Ottery St Mary, and so on. And there are numerous indulgences and bequests in wills for the repair or rebuilding of leper hospitals and important roads between market-towns.

The evidence for the rebuilding of churches and bridges in the period 1400–50 is overwhelming; and the work seems to have been at its height in the very years of the tax reductions – the 1430s and 1440s. To all this we can add a considerable amount of domestic building of a substantial kind. In many parts of Devon one comes across the surviving examples of small manor-houses built in this period, as at Little Hempston, just outside Totnes, or at Traymill, in the Exe valley between Tiverton and Exeter, or Wortham in the western parish of Lifton. These houses are all the work of small gentry and date largely from the early years of the fifteenth century. It is natural that few domestic buildings of this distant period should survive, and that their cumulative evidence should be small beside that of the parish churches, but such as it is it lends additional weight to the belief that this was a time of fairly general prosperity in the Devonshire countryside, if not in most of the towns.

For building on this scale, all over Devon, can only indicate some considerable degree of prosperity, and not merely the absence of depression. The rebuilding of the parish church, or of some great stone bridge, was the most formidable and costly enterprise that any medieval parish could undertake. The capital cost of such an undertaking is something we can appreciate today when, in the impoverished twentieth century, we approach a similar work of physical reconstruction after a great war, and find it almost beyond our resources. Even if medieval parishes were sometimes aided by funds from outside, under the stimulus of indulgences, the simultaneous construction of a great number of churches and bridges, such as we find in the 1430s and 1440s, indicates a high level of prosperity in the South West (for much work was also going on at the Cornish end of the diocese).

The most striking instances are perhaps those of Totnes and Plymouth. Both these towns had received substantial reductions in their tax assessments in 1433 and in 1445, but they were nevertheless able to rebuild their parish churches on a splendid scale during these very years. It is gratifying to think that the money which might have gone to finance the futile wars of Henry VI's reign was spent instead on the towers of St Mary at Totnes and St Andrew at Plymouth, and that we can still see them today, survivors into the Dark Age of the twentieth century.

The causes of this comparative prosperity in Devon during the greater part of the fifteenth century are not yet wholly clear. Some of it arose, as we shall see, from the growth of the cloth trade; some perhaps from the revival of the tin trade on and around the moor.

Exports of Devonshire cloth show a remarkable and sudden rise in the very years when church-building was most active, with an almost uninterrupted period of prosperity from 1430 until the early 1460s, when a sharp decline set in for some ten or a dozen years. It is true that we depend solely upon the figures of cloth exports for our knowledge of the state of trade at this time, and we do not know the size or state of the home market, which may have been more important. With this important qualification, if we take the total exports of cloths from the ports of Exeter-Dartmouth and Plymouth-Fowey, which between them included all the lesser ports of Devon and Cornwall, we shall see the movement of the South-Western cloth trade decade by decade:

*Exports of Broadcloths from
Devon and Cornwall, 1400–80*

1400–10	3,109 cloths
1410–20	7,118
1420–30	6,228
1430–40	19,100
1440–50	26,774
1450–60	17,010
1460–70	11,654
1470–80	13,812

These statistics are compiled from the tables based upon the enrolled customs accounts and published elsewhere.* There are some small gaps in the yearly accounts from time to time, for which no allowance has been made, but they are too small to affect the significance of the figures as a whole. Further, all cloths are reduced to terms of broadcloths partly for ease of comparison from decade to decade and also because the customs accounts do likewise for official reasons. Kerseys came to be exported in large numbers towards the end of the fifteenth century, but they were not separately distinguished in the customs accounts. They were rated for the subsidy at three kerseys to the cloth 'without grain'. Thus the Devonshire figures contain a large number of kerseys concealed under a general heading; but the figures as they stand serve to show clearly enough the movement of trade.

The bulk of these figures represent Devonshire production, although the Cornish ports are included in the totals for Plymouth-Fowey. Over the whole period Plymouth-Fowey handled slightly under one-third of the total exports of cloth from the South West, rising to rather more than 40 per cent in the boom years of the 1430s; but probably the greater part of

* Power and Postan, *English Trade in the Fifteenth Century*, pp 337–9, 352–4. The port of Exeter-Dartmouth included all the lesser ports of Devon (including Barnstaple on the north coast) except Plymouth. The figures for the first few years of the century seem to include Plymouth also (see Power and Postan, op cit, p 337 footnote 2).

this consisted of the export of Tavistock cloths through the port of Plymouth. The Cornish contribution to the export trade in cloth was small, probably negligible.

The cloth export trade of the South West more than doubled in the first years of the fifteenth century, growing slowly up to about 1418, when a pronounced depression set in which lasted until 1430. Then, in 1430–31, a remarkable rise set in at Exeter and Dartmouth, with the Plymouth figures following suit three years later (1433–4), both reaching a temporary peak in 1439–41. During the whole decade 1430–40 the cloth exports from the South West were more than three times the volume of those exported in the previous decade. After a slight setback in the early 1440s (hardly noticeable at Plymouth, but more so at Exeter and Dartmouth), the export trade grew even more vigorously to a climax in 1448. Large though the exports of the 1430s had been, those of the next decade were nearly half as high again, and more than four times the level of the 1420s.

There was a sharp drop in all the South-Western ports in 1449–51, Exeter and Dartmouth then recovered, and exports continued at a high level until 1464–5; but at Plymouth the slump lasted until 1453 and there was only a partial recovery throughout the later 1450s, ending with an almost complete collapse. Between 1462 and 1464 the Plymouth cloth trade nearly vanished, but it revived slowly and continued in a depressed state until the end of the 1470s. At Exeter and Dartmouth the years 1465–75 were years of comparative depression, the lowest level being reached in the early 1470s. Then came a dramatic recovery in 1476–7, and by the early 80s another boom was well under way. At Plymouth-Fowey the boom did not become evident until 1481–2, and even then it was not so marked as at Exeter and Dartmouth.

What is also very evident from the figures is the greatly increased share of alien merchants in this later boom. Whereas in the earlier peak-year of 1447–8, alien merchants had handled only sixty-one out of the total of 4,509 cloths exported from the South West, in 1481–2 they exported the equivalent of 2,560 cloths out of a total of 7,368 – well over a third of the

trade. But over the entire period 1400–80 they had handled
only 7 per cent of the total cloth exports from the South West.
Local merchants, the men of Tavistock, Totnes, Ashburton,
Exeter, and Barnstaple, handled 93 per cent of the trade
through the ports.

This point is of obvious importance in our examination of
the building activity in Devon during the fifteenth century, for
it means that the greater part of the profits of the rising cloth
trade remained in the coffers of Devonshire townsmen; and it
was out of this fund that so much of the church-building of the
1430s, 1440s, and 1450s was financed. We must not press this
economic argument too far; but the stagnation of the cloth
trade in the 1420s and the boom in the 1430s and 1440s are too
striking to be ignored in the light of all the architectural evidence we have uncovered. Apart from the stagnation of the 20s,
the Devonshire cloth trade experienced no general depression
until the 1460s, and even then cloth exports for the decade were
nearly twice what they had been in the earlier depression.

The evidence from the Devonshire tin trade is less decisive,
partly because the figures of production in the fifteenth century
are irregular and relate usually to isolated years.* Devonshire
production was only a small fraction of that of Cornwall: in the
early years of the fifteenth century it was generally less than
one-tenth. But within its own boundaries its fluctuations could
bring prosperity or depression over a wide area, and the figures
are worth looking at briefly for this reason. In 1400 the production of tin in Devon totalled nearly 129 thousandweight; in
1412, the next figure we have, production amounted to just
under 108 thousandweight. Low though these figures are when
compared with those for Cornwall, the fact remains that they
are much higher than any recorded for Devon in the thirteenth
century, and they are twice as high as those for the years
1294–1301. The later figures, up to 1450, are very few and
vary widely. On the whole, they suggest production at a low
level, except in 1447 which seems to have been a peak-year, as

* Cf, Lewis, *The Stannaries*, pp 253, 260, 274.

it was in the cloth trade. In that year production in Devon reached a total of nearly 203 thousandweight, probably the highest figure since the twelfth century, since the early boom days when production had jumped spectacularly year by year. Production in the next two years was the lowest for any years on record, but in 1450 the trade fully recovered and from that year onwards tin production in Devon showed a steady upward trend, reaching a temporary peak in 1472 at nearly 243 thousandweight.

The average of the five years for which we have figures between 1450 and 1469 is 134 thousandweight, a consistent level of production that had not been known for exactly 400 years. From 1472 to 1496 the average of six years when figures are available is much higher – 229 thousandweight – with production still rising steadily as the century ended, towards a peak of more than 470 thousandweight in 1515.

Thus, although it would be perhaps an exaggeration to speak of a boom in the Devon tin trade in the second half of the fifteenth century, production rose steadily from the year 1450 onwards, just when the cloth trade was beginning to slacken, and it compensated to some extent, at least, for that falling-off. Between 1450 and 1495 Devon tin production doubled, and reached the level of one-quarter of the Cornish output. By 1515 production had almost doubled again, and for many years (1515–30) stood at more than one-third the Cornish output.

Nor were the benefits of this trade narrowly confined to the moor and its fringes. Hundreds of investors all over Devon, from the bishop of Exeter and the earl of Devon downwards, put their money into tin works and the profits of the trade were widely distributed. The revival of the tin trade after 1450 is an important factor in the economy of the county for the next three generations. Not until the 1540s did it begin to fail again, and then it dwindled steadily for the rest of the century; but by then the Devonshire cloth trade was taking on even more vigorous life with the introduction of the New Draperies, and the balance was once more redressed.

During the fifteenth century, then, and especially after 1430,

the cloth trade, and then the tin trade, together kept Devon relatively prosperous, or at the worst free from the depression
that had fallen upon the agricultural Midlands. The profits of
these two trades helped to build several of the finest churches in
Devon during the fifteenth century and the early sixteenth. We
do not know how far the purely agricultural wealth of the
county may have helped, or how far Devon agriculture shared
in the general depression of the first three-quarters of the
fifteenth century: that is another aspect of Devonshire history
which awaits the specialist inquirer into the manorial accounts
of the period.

The Reassessment of 1489–90

In 1489–90 the country was again reassessed for a tenth and a
fifteenth. The same overall reduction was allowed to each
county as in 1445, but this sum was somewhat differently apportioned inside each county. In Devon the boroughs were
allowed a little more in the way of reductions, the main change
being at Plymouth. Here, the borough of Sutton Prior and the
tithing of Sutton Vautort had apparently coalesced into one
town by the beginning of Henry VII's reign, and they are
treated as one in the particulars of account among the 'Cities
and boroughs'. The united assessment of the two places was
£34 12s 8d, only a little less than that of Exeter; but whereas
Exeter's revised assessment allowed for a reduction of £8 (it
had been £10 in 1445) the revision at Plymouth allowed for a
reduction of £12, or more than one-third off the original figure.
Torrington and Barnstaple were allowed slightly greater reductions than they had previously had; in the remaining
boroughs the changes were small, a few shillings up or a few
shillings down.

The ancient demesne was expected to pay more than it
had done in 1445: then it had been allowed a reduction of
£23 11s 4d, now it was allowed £16 6s 4d, a change which
almost exactly compensated for the increased allowance to the
boroughs. In 1489–90 the taxable capacity of the county was
distributed as follows:

	Full Quota			Reduction			Net Yield		
	£	s	d	£	s	d	£	s	d
Cities and boroughs	169	16	7	46	5	8	123	10	11
Ancient demesne	81	18	5	16	6	4	65	12	1
Hundreds	702	0	0	87	7	2¼	614	12	9¾
Totals	953	15	0	149	19	2¼	803	15	9¾

The reductions in the hundreds show no significant change
from those of forty-five years earlier. The largest reductions of
tax (more than one-sixth of the original quota) were in Plympton, Roborough, and Ermington hundreds, in the extreme
south-west of the county; in Crediton, West Budleigh, and
North Tawton hundreds in the centre; and in Exminster, Clyston, East Budleigh, and Colyton hundreds – the country to the
south and east of Exeter. Only in three small hundreds – Crediton, West Budleigh, and Clyston – did the average reduction
for the whole hundred exceed 20 per cent. Crediton was still
the worst-hit borough: its new assessment was less than half
that of 1334, and the rural area around it – the hundred of
Crediton – was reduced by 30 per cent. The decline of Crediton from a respectable market-town in the early fourteenth century to a decayed, overgrown village 100 years later is partly
associated at least with the decline in the agricultural wealth of
all the countryside around it. This countryside contains some
of the richest land in Devon: one can only suppose that it had
been particularly hard hit by the plague and had only partly
recovered as late as the end of the fifteenth century. And yet
this decayed town, which was excused three-quarters of its tax
in 1445, had just finished building one of the most magnificent
parish churches in Devon!

Only one final comment is required upon this picture of the
county towards the end of the fifteenth century, and that is that
the clothing towns of East Devon had not yet appeared. Tiverton, that was to be the most opulent of them all 100 years later,
was still a feudal agricultural centre, largely dependent for its
economic life on the Courtenays' great household at the castle.

Its small assessment of 40*s* in 1334 was still halved as late as
1489–90, and Bradninch and Cullompton are no less incon-
spicuous. Their turn had yet to come, with the rise of the New
Draperies in the next century.

The assessment for tenths and fifteenths had been, in 1334, a
reasonably accurate and just valuation of movable property
throughout England. Thereafter, the changes induced by
plague, and by the depression in agriculture and trade, ren-
dered it increasingly unreal as an indication of where the
wealth lay. The comprehensive revision of 1445 was a serious
attempt to bring some semblance of reality back to the figures,
but in Devon, at least, it seems hard to justify some of the
reductions that were allowed. Its principal defect as a valuation, however, was that no increases in the 1334 figures were
provided for, and by the end of the fifteenth century it had
ceased to present anything like a true picture of the economic
state of the country.

The assessment continued to be used until 1623, together
with the reductions allowed in 1489–90 (apparently without
further revision), but it was so blatantly unreal as a measure of
personal wealth by the beginning of the Tudor period that
under Henry VIII a new form of tax, the subsidy, was introduced. It is to this that we must turn if we want a clear and
undistorted picture once more of the distribution of wealth in
England, above all to the comprehensive subsidy of 1524–5,
which swept almost everyone into its net.

CHAPTER TEN

The Farm-Labourer through Four Centuries

THE HISTORY of the farm-labourer is almost un-known. Perhaps we can never know much of it before the days of the reports to the Board of Agriculture, beginning with Fraser's report in 1794. It is not that he has no history, but that it is unrecorded until comparatively recent times. The doings and business affairs of every other class of society appear in records of one sort or the other, public or private, and we can learn something about them by the patient accumulation of facts. But of the agricultural labourers and their families, that great anonymous class, we learn little save generalities before the nineteenth century. Not until the Report on the Employment of Women and Children in Agriculture, presented by the special assistant Poor Law Commissioners in 1843, do we hear them speaking for themselves and learn something of their lives behind the arid generalities of official statistics.

Yet they have been a large class in the Devonshire country-side for some centuries. If we examine the comprehensive subsidy of 1524, which assessed men on their lands, their goods, or their wages, and count those who were assessed on their wages – most of whom we can regard without question in the rural parishes as farm-labourers or farm-servants of some kind – we find that they numbered rather more than one-third of the total population. From parish to parish the proportion naturally varied. In a few parishes it rose to two-thirds, in a few more it was a half. But, generally speaking, there is a high degree of consistency in the figures in each district, and the average for forty-four parishes scattered all over the county was 36 per cent. Some of these wage-earners were labourers in crafts and trades other than farming, but we shall not be far wrong if we put the number of farm-labourers in Devon in the early sixteenth century at just about a third of the whole rural population. In the Midland county of Leicestershire at the same date they were about a fifth of the rural population, a difference which epitomizes much of the difference in the agrarian history of the two counties before that time.

The Elizabethan statute of 1563 required the justices in each county to fix maximum rates of wages from time to time. From this time onwards we can speak with some authority of the farm-labourers' wages. The Devon county records do not begin until 1592, and the earliest surviving wage-assessment among them is that for 1594; but among the records of the city of Exeter there is an assessment which takes us back another thirty years, possibly to the first assessment made under the act of 1563. In 1564 the maximum rates of wages for labourers in husbandry were fixed by the Exeter justices at 6*d* a day between September 30th and March 1st, and 8*d* a day for the rest of the year, without food and drink. With food and drink provided the maximum rates were 3*d* and 4*d* respectively for the two periods. In the corn and hay harvests the maximum rate was fixed at 10*d* a day without food and drink, or 5*d* where it was provided. Women got 4*d* a day at harvest-time, or 2*d* a day where food and drink were provided.

A considerable number of farm-servants lived in, and for these special rates were provided. A bailiff or chief hind was not to take above 40*s* a year, and ordinary labourers not more than 20*s* to 30*s* a year, according to age. Women servants over 16 could not take more than 16*s* to 20*s* a year, according to age.

The Exeter justices had made no change in these maximum rates even by 1588, when they reissued the old rates, despite the serious rise in the price of all foodstuffs in the interval. There is no reason to believe that the Exeter rates, for farm-labourers at least, were any higher than those prevailing in the country at the same date, for there was no sharp distinction between town and country in this respect. The county assessment of 1594 shows some appreciable advances in the rates over those retained in Exeter in 1588; but almost certainly the city justices followed suit with their rates in 1594.

In the Devon assessment of 1594, the justices fixed the maximum wages for labourers in husbandry at 7*d* a day without meat and drink from November 1st to February 2nd, and at 8*d* a day for the remainder of the year. Where meat and drink were provided, the rates were fixed at 3*d* and 4*d* a day for the two periods. The great exception was harvest-time, when exceptionally long hours might be worked, and then the labourer might take 1*s* a day, or 6*d* with meat and drink. All labourers at task-work might take as they could agree with the employer. Thus the farm-labourer earned 4*s* a week for three-quarters of the year, and 3*s* 6*d* during the three winter months, provided he was in full employment six days a week all the year round, an unlikely state of affairs.

A bailiff or chief hind was not to take more than 53*s* 4*d* a year over and above his keep. A farm-servant of between 16 and 20 years of age was not to have more than 30*s* a year and his board and lodging, and above the age of 20 40*s*. Women were paid less, as always. Under the age of 14 a girl living in received nothing but food and clothes; from 14 to 18 she got 12*s* a year, and above 18 she got 16*s* 8*d*. At the hay harvest a woman in for the occasion could earn 6*d* a day without food and drink, or 2*d* a day with it. At the corn harvest, her maximum rates of pay were 7*d* and 3*d* respectively. At all other work a woman could earn 5*d* a day without food and drink, or 1*d* a day with it.

Hooker, in his *Synopsis Chorographical* of Devonshire, written about 1599 or 1600 – from which both Westcote and Risdon borrowed at times almost *verbatim* – gives us a passing glimpse of the labourer at this time. It is only a brief flash in the long darkness of Hodge's history, but all the more valuable because it is so rare. Talking of the degrees of people, Hooker comes to the fourth class – 'the dayle laborers that do serve for wages' – and he speaks of the hard existence and pitifully low standard of living of the labourers in the tin works.

Though the farm-labourer is 'also a dayly laborer at husbandry'
he

> serveth at more ease and more delycatly. Notwithstanding
> they be both [that is, both tin-workers and farm-labourers] of
> a mightye and a stronge bodye, hable to endure all laboures
> and paynes: and upon the holie dayes and tymes of leasure
> they do geve theym selffes unto such exercises and pasttymes
> as wherewith they do rather inseme theire bodyes with hard-
> enes and strengthe, then otherwyse. As with shotynge wras-
> telynge and hurlynge and they so well framed to any kind of
> service, as they will sone atteyne to the use and knowledge
> thereof and as experiens teacheth that a small treyninge will
> sone frame them to whatsoever he be imployed whether it
> be to be a seylder [soldier] or a perfect servinge man. And
> albeit theise laborers be of the most inferior in degree yet
> they be liberi homines and of a free condicion no villanes no
> bonde slaves.

Although it was a punishable offence to offer more wages
than the official maxima, or to take them, there is evidence from
other counties that both masters and men did so not in-
frequently. It seems it was so in Devon also, for in October
1601 the justices ordered the constables to ascertain the names
of all masters and men who gave or took more than the official
maximum rates and to report them to the justices. The matter
was evidently regarded as serious as five sub-committees were
set up to deal with such reports in the different districts. It is
still a matter for research among the Devon county records
whether any action followed the setting up of this machinery.

The rates fixed in 1594 remained unchanged for the rest of
Elizabeth's reign. The next rate which survives was settled by
the county justices at Exeter in April 1654 and shows only a
small advance on the wages of sixty years earlier despite the
very considerable rise in the cost of living in the meantime. The
maximum wage for a farm-labourer all the year round was
fixed at 10*d* a day without food and drink. With food and drink

he was to have no more than 3*d* in the three winter months, and 4*d* a day during the rest of the year. In other words, the labourer who did not receive his meat and drink could earn 5*s* a week all the year round if in full employment, as against an average of slightly under 4*s* a week in 1594. His wages had advanced by only a little over 25 per cent in sixty years, whereas the cost of foodstuffs at least had risen by something like 50 per cent in the same period. But the maximum rates at the corn and hay harvests remained unchanged, so that the advance in his annual income was less than 25 per cent in the end.

Bailiffs and chief hinds got £4 a year, as against 53*s* 4*d* sixty years before. Farm-servants of 16 to 20 years of age got up to 40*s* a year (30*s* formerly) and above 20 years of age 53*s* 4*d* (40*s* formerly). Girls of 14 to 18 who lived in got 16*s* instead of 12*s* a year, and women over the age of 18 23*s* 4*d* instead of 16*s* 8*d*. The rate fixed for this group specifies the age between 18 and 30, and nothing beyond, as though in the seventeenth century no woman above the age of 30 was likely to be capable of working in the fields. Women 'labouring at hay' could earn 6*d* a day without their meat and drink, or 2*d* with it; in the corn harvest, rates were 8*d* and 4*d*. The hay harvest brought in no more to a woman than it had done to her grandmother sixty years before; only in the corn harvest could she earn another 1*d* a day. At all other work in the fields she could earn 5*d* a day without food and drink, and 2*d* with it. It will be observed that the rates are very nicely calculated. The wages of masons, carpenters, and others employed in the building trades were actually left unchanged from those of 1594.

It seems likely that this 1654 assessment was a repetition of one which had been fixed many years earlier, for two years later the justices fixed new maximum rates which show appreciable advances for some classes of workmen at least. The winter rate for day-labourers was kept at 10*d* without meat and drink, but was raised to 4*d* with it; but the summer rate (that is, for the nine months from February to November) was raised from 10*d* to 11*d* a day without meat and drink or 5*d* with it.

The harvest rate was kept at 1s a day, or 6d if food and drink were provided – no change here since 1594. The bailiff's wages went up from £4 to £6 a year, however, and those of farm-servants over 20 years of age from 53s 4d to 80s.

The wages of the women who lived in were also advanced considerably, but those of men under 20 were reduced from 40s to 20s for some reason. Women brought in for the corn or hay harvest still got no more than they had done in 1594 – 6d a day – except where they were provided with their food and drink and then they received 3d instead of the old rate of 2d. It is probable that most men and women received their food and drink at harvest-time so that there was, in fact, a slight increase in the wages of women at harvest, though not of the men.

In a full six-day week the farm-labourer could earn 5s a week during the three winter months, and 5s 6d a week during the rest of the year, in the latter part of the seventeenth century, rising at harvest-time to 6s a week. These are the wages without food and drink. But this clearly overstates the labourer's income, for he was employed – where he did not live in – by the day and not the week, and he could not reckon on six days work every week of the year. His average weekly income over a whole year was something less than the official rates would suggest.

Richard Dunning, who published in 1685 his *Plain and Easy Method showing how the office of the Overseer of the Poor may be managed, whereby it may be £9000 per annum advantage to the County of Devon, without abating the weekly relief of any Poor*, tells us that a Devonshire day-labourer could earn 5d a day all the year round, and his food and drink worth another 5d a day. In other words, the day-labourer averaged about 5s a week all the year round. His wife could earn her food and drink, worth 3d a day, and 1d a day above that.

The official maximum rates may have risen to 1s a day for the non-winter months by the 1680s, as John Cruwys, the squire of Cruwys Morchard, was paying his labourers regularly at that rate in 1687 and 1688. He also supplied to most, if not all, of his craftsmen and labourers wood, cheese, butter, milk, bread, bacon, and wheat. Women got 7*d* a day at the corn and hay harvest at Cruwys Morchard.

The Devon county records contain a good series of official wage assessments for the years between 1700 and 1778. For the 1790s we have the printed evidence of Fraser (1794) and Marshall (1796). During the whole of this time the wages of the farm-labourer did not change perceptibly, although after 1766 the cost of living had risen steadily. No wonder Fraser and Marshall, and a little later Vancouver, describe the position of the Devonshire labouring families as they do, poverty-stricken and degraded, and no wonder the poor-rates had risen so dramatically all over Devon since the middle of the century.

Up to 1732 the official winter rate of pay was 11*d* a day without food and drink, 5*d* with it. The non-winter rate was 1*s* a day, or 6*d* with diet. From 1733 to 1778 the rate was fixed at 1*s* a day all the year round, without meat and drink. With their food provided, labourers could get 5*d* a day in winter, and 6*d* a day during the rest of the year. The harvest rate for men for the whole period 1700–78 was 1*s* 4*d* a day without food and drink, or 8*d* a day with it. Women could earn 6*d* to 8*d* a day at the hay and corn harvests, or 3*d* to 4*d* a day if they got their diet.

Even after the wars began, and the cost of living began to rise more swiftly, the labourer's wages did not rise by even 1*d* a day for some years. When Fraser and Marshall wrote, the day-labourer was still getting only 1*s* a day and an allowance of cider (which did not help his wife's housekeeping). Fraser tells us the wages were 1*s* a day and a quart of cider. Harvest wages were much the same, but the cider was then unlimited. The hours of work – a subject which has hitherto escaped all notice – were from six in the morning until six in the evening in the summer, and from seven till five in the winter. Marshall says much the same two years later, except that in the corn harvest the labourer got 1*s* and full board. In addition, many farmers let their labourers have corn at a fixed price well below the market-price and tried to give them piece-work. Even so, it seemed to him that the wages were low in view of the great rise in the cost of living, and that what the farmers saved by not paying adequate wages they more than lost in pillage and high poor-rates.

The standard of living of the farm-labourer had been steadily going downhill since Elizabethan days. In the 200 years between 1554 and 1796 his money-wages had only risen from 8*d* a day to 1*s* for the greater part of the year, a rise of 50 per cent. But the cost of living had something like trebled during the same period. Even with meat and drink provided, the increase was no greater, from 4*d* a day to 6*d*. Those who lived in were much better off. According to Marshall 'prime men servants' could get £8 a year in 1796, and the others £6 a year. Thus the wages of bailiffs and chief hinds had exactly trebled, and so had those of other men farm-servants living in. The wages of women living in had risen from 16*s* 8*d* a year to £3 or £3 3*s* 0*d*: they had nearly quadrupled. Moreover, the food, drink, and clothes of those living in were all provided, and the great rise in the cost of these items of expenditure, which hit the day-labourer even harder and harder, affected their pockets not at all. The farm-servants who lived in were as well off as their Elizabethan forebears had been; but the day-labourer and his family were incomparably worse off.

When Sir Frederick Morton Eden produced his report on *The State of the Poor* (1797) he described the parish of Clyst St George as it was in 1795. He found a sorry state of affairs. All the men of the parish were agricultural labourers. They generally received 1*s* a day and cider, though a few farmers gave 1*s* 2*d* a day and cider. During the corn harvest meat was added to the earnings.

No labourer can at present maintain himself, wife, and children on his earnings. All have relief from the parish in money, or corn at a reduced price. Before the war wheaten bread and cheese, and about twice a week meat, were their usual food; now barley bread and no meat. They have of late made great use of potatoes. An industrious healthy man can earn 8*s* a week by piece work on an average throughout the year. Labourers' children are often bound out as apprentices at 8 years of age to the farmers. Prior to the present scarcity a labourer, if his wife was healthy, could maintain two young children on his 6s a week and liquor without any parochial relief. A very few years ago labourers thought themselves disgraced by receiving aid from the parish, but this sense of shame is now totally extinguished.

South Tawton was a more fortunate parish than such purely agricultural parishes as Clyst St George since the serge manufacture gave constant employment to nine-tenths of the women (all of the poorest class) in spinning wool. Though spinners could not earn above 6d or 7d a day, a woman's annual earnings amounted to about £9 2s 6d, a half of her husband's income as a farm-labourer. He earned 1s 2d a day on the land, or £18 5s 0d a year. Even so, the labourer's usual diet was milk and potatoes, barley or wheaten bread, and only a little bacon. While the Devonshire serge industry lasted the supplementary earnings of women and children in spinning in some villages kept the labouring family out of the workhouse. But when this trade collapsed generally in rural Devon during the course of the Napoleonic Wars, as the war engulfed one foreign market after another, the whole family became dependent on the earnings from the land. The worst distress came after 1815, but it was bad enough in most Devon parishes long before that.

By the time Vancouver reported to the Board of Agriculture in 1808, the farm-labourer's wages had risen generally to 1s 2d a day, but his harvest pay was no better. At harvest he got 1s 2d a day and liberal food and drink. This wretched wage of 7s a week hardly changed for the next thirty or forty years. When Peel inquired into the wages of agricultural labourers in 1844* the answer he got from Devon was that in the north of the county wages had in general remained constant at 8s a week since 1837. A few farmers gave 9s, but a much greater number gave only 7s still. In very dear seasons some farmers supplemented their labourers' earnings with corn at a reduced

*Peel Papers, BM Add Mss 40536, fo. 64 and 40587 fo. 180

price, but such men were not very numerous. Indeed the
farmers of North Devon were mostly small men themselves and
were having a hard time of their own, and had done for many
years. Around Exeter the average wage between 1837 and 1844
was 7s 6d a week and cider worth 1s, while round Kingsbridge,
in the fertile South Hams, wages until two years previously had
stood at 9s a week, with cider worth another 1s. In 1842 they
were reduced to 8s and cider.

It is just at this time that the special assistant Poor Law
commissioners were appointed to inquire into the employment
of women and children in agriculture. They reported in 1843.
A good deal of their evidence comes from Devon, where medical officers and parsons gave evidence, as well as a number of
farmers. But for the first time we hear also the voice of the
labourer and his wife, telling us about their lives of unending
toil for their pitiful wages, and of their hardships as farm-
apprentices in their young days. Let Mary Puddicombe, the
wife of Samuel Puddicombe of Exeter, labourer, speak for herself from the pages of the commissioners' report:

My father was a farm-labourer at Bridford. I am 41. I
cannot read or write. I was apprenticed to Matthew Col-
eridge, of Bridford, when I was nine years old. My master
died when I was 14; I was not apprenticed afterwards. When
I first went, there were two boys and a girl apprentices; when
my master died, there were three girls and four boy apprentices. The girls slept in our master's daughter's room,
the boys in another room. We had to go through the boys'
room to our room. Three of us slept in one bed: the four boys
slept in one bed.

The family got their dinner all together, and supper too.
There was no difference in the meat, and we always had
wheaten pudding. There was wheaten bread ready, if anybody came in. I lived much better there than I should have
done at home. We might go to the bread and cheese when-
ever we liked, any of us. We were not clothed very well. I
didn't go to church for a long time, not for three years, and

then because the clergyman interfered: then we got better clothes for Sunday. We were never taught to read prayers, and we never said our catechism: people were not so strict in those days as now. It is a good thing for children now that they are brought up to education. It is a good thing for children to read and write; it keeps them out of mischief. Most all my children go to school.

I used to be employed when I was apprenticed in driving bullocks to field, and fetching them in again; cleaning out their houses, and bedding them up; washing potatoes and boiling them for pigs; milking; in the fields leading horses or bullocks to plough: maidens would not like that work now. Then I was employed in mixing lime and earth to spread, digging potatoes, digging and pulling turnips, and anything that came to hand, like a boy. I reaped a little, not much: loaded pack-horses; went out with horses for furze. I got up at five or six, except on market mornings twice a week, and then at three. I went to bed at half past nine.

I worked more in the fields than in the house. When my master died, I went as servant at Blackiston for two years. I was treated very bad there: the people beat their servants. I used to be beat black and blue. The servants beat me; my master used to bang me. I never was much hurt. I never complained to a magistrate. I told my father and mother, and they told me to be a better maiden next time. Apprentices were treated worse: two, without fathers to look after them, were beat with a stick for anything that happened. One maiden had her arm cut to the bone with a stick the young master cut out of the hedge at the time, for not harrowing right, for not leaving enough for a harrow to go back again. That went to a justice: master was fined 5l., and had to pay the doctor's bill. The 5l. was given away in bread to the poor. The parish did not bind any apprentices after that.

I married at 19; my husband was 24. We have got six children; the eldest a boy of 22. He was apprenticed when nine to Mr Emmens, of Bridford, until he was 21. It was a

very good place indeed: the boy was always comfortable; he
liked being with his master.

I worked in the fields many years after I married; lately I
have done washing. I think washing is harder than working
in the fields.

I think it was a good thing for young boys and maidens to
be apprenticed; now they are not brought up to learn anything. If they are bound out, and get good places, they can't
do better; but bad places are very bad. Apprentices were not
so well attended to as they are now; they were sometimes
very badly treated.

Mary Puddicombe's experience was much the same as that
of most labourers' wives. There were good masters and bad
masters in every parish, and there were good and bad apprentices. The evidence from Devon is generally mixed like
this. Sometimes the shadows in the picture fall more heavily,
and sometimes it is the light which predominates. But how one
gets from her simple clear language the feeling of a girl's life on
a farm 100 years ago! – loading pack-horses, going out with the
horses on the wildish Bridford farm to get furze to burn in the
farmhouse kitchen, up at three in the morning on Exeter
market-days, pulling turnips with numbed fingers on the hillside fields, milking the cows, leading the bullocks at the
plough: the hard labouring life.

Let us hear the story of Charles Medway, labourer of Doddiscombsleigh, as the report officially describes him – Charley
to all his friends in the village pub, no doubt:

I was born at Bridford. My father and mother were
farmers' labourers. I am 39 years old. I was apprenticed to
Mr. Smallridge, of Bridford, a farmer: he had a farm of 230
acres.

I was first put out at six years old to a place to fetch cows,
water, etc. I was afterwards, between seven and eight, apprenticed. My master died one year before my time was out;
I served the rest out with his widow. There were three or

four other apprentices at the same time; two of them girls. It was a very good place, as good a place as a person could wish to be in: plenty of meat and drink. As for work, why people must work, and there was plenty of that. The boys lodged with the master's sons, in the same room; the girls slept in another room with the master's daughters. There were 21 of us in the family all at one time. I was clothed pretty well. I had two suits, one for Sunday and one for week days. I always went decent to any place on a holiday. There was never any serious disagreement between master and mistress and their apprentices; a few words, perhaps, but none of them ever went before a magistrate. I was living much better in the farm-house than I might be at home.

I married at 28. I have got four children; the eldest is a boy of 10. He lives in a farm-house; he works for his meat, drink, and clothes and lodging, but he is not apprenticed.

I think it is a good thing for boys to be apprenticed. They used to be beat sometimes where I was; a stick or whip was used. We didn't like it, but now I think it was necessary. Where there are several young people together they must be done so to keep them in order. My young boy is now beat in the same way, but I don't think it is a matter to find fault with. He always tells me of it; if I thought it serious I would take him away directly.

I learned to read in the farm-house. Master took care we should read of winter nights, on Sundays particularly. All the apprentices were brought to the reading in the same way. I went to church twice on Sunday generally. I said my catechism every Sunday to my master; he made his sons and daughters attend to us. I was confirmed: master was always anxious about that with his apprentices.

My wife was an apprentice at Bovey Tracie. I never heard her say that she was badly off in any way. She was 27 when we married.

I think apprenticeship a good thing: a labourer gets rid of children, and the children are better off, in a good place. I was in a good place, but I was lucky. I know many places

where I should not like a child to be sent to: the children in
such places have no clothes to wear; they are beat and half-
starved. There are many such places; but generally speaking,
places are good.

He had been fortunate as an apprentice: the picture he
paints of those early days is pleasant enough. But Mary Rend-
alls had had a bad place. She ran away once when her master
beat her, back to her father, but he dared not keep her for fear
of being summoned.

When I was an apprentice, I got up as early as half-past
two, three, four, or five, to get cows in, feed them, milk them,
and look after the pigs. I then had breakfast, and afterwards
went into the fields. In the fields I used to drive the plough,
pick stones, weed, pull turnips, when snow was lying about,
sow corn, dig potatoes, hoe turnips, and reap. I did everything that boys did. Master made me do everything. I took a
pride to it, when I used to reap, to keep up with the men.

My mistress was a very bad temper; when bad tempered
she treated me very ill; she beat me very much; she would
throw me on the ground, hold me by the ears, kneel upon me,
and use me very ill; I used to scream. This has happened
several times a-week. I have not been free from sore from
one week to another. I have still marks upon me from kicks.
At other times she treated me pretty well. When she was
violent, we had not enough to eat.

Farmers differed as widely in their views about the value of
apprentices on the farm. Here is one side of the case as put by
Mr Edwin Troode of Exminster, who had not a good word to
say for anybody and paints a most unpleasant picture of himself
in the process.

I am tired of apprentices; I find it answers better to pay
regular wages; you have no control over apprentices; you
can't dismiss them; they are a mere plague; but you can

dismiss a paid boy or girl when you like, if they don't do their work properly.

Living near Exeter, when the girls are getting up to be girls, they will have their relations come over to see them on a Sunday; and some smart girl will soon make her ashamed of feeding pigs, and girls must feed pigs.

Unless you can chastise apprentices, they are up to all sorts of bad conduct; and if you have to take the horse-whip, that is unpleasant. I have had boys say to their mistress, when ordered to do work, 'that they would be d—d if they would,' and then I have been obliged to give a cut or two with the whip. They are a great plague to their mistresses. Some sort of girls are much better as servants at wages. They must do their work properly, or they are dismissed, and then they are called to account and punished at home.

Apprentices are indifferent to work; if they don't like things they spoil them; there's no depending on them. They are so much trouble, I will never have another. I have paid 10l. not to have one more than once. People about here won't take them. Servants won't live with apprentices.

I think the increased facilities of getting magistrates to interfere works badly. I think moderate chastisement, in the hands of the master, better. I had an apprentice who, I found, did not go to church though sent, and was out late at night. I applied to a magistrate; the boy was sent to the treadmill for a week, and whipped twice; but that only made him worse than before; nothing hurts a boy like punishment of that kind. I had another apprentice, a girl, who stayed out all night; nothing could be worse; Mrs. Troode scolded her, and the girl threw some potatoes at her; I came in at the moment and struck her with the horse-whip. The girl's parents applied to an attorney in Exeter, and the case was brought before magistrates; I was fined 1l. Upon this I ordered all my apprentices out of the house, for I found I could not have the proper control over them.

It is a difficult question, I dare say; magistrates cannot interfere properly; they never can know the facts of a case, when they are not very important; there may be a long course of harassing ill conduct on one side that is not the subject of interference, whilst the slightest act of retaliation may expose the master to unpleasant complaints and observations. But without the power of going to a magistrate, the apprentices' places, I think, would be very bad to what they are; – that would not do. But the matter between master and apprentice is not fairly understood by the magistrate; the distorted accounts get into newspapers. I have had 50 apprentices and more, and not one half have turned out well. The apprentices think they are always put upon. They don't find out their error till too late.

It is a very responsible thing to have so many children put upon you to bring up. Apprentices are much more independent than they were. The parents find they can get to the magistrates more easily; and they interfere more than formerly. Parents will tell their children that their masters are not to do this and that. 'If they do, I'll bring him before his betters for it.'

At 18 or 19, young lads, when they begin to get useful, will think it hard they are not paid for their labour, and they won't do their work, and they try to do you petty injuries. I have had horses misused by them, and if I have spoken about it, have been answered, 'D—n the horses, what do you put me to 'em for?' I have known of incendiary fires by apprentices, to revenge themselves upon their masters.

If apprentices behaved properly, it was a better thing for them than now when they work for wages. They were under control. Parents find that at the age of 16 or 17, their children are no longer under their management. Parents, when I hire a boy now, will tell me to correct him, and not mind giving him a cut with a whip. And parents advise their children to behave properly, for unless they are employed they must maintain them. Children formerly were bound out at seven.

Girls don't like going out to work – they like being at home, and in-doors better. But I don't know what they will do. Formerly, when apprenticed, they were forced into fields; for if the mistress had not always work enough indoors, of course they went out of doors. Still I think it better for girls not to go into the fields. They can't be looked after, and that is a bad thing in apprenticeship; they get with the boys, and there are opportunities for the worst mischiefs.

I think the small farmers were best for apprentices when they worked with them. The apprentices fared worse altogether, but it was a better school; they saw work well done, and were obliged to do it themselves.

Apprentices are now always much better off than if they remained at home with their parents, in everything, food, clothing, and lodging. If you have many apprentices, you are sure to have one bad one at least, and he, like a bad sheep, affects the whole flock. The poor regret binding out, for their children are not supported for them.

I don't employ any young women in my farm-work. I like married women better. I have six or seven now, and they are all between 40 and 60. Here the women work all the year round; in winter they are employed in digging up turnips, and in the threshing. I pay them half men's wages. My labourers earn 12s. a-week, all things taken into account.

So much for Mr Troode and his treadmills and horsewhips. The other side of the same medal is presented by Mrs Tuckett, farming her husband's farm at Dunsford: how eminently good and sensible she sounds and what an attractive picture she succeeds in painting unwittingly of herself and her farmhouse.

My husband farmed the farm I now occupy. We have had 17 apprentices who have served their time with us; I have now an 18th, who is just finishing his time, with five others now in the house. Of the 17, 5 were girls, the rest were boys. We never had anything wrong happen with any one of them; I mean we never had any serious misconduct, no breaking of indentures, no complaints of any kind. When my husband died there were six apprentices in the house; they could have been all assigned, if they pleased, but they all chose to stop with me.

My house is conducted in the old-fashioned Devonshire way. Myself, the servants, and apprentices, all get meals together, and all have the same things; breakfast, dinner, and supper. Between breakfast and dinner the boys and girls always have luncheon; boys take it out with them into the fields, – bread and cheese, and cider in their kegs. Every boy has his keg for cider.

I always made it a point not to let apprentices keep out after seven o'clock, except on particular occasions, and then never later than nine. As a rule, I never let them, particularly girls, go to fairs and wakes; there are no places so dangerous for girls. The girl whose time is now about expiring never was but at one fair in her life. I always have them to regular reading on a Sunday, and to say the catechism and prayers; the little ones I always take care are at their books on that day. They can't go to the Sunday-school, it is too far off, and too early, as the boys must look after the cattle on Sunday as well as on other days.

They get little sums at times; people coming to the house want their horses held, and they get 2d. for it. When their money gets to 2s. 6d., the rule is not to break it without my leave; when it reaches 5s. the same rule, and so on; so they always have a little money in hand when their time is out. The last girl that left me went into a place, and had a small sum saved in this way, and had no occasion to draw wages till they were due, as is often the case. When their time is out I give them a certificate of good conduct; that helps them to get good places, particularly girls.

I give them five days holiday in the year; three at Christmas and two at Easter; and I give them little amusements then, and at other times. It keeps them cheerful, and makes them like the place; and they always enjoy themselves. At those holidays they go home sometimes for the day, but I never allow them to sleep out. Their parents come to see them when they like, and there's always something to eat and a glass of cider for them.

I have watched my apprentices in after-life, and never had but one that got into any difficulty; that was setting a wire for a hare. All the rest have done well. One, whose time was out 26 years ago, has always been to see me regularly every Christmas-day since. The young men have not married before 27 or 30, and the young women not till a proper age; not like the young girls who are lazing about the village without anything to do.

I think apprenticing, with a premium, a bad thing. There are many little farmers, who take them merely to get the money, and have no proper work for them, and don't care what becomes of them. It can't be wondered at if these apprentices turn out bad. I know a case where one took three nearly at the same time for the premiums; they were badly treated; the girls were driven into the fields, and were left to get on as they could. The magistrates interfered. This system of apprenticeship, in such cases, drives girls into the fields, which is a very bad thing. In some places the parents set the children against their masters. Children are induced to take meat, etc., home to their parents, and it makes them thieves. I haven't a lock in my house where victuals are kept. Everything is open.

I always keep up one system; the children learn it directly they come, and soon like it. I always look after them myself, and never let anything wrong be done without checking them. I never let the girls be with the boys; they are not allowed to go into the fields or the stables; when that's allowed bad consequences must follow. Girls who work in the fields cannot work indoors; they get into all sorts of bad habits, learn bad language, and very bad things often happen. That is so with girls who are not apprenticed, and who are under no restraint; a big girl don't mind her parents when she has been brought up to do nothing regularly. This happens also when apprentices are not strictly looked after; when farmers, who are gentlemen, have them, then the girls and boys are mixed together, and everything follows that's bad.

I think that apprenticeship makes boys and girls much better able to conduct themselves after they grow up. A girl in a cottage, living at home, and working in the fields, can learn nothing; the girls in my house do all the house-work, and at one-and-twenty are fit to go to service, as they generally do. If they choose they have plenty of useful experience, and learn habits of order. I am afraid the doing away with the apprenticing of girls, for girls won't be taken as now though boys will, will be a bad thing for them. It will force girls to keep at home with their parents, and the life they lead there is very bad; there is no control over them, and they are at fairs and wakes; and in all kinds of mischief, and they soon get into difficulty, and are obliged to marry to hide it, whilst they are still children.

I think that apprentices are better off in all respects than children at home; especially in their moral habits. I am certain of it.

Under the old system, girls were driven into the fields to work, because their masters had not enough for them to do in the house. That was bad; I am certainly against girls going into the fields; sometimes, perhaps at hay-time, my girls have been out, but I always kept them in a little set, away from the other people, not to hear their talk.

The system of apprenticing 'parish' children to husbandry was almost peculiar to Devon, or at least much more universal in Devon than in any other county. It was done under the great Elizabethan stature of 1601, and apprenticeship indentures to husbandry survive for the seventeenth, eighteenth, and early nineteenth centuries in many Devonshire parish chests. Vancouver thought highly of the system, despite its undoubted abuses, and wished to see it extended to other counties. But the general weight of opinion was turning against it. By 1843 a number of parishes had already dropped it, and Mr Alfred Austin, the assistant commissioner who reported on the South-

Western counties, came down heavily against it despite the
excellence of Mrs Tuckett's household and of other farmhouses
in the same district. There were certainly far worse abuses
brought to light in this report – the infamous 'gang' system
practised in Norfolk, for example, hardly distinguishable from
slavery. The evidence of the Norfolk labourers about the
misery of their children in those slave-gangs is heart-breaking.
All over England the farm-labourer was degraded and oppressed, in these middle years of the nineteenth century, to a
degree for which it is hard to find a parallel in his long history.
Certainly his Elizabethan ancestors had been much better off in
all respects.

When James Caird wrote about Devonshire agriculture in
1850 he found the labourer's wages were still 7s, 8s, or 9s a week,
with three or four pints of cider daily; but taskwork was much
encouraged and by this means better wages were earned. The
labourer could not have lived if he had not enjoyed many ad-
vantages in kind. In Devon he often had an allotment, sometimes as much as an acre of ground, on which he could produce
300 bushels of potatoes. Generally the allotments were rather
less than half an acre and grew other vegetables besides potatoes, and frequently a little corn. Where a labourer had no
allotment, his master frequently allowed him a small piece of
ground, called the potato-ground, about a quarter of an acre
rent-free. In many instances the master dressed the ground and
carted home the dug potatoes. A great number of Devon
labourers also kept a pig; it was generally reckoned that this
was worth 6d a week to the family. With a good master, the
labourer might also get fuel for the gathering, run for his pig
and poultry in a grass field, barley, wheat, butter, and scalded
milk for the fetching. Many also had a cottage and garden rent-
free.

The earnings of his wife and children were also an important
part of the labourer's income. These came mostly from farm-
labour at harvest and other special times, but in many Devon
villages the labourer's daughters earned considerable sums at
lace-making. There was a great diversity in the circumstances

of labouring families even at the worst of times. In 1843 it was reckoned that some families were making not less than 18s a week, all things considered, for a good bit of the year; but at the other extreme there were families with nothing more than the bare money-wages of the husband – 8s, 9s, or 10s a week according to the season.

Occasionally, but all too rarely, a labourer managed to escape from this bondage of his forebears and to make a new life. One of the labourers who gave evidence to the assistant commissioner in 1843 was George Moxey of Shillingford. He had been apprenticed to a farmer at the age of nine and had had a good place. He was never ill-used by his master and had plenty to eat and drink. All ate together and had the same food. 'I always had a bellyful; if short one day I made up for it the next.' He had attended the day-school up at Whitestone until he had been apprenticed. Although this was the end of his formal schooling (at nine!) he had a good master who made him keep up his scholarship by reading the catechism and the Testament on Sunday nights in the farmhouse. His master had also had him confirmed. Altogether it had been a good upbringing for a labourer's child, but he added that other places were not as good. 'I have heard other apprentices speak differently of their places to what I do.' Yet he and his wife had a hard life, though he described it without complaining. In contrast to George Moxey, there was William Moxey who must have been a close relation as he was born in the next parish in 1780 and worked as an agricultural labourer at Whitestone. But he escaped from Devon, joined some relatives in London as a journeyman baker, began business by selling a single sack of flour on his own account, and became an extensive flour merchant and baker. When he died in 1833 he left £40,000.* Such success stories are exceedingly rare. In Victorian England the dice were too heavily loaded against the labourer from the start.

* Whitestone Memoranda, compiled by the Rev Charles Brown, Rector of Whitestone about 1830–48. M S in the D C R S library, City Library, Exeter.

Index

THE MOST SOUGHT AFTER SERIES IN THE '70s

These superb David & Charles titles are now available in PAN, for connoisseurs, enthusiasts, tourists and everyone looking for a deeper appreciation of Britain than can be found in routine guide books.

BRITISH STEAM SINCE 1900   W. A. Tuplin   45p
An engrossing review of British locomotive development – 'Intensely readable' – *Country Life*. Illustrated.

LNER STEAM   O. S. Nock   50p
A masterly account with superb photographs showing every aspect of steam locomotive design and operation on the LNER.

THE SAILOR'S WORLD   T. A. Hampton   35p
A guide to ships, harbours and customs of the sea. 'Will be of immense value' – *Port of London Authority*. Illustrated.

INTRODUCTION TO INN SIGNS
Eric R. Delderfield   35p
This beautifully illustrated and fascinating guide will delight everyone who loves the British pub. Illustrated.

THE CANAL AGE   Charles Hadfield   50p
A delightful look at the waterways of Britain, Europe and North America from 1760 to 1850. Illustrated.

BUYING ANTIQUES   A. W. Coysh and J. King   45p
An invaluable guide to buying antiques for pleasure or profit. 'Packed with useful information' – *Queen Magazine*. Illustrated.

RAILWAY ADVENTURE   L. T. C. Rolt   35p
The remarkable story of the Talyllyn Railway from inception to the days when a band of local enthusiasts took over its running. Illustrated.

THE PAN BESTSELLERS OF LITERATURE

A series of the most popular books by the world's great authors. Each volume is completely unabridged and contains analytic introduction: the additional notes will be of interest to the general reader and of value to the student.

OLD ST. PAUL'S	Harrison Ainsworth	30p	(6/–)
PRIDE AND PREJUDICE			
	Jane Austen	20p	(4/–)
NORTHANGER ABBEY			
	Jane Austen	17½p	(3/6)
PERSUASION	Jane Austen	20p	(4/–)
EMMA	Jane Austen	30p	(6/–)
THE OLD WIVES' TALE			
	Arnold Bennett	37½p	(7/6)
LORNA DOONE	R. D. Blackmore	37½p	(7/6)
JANE EYRE	Charlotte Brontë	25p	(5/–)
WUTHERING HEIGHTS			
	Emily Brontë	20p	(4/–)
THE MOONSTONE	Wilkie Collins	30p	(6/–)
NICHOLAS NICKLEBY			
	Charles Dickens	42½p	(8/6)
THE THREE MUSKETEERS			
	Alexandre Dumas	37½p	(7/6)
TOM JONES Henry Fielding, Edited by			
	W. Somerset Maugham	30p	(6/–)
MR MIDSHIPMAN EASY			
	Captain Marryat	25p	(5/–)
THE CHILDREN OF THE NEW FOREST			
	Captain Marryat	25p	(5/–)
SHORT STORIES	Guy de Maupassant	30p	(6/–)
NOVELS OF THOMAS LOVE PEACOCK:			
HEADLONG HALL, NIGHTMARE ABBEY,			
THE MISFORTUNES OF ELPHIN,			
CROTCHET CASTLE		30p	(6/–)
THE CLOISTER AND THE HEARTH			
	Charles Reade	37½p	(7/6)
KIDNAPPED	Robert Louis Stevenson	17½p	(3/6)
TREASURE ISLAND	Robert Louis Stevenson	17½p	(3/6)
VANITY FARE	William M. Thackeray	37½p	(7/6)
DR THORNE	Anthony Trollope	37½p	(7/6)
THE LAST CHRONICLE OF BARSET			
	Anthony Trollope	52½p	(10/6)
TOM SAWYER AND HUCKLEBERRY FINN			
	Mark Twain	30p	(6/–)

A SELECTION OF POPULAR READING IN PAN

FICTION

SILENCE ON MONTE SOLE	Jack Olsen	35p
COLONEL SUN A new James Bond novel by	Robert Markham	25p
THE LOOKING-GLASS WAR	John le Carré	25p
THE FAME GAME	Rona Jaffe	40p
CATHERINE AND A TIME FOR LOVE	Juliette Benzoni	35p
THE ASCENT OF D13	Andrew Garve	25p
THE FAR SANDS	Andrew Garve	25p
AIRPORT	Arthur Hailey	37½p
REQUIEM FOR A WREN	Nevil Shute	30p
SYLVESTER	Georgette Heyer	30p
ROSEMARY'S BABY	Ira Levin	25p
HEIR TO FALCONHURST	Lance Horner	40p
THE MURDER IN THE TOWER	Jean Plaidy	30p
GAY LORD ROBERT	Jean Plaidy	30p
A CASE OF NEED	Jeffery Hudson	35p
THE ROSE AND THE SWORD	Sandra Paretti	40p

NON-FICTION

THE SOMERSET & DORSET RAILWAY (illus.)	Robin Atthill	35p
THE WEST HIGHLAND RAILWAY (illus.)	John Thomas	35p
MY BEAVER COLONY (illus.)	Lars Wilsson	25p
THE PETER PRINCIPLE	Dr Laurence J. Peter and Raymond Hull	30p
THE ROOTS OF HEALTH	Leon Petulengro	20p

These and other advertised P A N Books are obtainable from all booksellers and newsagents. If you have any difficulty please send purchase price plus 5p postage to
P.O. Box 11, Falmouth, Cornwall.
While every effort is made to keep prices low, it is sometimes necessary to increase prices at short notice. PAN Books reserve the right to show new retail prices on covers which may differ from those previously advertised in the text or elsewhere.